WITHIN *the* REACH *of* ALL

AN ILLUSTRATED HISTORY
of BRANDYWINE PARK

Susan Mulchahey Chase

*To Pattie and Bob —
with all good wishes —
Susan Mulchahey Chase*

Published by the
Friends of Wilmington Parks

2005

ISBN 0-9774252-0-7

Book Design: Suzanne DeMott Gaadt, Gaadt Perspectives, LLC
Copy editing: Susan Randolph
Printing: Boyertown Publishing
Map illustration by Tim Crawford

Financial support provided by New Castle County, The Laffey-McHugh Foundation, and The Fair Play Foundation.

Contents

The Board of Park Commissioners

endorses parks as "public breathing places" that were especially desirable for
"those in moderate circumstance ... who must confine themselves to the crowded streets,
except an occasional stroll in the suburbs, or a holiday ride. A Public Park abolishes all these distinctions
(between rich and poor) and puts wholesome and rational out door enjoyment within the reach of all."

Report of the Board of Park Commissioners of Wilmington, Del.
for the Year Ending December 31st, 1895

Acknowledgements

No project like this is accomplished alone and I must acknowledge the contributions of several people who made my job easier. Ellen Rendle and Constance Cooper at the Historical Society of Delaware, the Delaware Public Archives staff, and the Wilmington Public Library reference room staff helped me find essential resources. Stanley Kozicki, Wilmington Department of Parks and Recreation, answered my questions on several occasions and John Kurth in the city's Planning Department passed along many useful references. State Representative Joseph G. Di Pinto and Charles Salkin of the Delaware Division of Parks and Recreation spoke with me at length about the park's transition to state management.

The Colonial Dames of America graciously opened their archives to me. Sharryn Johnson of St. Ann's Church and John McNesby of the Catholic Diocese of Wilmington, Scott Sendrow of the New York City Parks Department, Dr. Stephen Grove of the United States Military Academy at West Point, Mari Matulka of the Metropolitan Utilities District in Omaha, Gary Rosenberg of the Douglas County Historical Society of Omaha, and Dr. Arthur Tucker and Dr. Susan Yost both of the Claude E. Phillip Herbarium at Delaware State University all supplied particular help that filled gaps in the narrative.

Nancy Menton-Lyons, Loretta Kapa, Edward M. Laverty, James T. Laverty, and Anne P. Canby, all of whom are related to people who played a part in Brandywine Park's history, provided welcome aid. I am indebted to Don Eros, Eldon du P. Homsey, Vincent Monardo, Nancy Schanes, and Phyllis Wilkes who provided materials for my use and to Dr. Carol E. Hoffecker who graciously prepared the forward for this history. Susan Randolph and Suzanne Gaadt were unflagging in their support as editor and designer respectively. I am deeply thankful for all the encouraging words and efforts these contributors made to this project.

These acknowledgements would be fatally incomplete without recognizing the enormous contribution that Kim Johnson, executive director of the Friends of Wilmington Parks, has made. I count myself indeed blessed to have so congenial, reliable, and energetic a collaborator.

I am hugely grateful to my husband, Bill, for his support of this work. He cheerfully ventured with me into the park to check a detail, joined in the work at the Public Archives, and ran interference to keep daily tasks at bay.

Finally, we all owe a huge debt of gratitude to the founding members of the Board of Park Commissioners whose vision resulted in the creation of Brandywine Park and the stewards who, over the intervening years, have cared for the park so faithfully.

Bird's-eye View looking west from Du Pont Building, Wilmington, Del.

Wilmington, shown here circa 1910, grew rapidly in the
19th century, creating crowded living conditions that made the
provision of Brandywine Park with its open spaces, leafy groves
of trees, and tumbling stream a welcome enhancement.

(Postcard from author's collection.)

Foreword

Colonial Wilmington was a port town that faced the Christina River. The town's main export came from the flour mills on the nearby Brandywine River. Unlike the county seats of New Castle and Dover, commercial Wilmington had no space designated to remain green. But, open land was not far away. Townspeople especially enjoyed walking along the rock-strewn, forested banks of the rapid-flowing Brandywine.

In the course of the 19th century, Wilmington grew to be an industrial city. By 1880 its population exceeded 42,000. Residential and commercial development appeared destined to envelope the Brandywine's banks. Fortunately, a group of Wilmington's prime business leaders intervened to save those scenic places from such a fate. Through their efforts the state legislature created the Board of Park Commissioners.

The Board of Park Commissioners acquired the properties adjacent to the Brandywine and developed that already beautiful space into a park that remains the crown jewel of Wilmington's park system and the envy of other cities. The commissioners continued their benevolent, far-sighted efforts for nearly a century. Only then were their duties transferred to a succession of government agencies that moved from city to county and finally to the State of Delaware, which maintains the park today. The state's partner in this endeavor is the Friends of Wilmington Parks, a nonprofit citizens group that carries on the tradition of the original park commission.

The story of the evolution of this extraordinary park is told at its fullest in this comprehensive historical study. The book is based upon a meticulous reading of the park commissioners' minute books, which are now located in the Delaware Public Archives in Dover.

This rich source has yielded some intriguing tales. None is more memorable than that of Jim, the dancing bear. Jim was a retired performer from the boardwalk in Atlantic City who spent his final years at the Brandywine Zoo. There, unprompted, he continued his craft, entertaining zoo-goers with his routine. Like Jim, Brandywine Park never fails to entertain and inspire, just as its founders knew it would.

Carol E. Hoffecker
Richards Professor of History
University of Delaware

William Poole Bancroft, an ardent advocate on behalf of a park

system for Wilmington, gave time, energy, funding, and land

to the effort to provide the city's residents with parks. He served

on the Board of Park Commissioners from its creation in 1883

until his death in 1928, providing leadership as the second

president of the Board from 1904 to 1922.

(Courtesy of Historical Society of Delaware.)

Chapter 1

FOUNDING FATHERS

In the 1895 *Annual Report*, the Wilmington Board of Park Commissioners provided a brief history of its "transactions" from the time the legislature established the board in 1883 to 1895. In the report the commissioners identified the beneficial effects that parks could have: "elevating the taste, promoting in the minds of the masses a love for the beautiful, giving a higher moral tone to all grades of society, bringing them in contact with the purest and most ennobling work of nature."[1] In this philosophy, the first commission members were following the same path that park commissioners throughout the country were also treading. The park itself, with its deliberate contrast to city streets, had the power to counteract the often harmful impact of urban living.

Nineteenth-century cities were uninviting places for the vast majority of residents. The crowded, noisy streets, fetid air, lack of trees, and dearth of greenery were, in the minds of many city dwellers, a vivid contrast to the rural countryside from which they had migrated and to which they looked for standards of decency and healthy living. In many cities of the period, municipal governments joined with local reformers to create urban parks to bring restorative nature into the city. If the city's atmosphere was degrading and dehumanizing, they reasoned, then nature, found in the small slices of countryside reproduced within the city parks, could restore both spiritual and physical vitality. Landscape architect Frederick Law Olmsted, a proponent of nature's power to counteract the city's negative impact, stressed to the park commissioners of Boston in 1870 the benefits of urban parks with a rural character. They should be, he wrote, places where people "may stroll for an hour, seeing, hearing and feeling nothing of the bustle and jar of the streets, where they shall, in effect, find the city put far away from them."[2]

Certain reformers regarded the "wicked" city as a place of moral pollution and held that in the face of degrading city conditions—crowded housing, poor sanitation, narrow streets, filthy air, incessant noise, numbing industrial jobs, and grindingly long hours and weeks of work—natural beauty could exert an elevating influence on the character of city residents caught up in the seemingly endless cycle of the unnatural urban environment. The parks' soothing tranquility in the midst of the untranquil city thus provided moral uplift to park visitors.

Many cities along the East Coast undertook park projects in order to afford residents relief from city living and working conditions. Most famous perhaps was New York City's

Central Park, begun in 1858 on a plan that Frederick Law Olmsted and his collaborator, Calvert Vaux, created. Closer to Wilmington, Philadelphia had established Fairmount Park in 1843, and Baltimore created its first large city park, Druid Hill Park, in 1860. In the years following the opening of Central Park, New York City added Prospect Park (1866) and Riverside Park (1875), Buffalo established Delaware Park (1869), and Boston created the first section of its "Emerald Necklace" park system with Back Bay Fens (1879).

A PUBLIC PARK FOR WILMINGTON

Wilmington too felt the impulse toward park building. The city was growing in the years after the Civil War and the growth began to encroach on the area along the Brandywine River. After some community discussion about the merits of a public square for the city and possible city acquisition of land on the Brandywine as a park, a group of interested citizens established a committee in 1868 to look into the development of a park along the river. A year later, the committee recommended to the City Council that the city acquire the land between Adams Street and Rattlesnake Run and stretching from Lovering Avenue to Brandywine Creek, including the millrace and urged that the acquisition extend "to such natural boundaries on the opposite side of the Brandywine, as may be deemed most desirable." The report compared the site with well-known parks of the day—Central Park, Fairmount Park, and Prospect Park—and noted that within the limits they designated, "we have all that is desirable in Park scenery, and all that is necessary for Park use,—running water, level lawn, grove, forest, playgrounds, walks, drives and beautiful vistas."[3]

The committee urged prompt action, both because increasing property values threatened to push up the price of the project and because they wanted to provide as quickly as possible the benefits that a park could have on "the culture, taste, and morals of the community." In their estimation, the creation of a park "adds materially to the attractions of a City" and had the effect "of elevating the taste, promoting in the minds of the masses a love for the beautiful, giving a higher moral tone to all grades of society, bringing them in contact with the purest and most ennobling works of nature."[4] Referring to parks as "public breathing spaces," the committee members considered them especially desirable for "those of moderate circumstances … who must confine themselves to the crowded streets, except an occasional stroll in the suburbs, or a holiday ride" because Wilmington offered no places "where the mothers with their children, or the aged people can stroll, away from the noise and dust of the City, without being trespassers."[5]

Public reaction to the report was mixed. In the *Wilmington Daily Commercial* of May 22, 1868, the public objected to the area along the river being turned to private use. "We protest against allowing the beautiful natural park along the banks of this stream being appropriated for building purposes," the newspaper reported. "The city must have this ground, and the sooner the better and cheaper. The banks of the Brandywine must not be monopolized by private residences, or cut up into private grounds. They must belong to the whole people, rich and poor."

Such support was not unanimous, however. As an account in the Board of Park Commissioners' *Annual Report* for 1895 described, the committee report generated interest, but "a few strong opponents had more weight than a large number of disinterested friends, and the members of The City Council,—induced to believe that the former voiced the sentiments of the majority, bowed down submissively to their will, and the endeavor failed."[6]

Because of this uncertainty, several years elapsed before the project made any appreciable progress. Discussions continued until 1883, when a group that included William Marriott Canby and William Poole Bancroft persuaded the state legislature to enact a bill providing for public parks for Wilmington. The bill also created the Board of Park Commissioners, made up of 10 appointed commissioners (William Poole Bancroft, George H. Bates, Thomas F. Bayard, Edward Betts, Francis N. Buck, George W. Bush, William Marriott Canby, Joseph L. Carpenter Jr., Henry A.

du Pont, and J. Taylor Gause) and four ex-officio members (the mayor, the president of the City Council, the chair of the Council's Finance Committee, and the chief engineer of the city's Surveying Department).[7]

The First Board of Park Commissioners

With the legislated authority to establish and manage a city park system, the men who made up the first Board of Park Commissioners brought to their new assignment both a commitment to create a park for the city and a wealth of leadership skills and organizational experience that boded well for success. Drawn from the local business and professional community, they were industrialists, bankers, attorneys, a real estate developer, and the head of a local freight line.

Several of the commissioners served together on boards of local philanthropic institutions. They shared leadership responsibilities for the Wilmington Institute and the Home for Friendless Children, the Ferris Reform School, the Associated Charities, and the Wilmington Fountain Society. They had also forged working relationships as members of numerous boards of directors of city banks and businesses. Various commissioners helped guide the business courses for Farmers Bank, Artisans Bank, and the Banking House Corporation as well as for the Wilmington City Railway Company, the Front and Union Street Railway Company, the Wilmington and Brandywine Cemetery, and the Board of Trade. All assisted in laying the foundation on which the city's park system would be built. It is clear, however, that four men—William Marriott Canby, William Poole Bancroft, Henry A. du Pont, and Joseph L. Carpenter Jr.—stood out from the rest in the contributions they made to the endeavor before them.

William Marriott Canby

When the board met for the first time on April 26, 1883, the members elected as their president William Marriott Canby (1831–1904). Canby had an initial four-year appointment to the board, an assignment that was

routinely renewed, and he remained president from his 1883 appointment until his death in March 1904. Educated at Quaker schools near Chadds Ford and at Westtown in Pennsylvania, Canby was a member of one of Wilmington's long-established families and a successful businessman. He was president of the Wilmington Savings Fund Society when he became president of the Board of Park Commissioners, and during his commercial career, he was a trustee or director of the Union Bank, the Delaware Fire Insurance Company, and the Wilmington and Brandywine Cemetery board. He was also one of the founders of the Delaware Western Railroad, later part of the Baltimore & Ohio Railroad system, of which he was a director.[8] He served as an early director of

William Marriott Canby, businessman and philanthropist, was the first president of the Board of Park Commissioners, 1883–1904. He is shown here on the left with Charles Sprague Sargent, director of the Arnold Arboretum at Harvard University. (Courtesy of the Claude E. Phillips Herbarium, Delaware State University.)

the Wilmington Fountain Society and a trustee of the Home for Friendless and Destitute Children. In 1872 the board of the Wilmington Institute, a precursor to the Wilmington Institute Free Library, elected him president, and in 1888 he was elected president of the city's Associated Charities, formed in 1884 to coordinate the work of existing charities and to distribute food and fuel to needy families.[9]

Canby was an avid and talented botanist who was well known in scientific circles. When he died, the *Botanical Gazette* observed that his death would be "a personal loss to botanists throughout the country."[10] He began collecting plants in the late 1850s, traveling far and wide to find specimens. In 1882 and 1883, he was the lead botanist on the Northern Transcontinental Survey, a natural resources study that the Northern Pacific Railway conducted in areas through which the railroad passed. In 1898 he joined John Muir, founder of the Sierra Club, and Charles Sprague Sargent, director of Harvard's Arnold Arboretum, on an expedition to the Appalachian Mountains. Three years later he joined Muir on an Alaska trip, and each journey produced additional plants for Canby's collection. He sold his first herbarium of 30,000 specimens to the College of Pharmacy in New York. He assembled another herbarium of 15,000 specimens, which he gave to the Natural History Society of Delaware, of which he was founder and first president.[11]

His reach was international, with some of the specimens he collected eventually becoming part of foreign collections.[12] He corresponded with Charles Darwin who found inspiration in Canby's studies of insectivorous plants, and declared that Canby's letter on the topic "fires me up" to finish work that Darwin had begun. Darwin's completed study contained three references to Canby and his successful scientific efforts.[13]

Canby was the primary link between the Board of Park Commissioners and nationally renowned landscape designer Frederick Law Olmsted, with whom the commissioners consulted early in the process of land acquisition for

Brandywine Park. After a decade of working together, miscommunications and misinterpreted actions ended the relationship between the board and Olmsted. The landscape architect visited Wilmington in December 1892, and his notes on the visit indicate his perception of a "mutual misunderstanding," apparently stemming from work that deviated from what the Olmsted firm had recommended. Olmsted seemed to think that the Board of Park Commissioners had taken charge of the park design work because they thought Olmsted's extremely busy schedule had left him no time for projects like Wilmington's parks. In 1893 Olmsted wrote an 18-page letter to Canby defending his firm's work and expressing his unhappiness at the course of events. Canby replied to Olmsted, assuring him that there had indeed been a misunderstanding and ending with an expression of admiration. Canby's words to the old and ailing Olmsted were ones of kindness and conciliation: "It is nothing to you that you have known me," he wrote, "but it means a great deal to me that I have known you. ... Long before you knew of me you had my sincere homage and it is more full and sincere now than ever before."[14]

Canby proved an able and dedicated leader to the first board. During his presidency, the first land for Brandywine Park was acquired, the first staff members were hired, roads were laid out and improved, walls were constructed, and amenities were added to the landscape, making the park an increasingly inviting destination for Wilmingtonians.

When Canby died in 1904 at the age of 73, commissioners recorded their sense of deep loss: "He will be greviously [sic] missed," the board's *Annual Report* recorded. "From the first organization until his death he was (the board's) President and in very many respects its leader. His appreciation of Nature [sic], his botanical and general scientific knowledge, and his executive ability rendered him especially useful, and no results at all like those that have been attained could have been reached without him."[15]

On a blustery December day in 1905, a "considerable" group of people gathered on the bluff behind Rockford Tower, where they dedicated a memorial to William

Marriott Canby—a seven-foot granite bench overlooking "Canby Vista," a vantage point offering a scenic view of the Brandywine Valley below.[16] He is memorialized in the larger world as well. People who have never heard of Canby invoke his name when they refer to Canby paxistima (*Paxistima canbyi A. Gray*, a dwarf evergreen shrub) or Canby blue grass (*Poa canbyi*) or Canby oak (*Quercus canbyi*) or any of the other dozen species bearing his name.

WILLIAM POOLE BANCROFT

Following Canby's death, his friend and cousin William Poole Bancroft (1835–1928) assumed the office of president of the Board of Park Commissioners, serving from 1904 until 1922. Bancroft is rightly known as "the father of the Wilmington Park system." In 1881 he complained that the city had "scarcely any provision for parks or open spaces of any kind—except cemeteries."[17] Two years later, he served with Canby and others on the committee that successfully lobbied the state legislature for the creation of a Board of Park Commissioners and the establishment of parks for Wilmington.[18] When the board was established in 1883, Bancroft was appointed to the board for an initial two-year term; yet he remained a commissioner until his death in 1928.

The Bancroft family had been in Wilmington since the early 19th century. In 1831 Joseph Bancroft began operating a cotton textile mill. His son William Poole Bancroft started work in the family's business at an early age and became a partner in the firm in 1865. When the company went from a partnership to a corporation in 1874, William was one of the incorporators and became vice president of Joseph Bancroft & Sons Company while his brother Samuel became company president.[19]

Although Bancroft's business acumen was considerable, he is best remembered for his philanthropy. His gifts to the park system were many and varied. During the years that Bancroft was on the Board of Park Commissioners, he donated more than 200 acres of land for city parks and parkways.[20] Among his gifts is Rockford Park, which remains closely associated with the Bancroft family. In 1889 Bancroft, along with his brother Samuel and their wives, donated 65 acres that made up the initial core of the park.[21]

During Bancroft's years as a park commissioner, if land that was well suited for park use came up for sale at a time when the city lacked funds to purchase it, Bancroft often acquired the property and held it with the expectation that eventually the city would purchase the land for its intended purpose. In 1899, for example, he paid $20,000 for several parcels of land along both sides of Rattlesnake Run, "subject to an understanding whereby the City agrees to purchase (the land) at the earliest opportunity," which the city did in 1905.[22] For several years Bancroft held nearly 97 acres of woodland and meadows on the southwest side of the city, protecting it from development. In 1917 Irénée and Pierre du Pont bought the parcel and donated it to the city, creating Southwest Park (now Canby Park).[23]

Bancroft's philanthropy included gifts of money for park plantings, for the care of park trees and shrubs, for road improvements, and for incidental surveying expenses.[24] He often underwrote an expense that he saw as a necessary enhancement for the park and noted that if and when city funds became available, the city could reimburse him. In 1911, when the $1,750 needed for playground operations was uncertain, Bancroft concluded board discussion on the issue by stating that if the city appropriation was insufficient and funds could not be found elsewhere, "I will see that, within the amount $1750.00, contributions shall be secured to cover the deficiency."[25]

Bancroft also gave generously of his time. From 1902 until 1921, he represented the Board of Park Commissioners on the Mayor's Advisory Board, which brought together the heads of several city commissions each month. The regular exchange of information at the meetings often led to productive collaborative efforts. He presented to City Council recommendations offered by the board, drafted park legislation, and negotiated with the Baltimore & Ohio Railroad when the company sought the cooperation of the Board of Park Commissioners in a project impinging on the park.[26]

Even the small details of daily operations did not escape Bancroft's notice. In 1910 Park Superintendent Edward R. Mack recorded in his superintendent's log that he met with Bancroft 33 times between January 24 and November 8, some of the meetings occurring at particularly important junctures in the park's evolution.[27] They met on May 5, 1910, the day before the superintendent accompanied Bancroft to a City Council meeting. Similarly, the pair met on June 14 and 16, immediately after Superintendent Mack's return from a playground conference and at the time that Mack was hiring the park system's first playground supervisor, Jennie Weaver.

William Poole Bancroft's support for other worthy endeavors included service to the Wilmington Institute as a significant benefactor. His gift of $20,000 freed the private subscription library from a crushing debt and allowed it to operate as a public library. He was an incorporator of the Delaware Hospital and served as secretary of the hospital board and as a general benefactor of Wilmington Friends School. His interest extended to public education, and he was a member of the Public School Committee for more than 30 years.[28]

Bancroft was a modest man, never seeking attention or acclaim as he went faithfully about his work. In the minutes of the March 2, 1910, Mayor's Advisory Board meeting, he requested that wording in the February minutes mentioning "his new Park land acquisitions" be corrected to read "*the* new Park land acquisitions." In May 1913, he wrote to the City Council about the board's financial shortfall, noting that "a member of the Board" had promised to meet the bills if necessary. He was that member of the board.[29] Patience seemed to come naturally to Bancroft. In April 1890, he wrote to the board president, William Marriott Canby, about a visit he had made with Francis G. du Pont to assess land near Rockford Park and the discussion the two had regarding acquisition of the land for park use. His patient negotiations paid off when, five years later, the DuPont Company donated the nine and a half acres that Bancroft wanted to add to Rockford Park.[30]

Bancroft was, in many ways, a visionary in his perception of the city, its development, and its needs. In 1916 he declared that the path of growth for Wilmington would be north along Concord Pike. Based on that prediction, his Woodlawn Company (after 1918, Woodlawn Trustees) purchased extensive acreage north of the Brandywine and along the west side of the highway's path.[31] Bancroft had established the Woodlawn Company in 1901 as a mechanism for improving housing for working families. Between 1903 and 1913, the company constructed 270 two-story dwellings to accommodate 390 families in the neighborhood along Union Street. The Woodlawn Company's successor, the Woodlawn Trustees, designated that profits from its work were to be used to promote parks and playgrounds and to provide support for local philanthropic and educational organizations. In recent years, the company has used the income from real estate operations to acquire and protect open space, much of it turned to park use.[32]

Bancroft Parkway, originally called Western Parkway, bears William Poole Bancroft's name in recognition of his vision for a system that included roadways linking the parks. Out of this vision came the Kentmere Parkway link between Brandywine and Rockford parks and the Bancroft Parkway link between Kentmere Parkway and Canby Park on Wilmington's southwest edge. His numerous land purchases in anticipation of later need testify to his enduring ideas about the city's needs. In January 1915, he articulated his ideas in a letter to the City Council. "It is said truly that we have more park land now than we can take care of properly," he wrote. "It would be practicable at this time to obtain all, or nearly all, the tracts suggested. … If they are not secured soon many of them can never be obtained. Let us get them now, even if improvement of them must in a very large degree be deferred for several years." After discussing certain practical and monetary aspects of the situation, he concluded, "I am willing to ask that, for the sake of Wilmingtonians of the present and the near future and of the hundreds of thousands who will be here in a few generations, we shall endeavor to secure, at the approaching session of the

Legislature, the power that will enable the City to go ahead with this work within the next few years."[33]

Henry A. du Pont

Henry A. du Pont (1838–1926), who graduated first in his class at West Point and who was awarded a Congressional Medal of Honor for distinguished service during the Civil War, was known to many as Colonel du Pont.[34] After leaving the military in 1875 to return to Delaware and become part of his family's black powder business (E. I. du Pont de Nemours & Company), du Pont managed sales and oversaw transportation for the company, including negotiations with railroads over rates. He rose to partner by 1878 and was one of three vice presidents when DuPont was incorporated in 1899.[35] In addition to his leadership roles within the company, he was also president of the Wilmington and Northern Railroad, a post he retained from 1899, when the Philadelphia and Reading Railway took over the Wilmington and Northern, until his death in 1926. Du Pont also served on the boards of directors of Union National Bank and the New Castle County Mutual Insurance Company.[36]

In 1895 du Pont was the largest stockholder when the DuPont Company donated nine and a half acres of land to Rockford Park.[37] He served on the Board of Park Commissioners for 26 years, until his political responsibilities and ambitions placed heavy demands on his time and he resigned in 1909. In a special election three years earlier, he had been elected to represent Delaware in the U. S. Senate, and he faced reelection in 1911, a contest he won. He served until 1917, after which he retired to his home at Winterthur to pursue his personal interest in family history.[38]

Joseph L. Carpenter Jr.

Joseph L. Carpenter Jr. (1841–1942) was the longest serving member of the original board, joining in 1883 and serving until his death in 1942. In October 1941, his fellow commissioners honored him on his 100th birthday with a resolution congratulating him on his "long life and splendid

Henry A. du Pont, graduated first in his class from West Point, earned the rank of colonel during the Civil War, and was awarded the Congressional Medal of Honor. He served on the board from 1883 to 1909. (Courtesy of Historical Society of Delaware.)

record of usefulness to the community." They noted that, as the years had passed, he had held the "respect and friendship of (his) fellow citizens in ever increasing numbers." Marking his death less than six months later, the board praised Carpenter for his "advice and counsel (which were) uniformly sound" and for the zeal with which he had served the board.[39] He was on the park board's Executive Committee from 1906 until 1942 and also served on the Park Extension Committee and the Rodney Square Committee, which oversaw use of Wilmington's downtown "park." Though the Board of Park Commissioners was Carpenter's primary public service, he also served on the board of directors of the Street and Sewer Department for six years in the early 1890s.[40]

Carpenter, who was in real estate, not only facilitated property trades but also undertook at least one development project—the Second Street Market House, which he built in 1876. He served on the Market House Board after it opened, first as treasurer and then as a board member. He was also president of Farmers Bank, and his banking connections extended to directorships on the boards of Artisans Bank and the Banking House Corporation. The responsibilities of the Board of Park Commissioners' Executive Committee were heavy because the committee met weekly, so Carpenter's other philanthropic works were necessarily limited, although he sat on the Almshouse Committee in the 1880s and served as a director for Ferris Reform School.[41]

OTHER MEMBERS OF THE ORIGINAL BOARD

Of the remaining six members of the original Board of Park Commissioners, Edward Betts, president of the First National Bank, served the shortest term, leaving the board at the end of his two-year appointment. He had a long and busy career in philanthropic causes in Wilmington, serving on numerous charitable boards over several decades. Betts, as a school board member in 1854, worked with the committee overseeing land purchase for new schools. He was also a member of the committee appointed in 1867 to assess Wilmington's needs for an increased water supply.[42] He was a director of the Wilmington Fountain Society in the 1870s and acted as treasurer for the Associated Charities board in the mid-1880s (serving with fellow park commissioner George W. Bush). He also served on the board of the Home for Friendless and Destitute Children in 1888 (with Bush and J. Taylor Gause) and as a director for the Ferris Reform School.

Thomas F. Bayard (1828–1898) was the commissioner who enjoyed the widest national reputation among the members of the board. He was elected one of Delaware's U. S. Senators in 1869, serving three terms.

President Grover Cleveland named him Secretary of State in 1885, a post he held until 1889. In 1893 President Cleveland named Bayard the first American ambassador to Britain. Prior to this appointment, America had sent ministers, not ambassadors, as representatives to foreign countries. Bayard returned to America in 1897 and died the following year. Scholars often credit him with forging the first strong links between the United States and England at a time when relations were strained as both America and England sought to extend their power around the world.[43]

In 1868 Bayard was on the committee that first considered the possibility of a park for Wilmington, and he brought to the Park Commission a long history of advocacy on behalf of parks. It was he who suggested that the board consult with Frederick Law Olmsted "or such other competent authority as he may see fit" when the first land purchases along the Brandywine were contemplated.[44] His suggestion and Olmsted's subsequent endorsement of the site provided the impetus needed to launch the city's park system.[45]

George H. Bates (1845–1916), a prominent attorney, was Speaker of the Delaware House of Representatives at the time he was appointed to the first Board of Park Commissioners. Bates served his profession as secretary-treasurer of the Bar Association of New Castle County and as the president of the Law Library Association. He sat on the board of directors of the Farmers Bank for several years and was also a director of the board of the Wilmington City Railway in the 1880s.[46] He was president of the Wilmington Institute in 1873, the year after William Marriott Canby held the same post, and he served on the board of the Historical Society of Delaware in 1888 with Thomas F. Bayard, who was a vice president of the society.[47]

Francis N. Buck (1842–1926), secretary and treasurer of Walton, Whann and Company, manufacturers of phosphate fertilizers, served the Board of Park Commissioners for over a decade, from his 1883 appointment until 1895. Aside from the park board, Buck's service was largely restricted to business. A neighbor on West Street of fellow park commissioners Edward Betts and George W. Bush,

Buck was a director and, in 1881, president of the Wilmington Board of Trade, an organization in which Bush and J. Taylor Gause were also active. He also served with Bush on the board of the Front and Union Street Railway Company and was director of the New Castle branch of the Delaware Farmers' Bank in the 1880s.[48]

George W. Bush (1824–1900), brought wide-ranging interests to his responsibilities as a member of the Board of Park Commissioners. Bush was vice president and then president of Artisans Bank as well as president of his family's freight line, which operated steamships between Wilmington and New York. He was also president of the Front and Union Street Railway Company when it was chartered in 1877 and president of the Electric Line, which provided steamship service between Wilmington and New York. Bush gave long board service to the Wilmington Board of Trade; the Banking House Corporation, serving as president in 1873; Delaware Fire Insurance Company; Wilmington City Railway Company; the Wilmington and Brandywine Cemetery; and the First National Bank of Wilmington.

Bush was also active in charitable organizations in Wilmington. In addition to being an elder of Central Presbyterian Church, he served on the board of the Wilmington Institute of which he was vice president in 1859 and president in 1863. He was an incorporator in 1863 of the Home for Friendless and Destitute Children and a long-term trustee of the home. He sat on the boards of the Wilmington Hospital and Associated Charities.[49]

J. Taylor Gause (1832–1898) was president of Harlan and Hollingsworth, one of Wilmington's leading manufacturing concerns, producing steam ships and railroad cars. He had risen within the company from a lowly clerical position in 1843 to become an equal partner in 1858, then rising to president of the corporation in 1888.[50] After retiring in 1896, he enjoyed but a brief respite. In 1898 his successor resigned, and he was again elected president of the company, a post he held for four months before his death in December 1898.

Like his fellow commissioners, Gause was active on the boards of other companies, and he served on the Board of Park Commissioners until 1897. He also devoted considerable energy to charitable service, at least in part because of the interest his wife took in philanthropy. In 1863 he was one of the original incorporators when the Home for Friendless and Destitute Children was established at his wife's behest. The home provided foster care for children whose fathers had gone into the army during the Civil War and whose mothers did not have the resources to care for them. The need for such care endured beyond the end of the war, and Gause remained a director on the home's board for more than two decades.[51]

In 1887 he assisted with the creation of the Homeopathic Hospital of Delaware, another undertaking spearheaded by the energetic Mrs. Gause.[52] Gause purchased the Hygeian Home and offered it to the founders of the new hospital free of rent for a year so that the Homeopathic Hospital (later Memorial Hospital) could get started. It opened in 1888. In addition, Gause sat on the board of the Associated Charities and was an original board member and vice president of the Ferris Reform School. In 1870 he was a director on the board of the Wilmington Fountain Society, and, two years later, he and his wife donated the land on which the society erected a fountain honoring the society's founder, Ferris Bringhurst.[53]

A devout Methodist, Gause was an active participant through his church in outreach efforts to and on behalf of Wilmington's poor. He joined with fellow industrialist Job Jackson in leading the campaign for the construction of Grace Methodist Church, dedicated in 1868 and offered in thanksgiving for God's many blessings on the people of Wilmington.[54]

The Philanthropic Victorians

The original commissioners gave extensive and long-term service to the park system and to the many philanthropic endeavors they undertook. Such dedication was the hallmark of both the Victorian ethic of service and of the Victorian belief that, by the proper application of resources, any problem could be solved.

Victorian society was divided into social classes, and each class had its own responsibilities. For the members of the upper classes, such as the first members of the Board of Park Commissioners, their status provided them with certain privileges but also placed upon them the requirement that they use the benefits they enjoyed for the good of less fortunate members of society. Thus they undertook efforts to provide shelter for destitute and friendless children, water for horses, and parks that would provide acres of lawn and groves of shady trees with the restorative power to ease the burdens of everyday urban life. The Victorians witnessed changes in technology that persuaded them it was possible to address any problem and solve it, to find a remedy for any malady. For the first commissioners, this meant applying energy, imagination, and patience to the problems of the late 19th-century city. Their assessment of the city's drawbacks led them to parks as the therapeutic intervention needed to counteract those shortcomings.

In addition, some of the impetus for good works came from the leadership of William Marriott Canby and William Poole Bancroft, men whose philosophy and approach was grounded in their Quaker roots. As members of the Religious Society of Friends, they believed in the equality of all people and took seriously their responsibility to better the conditions they saw in the surrounding city. Such beliefs tempered their approach to the people with whom they dealt and gave an impressive tenacity to their pursuit of the goals they set for themselves and for the park. Canby's kind and generous words to Frederick Law Olmsted in response to Olmsted's long and complicated letter speak volumes about Canby's compassion for the elderly, ailing Olmsted. Bancroft's unfailing courtesy and modesty, demonstrated repeatedly in his refusal to take credit for many acts of generosity, likewise suggest a worldview that shunned glory for oneself and valued the final good outcome.

By living up to their social responsibilities and by applying the notion of the improvability of people through the provision of a suitable salubrious environment, these 10 philanthropists were generous with their time and resources. Their initial efforts were not without challenges, but persistence and a firm self-confidence marked their path forward as they crafted the foundation on which an entire park system would be built.

Chapter 2

Land and Money

It was clear to the citizens proposing the creation of a park that Wilmington needed green space, and their vision of the importance of an open, public "pleasure ground" was realistic. Between 1850 and 1880, the city's population more than tripled, increasing from 13,979 to 42,478, which meant that there were more than 4,000 people per square mile. This urban growth proceeded largely unplanned and unchecked.[1]

Many residents lived in row houses on narrow streets laid out in an inflexible urban grid. Many of the dwellings measured 15 to 20 feet wide and extended 30 to 40 feet from front to back for a total of 900 to 1,600 square feet of living space. These homes featured four rooms: a kitchen and parlor on the first floor and two bedrooms on the second floor. A privy occupied a corner of the back garden. It was not unusual among working families for six or eight people to live packed into such houses. With dwellings filled to overflowing, entire urban districts struggled under uncomfortably crowded conditions.

Laboring families worked long days that stretched into long working weeks. Factory employees put in 10- to 12-hour days from Monday through Friday and at least half a day's labor on Saturday. In 1913, when William Poole Bancroft offered an account of his early years in his family's textile mill, he wrote that factory employees worked 70 hours per week, with the workday ending at 6 p.m. on weekdays and 4 p.m. on Saturday.[2] There were no paid vacations, and the refreshment of leisure time had to be squeezed into the few hours available on Saturday afternoons and Sundays. The small but growing class of white-collar workers fared only slightly better, working nine-hour days six days per week.[3]

The proposed park site in the midst of the city offered a respite close at hand. While many Wilmington streets were treeless and dusty, there was cool shade along the river. If the city surrounded dwellers with noise and crowds, the water's edge offered the sound of birds and space to walk and breathe in solitude. A rich variety of trees covered the rocky hills, the river's constant splash was a much-sought-after contrast to urban noise, and the fresh breezes were a sweet contrast to the filthy air of an industrial setting. A few hours of leisure in the park was an effective antidote to numbing industrial jobs and grindingly long hours and work weeks.

Planning for a Park

When the board convened for the first time on April 26, 1883, and elected William Marriott Canby president, the group's primary initial objective was to acquire land along the

After Frederick Law Olmsted, landscape architect and planner, visited Wilmington in 1883, his wholehearted endorsement of a park site along the Brandywine provided the needed impetus for the creation of Brandywine Park. (Courtesy of the Library of Congress, LC-USZ62-36895.)

Brandywine within the city "before it should be built upon, or its natural scenery otherwise destroyed or impaired."[4]

The commissioners considered the first steps needed to acquire the land for a park along the Brandywine River, a mile stretch running from a suspension pedestrian bridge near the Jessup and Moore Paper Company's Augustine Mills upstream to the Market Street Bridge downstream. On the table at the same time was Bancroft's offer of 48 acres west of the city. While no action was taken in regard to the Brandywine site, the board issued a formal recommendation that the City Council accept Bancroft's generous offer.[5] Seven months later, in November 1883, the board met again, but the City Council had not yet acted on the recommended land acquisition. The commissioners' determination alone was not enough to meet the land acquisition challenge—either along the Brandywine or west of the city near Bancroft's textile mills. Commissioner Thomas F. Bayard moved that the board authorize the president to seek the advice and council of Frederick Law Olmsted ("or such other competent authority as he may see fit").[6] With the

commissioners' approval, Canby responded promptly, and at the December 1883 board meeting, he reported that Olmsted had been to see the potential park sites in Wilmington. Canby told the board that although Olmsted's report had yet to arrive, the park designer recommended "the purchase as soon as possible of the land on both sides of the Brandywine River within the City limits, as the most eligible for Park purposes."[7]

Olmsted had established a long and enviable record of success in park design by 1883 when he came to Wilmington. After his successful design for New York's Central Park (begun in 1858), he prepared plans for other New York parks—Prospect Park (1866), Fort Greene Park (1868), Morningside Park (1873), and Riverside Park (1875) as well as two parkways for Brooklyn in 1868. Outside of New York, he created designs for Buffalo's Delaware Park (1869), South Park in Chicago (1871), Mount Royal in Montreal (1877), and Detroit's Belle Isle (1881). He also prepared plans for parkways in Buffalo in 1870 and a decade later laid plans for Boston's "Emerald Necklace," a series of parks and parkways threading through the city.

On December 22, 1883, Olmsted visited Wilmington's two potential park sites: first, the stretch of land along the Brandywine that had been the focus of so much attention and, second, the 48-acre parcel that Bancroft was offering to donate if certain stipulations could be met. Olmsted's long, detailed, and determined letter to the Board of Park Commissioners endorsed wholeheartedly the river site as the parcel that the commissioners should make their top priority. While he admired the Bancroft land as a possible park, he preferred the river site because it was in a largely natural state, requiring little work to make it suitable for park use. It was also near densely populated neighborhoods so it could easily provide the benefits it was intended to offer.[8]

Reminding the Board of Park Commissioners that parks were vital to the health of city residents and underscoring to the men their responsibility to safeguard the lives of Wilmington's citizens, he wrote that "the artificial circumstances of a city—walls, windows, roofs, flags,

The Brandywine, captured in this 1897 image,
looks remarkably the same in the 21st century.
(Courtesy of the Historical Society of Delaware.)

pavements, plants in pots and gardens, all sorts of fabrics, and the constant evidence of work, intercourse, and traffic—gradually and insensibly have a wearing and depression effect" on city dwellers. Once individuals have escaped the artificial, he advised, they must turn to nature "working in a large, free, generous, and spontaneous way" to provide the desired "counteracting influence."[9]

Olmsted articulated a vision (shared by board members) emphasizing the essential importance of parks to the moral and physical health of the city and on their personal duty as park commissioners to do all they could to make that vision a reality along the Brandywine. The area, already the site of numerous leisure-time outings by city residents, seemed perfect for park purposes, with all the features that Olmsted's style prized—the "natural scenery" provided by the rocks, trees, open spaces, and running water of the river. Olmsted warned them to act promptly lest someone else acquire the property and put it to private use, something that he had seen happen elsewhere. "I have as often heard bitter expressions of condemnation of the seemingly insane shortsightedness that allowed these opportunities to be lost," he warned, "But in no one of these cases has there been as much to save, as at moderate cost, as there will have been in Wilmington."[10]

With Olmsted's stern advice in mind, the members of the Board of Park Commissioners turned their collective energy and efforts to the twin tasks of finding the necessary funding for their project and acquiring the acreage that would become Brandywine Park.

NATURAL FEATURES

That Frederick Law Olmsted was enthusiastic about the Brandywine River site should come as no surpise. In his writing and his work, he identified the characteristics he considered important in an urban park. Olmsted sought to combine park elements into as natural a landscape as possible, in the belief that observation of nature could soothe and refresh those whose lives were spent in the midst of urban life's noisy confusion. When Olmsted observed the proposed park site in Wilmington, the elements that he valued were present in the river, the rock outcroppings, the trees, the hills, and the undeveloped spaces.[11]

The most obvious natural feature in the park is the Brandywine River. In slightly more than a mile, between the upstream end of the park near the Swinging Bridge and the downstream end at Market Street, the stream falls approximately 20 feet, passes over two dams, and tumbles over the stone remnants of a third dam.[12] The falling water and the

DOG HEAD ROCK, BRANDYWINE PARK.

Dog Head Rock once overlooked the north millrace. The rock is still there but the race was filled with earth in the late 1950s. (Postcard from author's collection.)

In 1902 the president of the Board of Water Commissioners presented to the Executive Committee of the park board a plan to install a sewer down Rattlesnake Run. The sewer was to extend to a point below the dam so that storm water runoff would enter the Brandywine below the headgates of the raceway. As the Water Commission's *Annual Report* for 1902 eloquently put it, "the discharge of Rattlesnake Run into the Brandywine a short distance above the head of the South Long Race, emptied so much filth into the stream at each heavy rain storm, that it was decided to divert its flow … and discharge it below the dam, where it would not effect the City's water supply."[15] Because water for Wilmington's homes and businesses came from the Brandywine via the south raceway, it was important to direct the pollution into the river at a place below where water was captured for delivery to the water treatment plant at Market Street. The storm water was carried across the race by a steel flume that also served as a footbridge.

calm ponds collected behind the dams testify to the river's historic importance as a source of waterpower for the flourmills that were once the heart of Brandywine Village. Today a focal point for leisure-time pursuits, the river has been the site of such active recreation as ice-skating, fishing, kayaking, and canoe slalom competitions as well as a place visited by painters, photographers, and poets for inspiration and quiet contemplation.

The park landscape also has several runs that make their way down the park's slopes to the river. The largest and best known is Rattlesnake Run, which follows the downward continuation of Clayton Street as it enters the park at Gilpin Avenue.[13] Rattlesnake Run was once an open stream, substantial enough to require a bridge near its foot to continue a walking path across the river. It has been subjected to a number of projects over the years, all intended to control the flow of water. In 1887, for example, the directors of the Street and Sewer Department asked permission to put a drain from the top of the run down to "a point below the third dam for the purpose of carrying the drainage of said run below the dam."[14] This was the first of several similar projects.

Rattlesnake Run experienced substantial erosion when there was heavy rainfall, and the rushing water made deep cuts in the sides of the little valley, washing heaps of gravel across the path. In 1996 the New Castle Conservation District hired landscape architect Rodney Robinson to undertake a remediation effort in Rattlesnake Run. Robinson's plan was executed in 2000, as workers regraded the site and created a series of small weirs and stepped terraces that caught the water in small pools to control its flow, thus limiting erosion and improving water quality before it reached the Brandywine. The resulting grassy meadows, carefully selected and maintained specimen trees, and meandering watercourse made Rattlesnake Run a friendlier and more beautiful part of Brandywine Park.

Elliott's Run is part of the topography of North

Brandywine Park. It takes its name from the Elliott family that once owned the land that the run drains, coming down to the river just upstream from the I-95 Bridge. As soon as the Elliott tract was added to the park in 1902, the park board made plans to construct a culvert to carry the run under North Park Drive so that the park road could be extended upstream. In 1905 the commissioners installed the culvert and soon added a separate footbridge with square stone piers and rustic log railings.[16] Over time, the concrete culvert and conduit were extended and what had originally been a small stream meandering toward the Brandywine was captured and directed to the river below.[17]

During the 19th and early 20th centuries, Wilmingtonians visited Brandywine Park to collect water from the springs there. Many city residents considered the spring water to be reliably pure and thus preferable to the water supplied by the city's Water Department. There were several springs at various locations around the city.[18] In 1909 an article in the local press declared "City Water Is Bad" and reported that residents near Brandywine Park "are among those who have refused to use the water and nightly many of them can be seen carrying water from the spring in that vicinity."[19] One of the springs was along South Park Drive, west of Van Buren Street. In 1911 the Board of Park Commissioners installed a "sanitary fountain" there and also diverted some of the water to the footpath near the raceway down the slope.[20] There were also springs near the zoo and a spring known as "Whiskey Run" on the hillside below Baynard Stadium. The Water Department periodically tested the spring water, and in 1962 the city's health commissioner finally condemned as unfit the last two springs still used by city residents.[21]

The park was the site of several quarries that at various times yielded granite for the construction of walls and roads in the park. During the late 1870s, Philip P. Tyre operated a quarry along the Brandywine below Alapocas Woods. He supplied granite used to rebuild the Mount Salem Methodist Church in 1879 after a fire and granite for the Street and Sewer Department to use for curbs along the

city's streets. In 1886 Tyre sold the quarry to the Board of Park Commissioners and moved his operations to a new location on Philadelphia Pike, north of the city.[22]

The quarry that Tyre sold continued to supply granite. By 1917 the D. L. Taylor Company quarried there under a lease arrangement with the park board. In 1918, when the board and the Jessup and Moore Paper Company decided to pave North Park Drive, the quarry supplied the stone. Within a decade, Hubbert and Company had the lease to quarry on a royalty basis from the Brandywine location. Quarrying continued at least through 1938.[23]

Under the direction of the Board of Park Commissioners, quarrying at other sites in the park provided materials for park projects and left behind sheer cliffs as evidence of the excavation. In 1898 the park commissioners sought to beautify the "rocky bluff" at the north end of the Washington Street Bridge. They ordered the removal of 1,500 cubic yards of rock and 3,400 cubic yards of earth, materials used to build walls along the south millrace between Market and West streets. Three years later, concerned about the shabby appearance of "the old quarry" area, the board undertook the construction of a masonry wall on the top of the rock ledge and a battlement that offered a view of the river below. The cliff top was also the site for a concrete and steel pavilion, later known as the Sugar Bowl, constructed at the same time.[24]

There was also quarrying on the opposite side of the Brandywine. In 1896, when workers were preparing the roadbed for sections of South Park Drive, they excavated rock later used as the foundations for park footpaths and for a massive embankment retaining wall along the Brandywine between Market Street and the foot of West Street.[25] In 1903 park work crews began grading Lovering Avenue, which bordered the park, and used stone excavated in the road project to build the wall that stands along the avenue near the foot of Franklin Street. The next year, the commissioners began construction of a retaining wall on Lovering between Harrison and Hancock streets. Because the rock taken out during the roadwork was insufficient to complete the wall, they opened a quarry in the bank below South Park Drive. The quarry survives next to the pavilion overlooking the race and the river. The commissioners also used stone from that quarry site for the flight of steps leading from Franklin Street down to South Park.[26]

Other quarrying operations left their mark on the park's landscape although they ceased before the area became a park. A rocky glen on the south side of South Park Drive, a few hundred yards upstream from where the drive intersects Van Buren Street, is the "old quarry hole" that became a rock garden in 1931 and the site for a horse trough that the Wilmington Fountain Society had relocated there two years earlier.[27]

Evidence of Industry

Two industrial enclaves bracketed the area along the Brandywine that Frederick Law Olmsted examined in December 1883. Downstream, the mills of Brandywine Village flanked the river, and upstream, the Jessup and Moore Paper Company operated at the other end of the proposed park. For many years, the river's water powered mills for miles above Wilmington, although by the 1880s steam had largely replaced waterpower. Near the foot of Adams Street, Timothy Stidham established a gristmill in the 17th century, and by 1822 a "cotton factory" occupied the site. All that remains is a range of scattered stones that are the surviving remnants of the dam that once diverted the Brandywine's water to power these earliest of mills.

By the middle of the 18th century, the flourmills of Brandywine Village occupied this area.[28] Quaker millers from Pennsylvania purchased land on the Brandywine, erected mills, and set about harnessing the power of the river. Their operations had an enduring impact on the appearance of Brandywine Park. In 1762 millers Daniel Byrne and William Moore, wanting to operate on the south side of the Brandywine, laid out the millrace course that still runs parallel to the stream. At the same time, William Marshall erected a dam at the start of the race to divert water that, when it reached the mills near Market Street, would cascade

some 20 feet to power the machinery. Seven years later, William and James Marshall dug a comparable race on the north side of the Brandywine and diverted additional water to turn the mill wheels on that bank.[29]

Brandywine Village was ideally situated for such an endeavor. The nearby fields of Pennsylvania produced abundant wheat for grinding into flour (called "superfine" because of its fine-ground quality), and the Brandywine reliably provided the water to power the milling equipment. In addition, the village stood at the point where the river stopped falling and became tidal. This made it possible for ships to sail from the Atlantic up the Delaware to the Christina, up the Christina to the Brandywine, and up the Brandywine to the mills, where they could be loaded with flour and sail away to the Atlantic and points beyond.[30]

The mills on the south side of the Brandywine ceased operations over several decades. In 1827 the city purchased a mill near the Market Street Bridge and used the location for a pumping station for water that it then distributed to city homes and businesses. By 1890 a series of fires had ended all milling on that side of the river. The city obtained rights to the water in the south millrace, and the water was rerouted directly to the pumping station. The substantial dam diverts water into the race, and the race, measuring 23 feet wide and 4 feet deep, continues to deliver water for treatment and distribution to Wilmington homes. The complex of buildings associated with water pumping and treatment occupies the site of the mills.[31]

On the north side of the river, milling operations waned in the early 20th century. In 1906, 1915, and 1917, the city, through the Board of Water Commissioners, made offers to William Lea and Sons (a milling company) for rights to the water in the north millrace. The company refused to sell unless the commission purchased their entire complex of mill buildings. Finally in 1923, the city obtained the rights to the water in the race without having to acquire the mill property. The mills burned in 1933, and the condominiums on Superfine Lane (built in 1984) stand upon their foundations.[32]

gustine Paper Mills on Brandywine, Near Wilmington, Del.

Starting in 1845, the Jessup and Moore Paper Company operated its Augustine Mill on the site now occupied by the Brandywine Park Condominiums. (Postcard from author's collection.)

Although the city maintained the north race for many years, it did not serve the same useful function as its counterpart on the opposite bank. In the late 1950s, the race was viewed as a liability rather than an asset. In 1959 the Executive Committee received a letter from a neighborhood resident suggesting that the "abandoned open sewer" in North Brandywine Park be filled in (a recommendation that accorded with the board's own plans). As it happened, the Board of Education had selected a nearby site on 18th Street for the new Shortlidge School. The demolition and excavation associated with the school construction supplied the materials needed to fill the raceway, a task completed early in 1960.[33] The Board of Park Commissioners later paved that portion of the race near the zoo and the Josephine Fountain for a parking area and roadway.

The Jessup and Moore Paper Company mill (also on the north side of the river at the upstream end of the park) was not the first industrial operation on the site. The buildings had previously housed a snuff mill and a flour mill before Augustus E. Jessup of Westfield, Massachusetts, and Bloomfield H. Moore, Jessup's son-in-law from

Philadelphia, purchased the property in 1845. The partners turned the mill, known as the Augustine Mill after Augustus Jessup, to the production of fine papers used in the printing of maps and lithographs. By the end of the 1880s, the plant employed 100 workers, produced 23,000 pounds of paper daily, and was one of the first industrial plants in Wilmington to have electric lights.[34]

In the late 1870s, the Philadelphia, Baltimore and Washington Railroad laid a railroad spur, the Brandywine Branch, through the park to link the Jessup and Moore mill with the railroad's main line, which ran parallel to the Delaware River to the east. Over the next century, the mill remained in operation, eventually under the ownership of the Container Corporation of America, and the spur was in use until 1982, when the factory closed. The Brandywine Park Condominiums now occupy the site, and portions of the rail line can still be seen near the zoo.

FUNDING

An important first hurdle facing the Board of Park Commissioners on the journey to building a park along the Brandywine was finding the money to make the necessary purchases. The board had met in December 1883 to receive Olmsted's endorsement for the purchase of the land along the Brandywine. When the Board of Park Commissioners next met in November 1884, Dennis J. Menton, an ex-officio board member due to his chairmanship of the City Council's Finance Committee, advised the commissioners that the $10,000 appropriated for parks for 1884 had been spent to cover other bills. Menton kept the issue of park funding before his fellow council members, and the City Council eventually established a committee to work with members of the Board of Park Commissioners on land acquisition.[35]

Even so, progress was slow. In April 1885, the General Assembly passed legislation allowing the Wilmington City

Council to issue bonds up to $150,000 for land purchases, and the following month the Board of Park Commissioners sent a resolution to the council asking that all the designated land be purchased within a year. Again in June 1885, the Park Commissioners sent a resolution to City Council, recommending immediate purchase of certain designated lands. They observed that, while the 1883 legislation creating the Board of Park Commissioners had given the board insufficient authority to achieve its goals, later legislation had given the necessary powers to the city and asserted that the people of Wilmington wanted the park to become a reality. The commissioners urged the council to act promptly because if there were a delay, the best land would not be available or would have been ruined for park use. Furthermore, they argued, both real estate prices and interest rates were low, making it an ideal time to buy land.[36]

In July 1885, a committee from the City Council

(chaired by Dennis J. Menton) and a committee from the park board visited various potential park locations, including the Brandywine site, and ordered a survey of the river parcels. The two committees agreed that Park Board President William Marriott Canby and council Finance Committee Chair Menton would collaborate to "secure the most favorable terms [for] the lands recommended for purchase."[37] On October 20, 1885, the committees again met jointly and Canby and Menton reported on the results of their meetings with landowners. Both committees agreed that the prices were too high. Canby and Menton were asked to make a careful estimate of the value of the lands proposed for purchase and to go back to the owners to negotiate a price reduction.

At the December 22, 1885, board meeting, Menton reported on the price and availability of land along the Brandywine, and the Board of Park Commissioners again

DENNIS J. MENTON

The legislation establishing the Board of Park Commissioners stipulated that the chair of the City Council's Finance Committee was to be an ex-officio member of the board, and, to the great good fortune of the new commissioners, they had Dennis J. Menton join their number in that capacity in 1884. Menton was a councilman between 1869 and 1886, representing the 10th Ward. His participation in the commission meetings helped sustain the City Council's interest in developing the parks, and his position as chair of the Finance Committee equipped him with knowledge and organizational links that proved essential to the initial steps

toward land purchases. It was Menton who, in June 1885, presented to City Council the park board's resolution recommending purchase of lands along the Brandywine.[49] He and William Marriott Canby (president of the park board) negotiated the initial land purchases. In 1902, when the J. Cloud Elliott estate offered to sell a key tract of land adjacent to North Brandywine Park, Menton accompanied William Poole Bancroft to the City Council meeting to present the Board of Park Commissioners' recommendation that the city accept the offer, which it did.

When Menton's term as councilman ended in 1886, he accepted an appointment to the Board of Park Commissioners. His work on behalf of

the city extended beyond land acquisitions. In 1889 he joined Canby and Bancroft on a trip to New Haven, Connecticut; Boston; Williamstown, Massachusetts; Rochester, New York; and Buffalo, New York. The trip was prompted by the commissioners' wish to "have a better idea of what was done in other cities under similar circumstances, and with a further view of studying by closer observation, the details of Park development."[50] Frederick Law Olmsted had planned parks for Boston and Buffalo, and in Rochester an Olmsted park was under development at the time. In 1897 Menton again accompanied fellow park board members to a convention of park commissioners and park engineers in recommended that City Council use its powers to borrow $150,000 to buy park land. The following February the City Council committee reported to council on the prices that Menton and Canby were able to negotiate, bringing the price for land for North Brandywine Park down from $101,578 to $63,548 and bringing the price for land for South Brandywine Park down from $137,562 to $48,375. The parcels also included 14 houses that would yield income until they needed to be removed so the properties could be put to park use. At the same time as the report, Menton, still a member of City Council, introduced an ordinance directing the council to issue $150,000 in bonds to purchase the recommended lands.[38]

Despite endorsement of the ordinance by the City Council committee, some councilmen opposed the land purchase. In addition to the risk of the purchases increasing taxes, council members argued that "if a park is established 25 or 30 police officers will be required to keep the people from running away with the rocks and bushes and that the park will have to be lighted by at least 50 lamps, which will not cost less than $21.75 each." Others objected to the cost of making the accumulated acres suitable for park use. "To put them in a safe condition," argued a council member, "would cost four or five times as much as is now asked for them."[39] Such objections notwithstanding, the proposal was approved on June 4, 1886, by a vote of 14 in favor and 8 opposed. Mayor Calvin B. Rhoads signed it into law four days later.[40]

Once the first purchases were made, a long period ensued during which the three parties—the Board of Park Commissioners, the City Council, and the General Assembly—fell into a regular pattern of interaction. They negotiated over legislation, bond sales, and the transfer of bond sale proceeds to the Board of Park Commissioners so

Louisville, Kentucky, a journey that took the party to Cincinnati and Indianapolis as well, where they saw other urban parks.[51]

Unlike his fellow park board members, Menton was a skilled laborer who worked with his hands. Born in Ireland in 1845, he came to America with his parents when he was five years old. He had been a ship joiner and eventually became a supervisor and foreman at the Harlan and Hollingsworth shipyard, a company he joined as an apprentice joiner at age 16. Like other members of the board, he served his community. He was a founding member and the first president of the Weccacoe Fire Company at the corner of Jackson and Second streets in Wilmington. He served St. Paul's Catholic Church as a trustee for over two decades.[52] At the end of 1913, when Menton retired from the park board after 27 years' service, the commissioners issued a resolution noting in particular his service on behalf of parks during his tenure on the City Council as well as his "continued interest and activity" as a commissioner in the intervening years.[53]

Menton died in 1922 at the age of 77, and the board marked his death in their minutes. "He was," they record-ed, "very effective in the negotiations and arrangements for the purchases of land for parks (in) the early days of the Park Commission."[54] When Park Superintendent Edward R. Mack wrote about Wilmington's park system in *Wilmington* magazine in 1929, he described the initial bond issue and land purchases, declaring that it was "largely through the efforts of Dennis J. Menton, a bond issue of $150,000 was passed and acquisition of land started."[55]

(Courtesy of Nancy Menton-Lyons.)

WILMINGTON, DEL. BRANDYWINE PARK, WEST STREET ENTRANCE.

The bridge over the south millrace at West Street was installed in 1898. Park superintendent Theodore A. Leisen wanted to construct a masonry bridge, but had to settle for a steel girder bridge instead because of cost. (Postcard from author's collection.)

that work on the park system could go forward. Once the state legislature approved the city's request to issue bonds, the park board continued the funding process by passing a resolution asking the City Council to issue and sell bonds for park improvements. After shepherding the legislation through to enactment, the board instructed the treasurer to ask the council for the appropriated funds, including the proceeds from bond sales.[41]

During the closing years of the 19th century and opening years of the 20th century, the entire board involved itself in issues of funding and in the necessary supporting legislation. Members gathered for special meetings to consider plans and draft legislation to present to the mayor and City Council for the issuance of bonds to support park work. Proposed projects and the cost of additional land purchases and park improvements repeatedly drove the members to approach legislators on both the local and state level for financial support. At its annual meeting at the end of 1909, the board established a Finance Committee of

three members to assist with the commission's work. Several long-serving members of the Finance Committee provided the Board of Park Commissioners with continuity and stability that aided negotiations with the City Council and with the state legislature. They guided the process of funding until the appropriations became a regular part of the city budget and no longer required the constant, eagle-eyed attention of representatives from the park board.[42]

By 1910 all the acreage for Brandywine Park was assembled, and the board's efforts to sustain funding focused on other parks, although financial support for improvements in Brandywine Park continued to occupy the commissioners. Bond issues for park development received the board's steady attention, but, with time, other sources of income—fees, regular appropriations, rental income, and generous gifts from donors—also helped meet the expenses of managing and improving the park.

LAND ACQUISITIONS

The initial land purchases along the Brandywine came within five months of the city's decision to issue its first bonds for park purposes. During those months, Park Commission President William Marriott Canby and City Councilman Dennis J. Menton inspected land, negotiated with the owners, and bargained the asking prices down from a total of $239,140 to $111,923, a level that the board found acceptable. In November 1886, the city acquired its first land plot, purchasing 13 parcels totaling 101.76 acres, 63.44 acres on the north side of the river and 38.32 acres on the south. By the end of the first year during which the Mayor and Council became owners of parkland, they had assembled 103.39 acres for the Board of Park Commissioners to manage as Brandywine Park.[43] By November 1887, the board was managing 126.39 acres that made up the start of Brandywine Park, 103.39 acres of dry land and 23 acres of riverbed.[44]

In 1892 Canby and Menton personally bought land between Wawaset Street and the south millrace from Adams Street to Van Buren Street to secure a right-of-way for the anticipated South Park Drive. The $14,000 purchase was made with the understanding that "funds would be provided the following year for their purchase by the city." Two years later, the City Council considered backing out of the understanding because the agreement to acquire the land from Canby and Menton had been made by a previous council, but in March 1894, ownership passed to the city and the much needed right-of-way was secured.[45] Certain questions were raised regarding whether the transaction had "something wrong in connection with it." A committee investigating whether Canby and Menton had received a commission from their work concluded that the men had not profited in any way by purchasing and reselling the land. Indeed, the committee applauded "the disinterested public spirit of Messrs. Canby and Menton who, without any compensation, have spent much time and labor in the improvement of the Public Parks of the City."[46]

Within 10 years of the first purchases, the total land in Brandywine Park totaled 140 acres, and by the time a new century began, it was 153.79 acres. In 1902 the Board of Park Commissioners was able to add the last substantial parcel of land to Brandywine Park, the Elliott tract. J. Cloud Elliott owned 20 essential acres on the north side of the Brandywine, between Elliott's Run and the Baltimore & Ohio Railroad. Without this land, the commissioners could not extend North Park Drive to connect the downstream end of the park on that side of the river with the upstream end where the pedestrian suspension bridge spanned the water. After Elliott's death in 1897, his executors agreed to sell the "missing piece" for $28,800.[47] With this last section in place, purchases of land for the park were largely complete. Although there were a few later additions, primarily small parcels along Rattlesnake Run, by 1910 the Board of Park Commissioners, mayor, and City Council had assembled the park's 179 acres.

THE STAGE IS SET

Writing in the *Board of Trade Journal* in June 1899, Park Superintendent Theodore A. Leisen was able to declare, "Few cities in this country are more fortunate in their possession of parks than Wilmington, Del." Wilmingtonians were lucky, he asserted, because they had "wild natural scenery, extending into the very heart of the city, and so situated as to enable one within a few minutes [*sic*] walk to lose all signs of city strife and turmoil, narrow streets and their crowded houses, and fulfilling the true mission of the large park—a place of rest from all impressions of daily toil."[48] It is hard to imagine a description that came closer to Frederick Law Olmsted's vision of the ideal urban park and its capacity to address the city's shortcomings. The initial labors of the Board of Park Commissioners appeared to be a confident step in the right direction. Next the commissioners faced the challenges of managing the park they had so optimistically launched.

The West Street entrance to the park linked South Park Drive and

the park's green refreshment with the grid of nearby urban streets.

(Postcard from author's collection.)

Chapter 3

MANAGING THE PARK

Although the character of the challenges facing the Board of Park Commissioners changed with time, their unrelenting nature did not. When one problem had been resolved, another arose to take its place. The commissioners treated the challenges as opportunities and applied their energies to good effect, participating in the creation of the park system in an intense, hands-on way. The men oversaw designs and plans, worked directly with Frederick Law Olmsted, set priorities, and arranged funding to pay for them. Between 1886 (when they bought the first land) and 1891, the commissioners acquired 63.48 acres of land for North Brandywine Park and 40.11 acres for South Brandywine Park, installed four "comfort stations" in the park, and began creating other parks within the city. A number of dedicated allies helped them along the path to success, to the credit of all concerned.

LEADERSHIP

The legislation establishing the Board of Park Commissioners provided little guidance on governance or policies, but the board members, experienced with other institutions, quickly elected William Marriott Canby their president and established an Executive Committee to transact business on the board's behalf between monthly board meetings.[1] Headed by the president and numbering usually three or four members, the committee met weekly and often prepared recommendations for board action. These dedicated men made decisions about park policies, actions, directions, and development. Working closely with the superintendent, they had plans drawn, gathered information, selected projects, authorized work, and oversaw park usage. While they routinely referred matters to the board, they themselves also made far-reaching decisions so the business of Brandywine Park and the Wilmington park system could go forward.

In most infant organizations, the directors manage all aspects of the organization's early operations. The Board of Park Commissioners followed that pattern. During the first full calendar year that they had land to manage, the commissioners decided on park rules, selected a surveyor to make a topographical plan of the park, and approved the Street and Sewer Department's request to lay a storm drain down Rattlesnake Run. In the ensuing months, they purchased park benches, installed lighting, hired a superintendent and four guards, and ordered uniforms for the park guards.[2] The Executive Committee occasionally held special meetings at the sites of particular projects, such as proposed retaining walls, the Brandywine swimming pool, roads, pavilions, and "plantations" of shade trees.[3]

Eventually, the commissioners had a suitable staff and a set of procedures that made their participation in many situations unnecessary, although they were still occasionally seized by fits of micromanagement. In February 1908, for example, the superintendent needed Executive Committee authorization in order to haul ashes to the approach to the Van Buren Street Bridge. Similarly, in 1921, the Executive Committee gave the superintendent "power to act" in regard to installing a railing on a set of park steps. After several seasons during which the park staff issued picnic permits, the Executive Committee suddenly decided in 1932 that the committee needed to review all permit applications.[4]

SAMUEL H. BAYNARD

In 1922, when William Poole Bancroft, now in his late 80s, resigned because of fragile health, the Board of Park Commissioners elected Samuel H. Baynard (1851–1925) as the new president. Baynard had joined the park board in October 1900. In the two decades prior to assuming the presidency, Commissioner Baynard was a special patron who took particular interest in North Brandywine Park, giving generously of his time and wealth to improve the area along 18th Street. Born in 1851, Baynard was a watchmaker by training; he eventually also served as president of two banks and director of a savings and loan. In 1891 he and several other entrepreneurs, including Bancroft, formed the North Side Improvement Company to develop land on the northern bank of the Brandywine. On 60 acres, they laid out the Boulevard (later Baynard Boulevard), subdivided the tract into building lots, and called the neighborhood "Washington Heights."[5]

Baynard's interest in city parks dates from the 1880s. In 1886 he was one of the councilmen, along with Dennis J. Menton, who persuaded the council to enact legislation enabling the initial land purchase for Brandywine Park. After Baynard joined the park board, he personally underwrote much of the cost of improving the Baynard Stadium area.[6] In 1912 the city graded 18th Street between

Samuel H. Baynard, businessman and land developer, was the third president of the Board of Park Commissioners, 1922–25. Baynard Stadium is named after him, a reflection of the time and resources he expended on improvements in that part of the park. (Courtesy of the Delaware Public Archives, Dover, Delaware.)

Van Buren and Franklin streets and left a 12-foot-high bank of soil along the road, obscuring any view of the park for two blocks. Baynard had the mound graded down to a "suitable level," moved the earth to an area west of Franklin, and created the foundation for what became the Baynard Athletic Grounds. "To this work," the board reported, "Mr. Baynard has given his personal supervision." The roadwork made it necessary to extend the Franklin Street sewer, and when no public funds were available for the extension, Baynard underwrote that cost as well. The earthmoving project, which took over a year to complete and involved relocating 40,000 cubic yards of earth, reconfigured an area that had allowed for only one baseball diamond so that it could accommodate three baseball diamonds and a football field.[7]

Three years later, Baynard offered to pay for further grading along 18th Street, but equipment problems and the onset of World War I delayed completion of the work. By 1920, when the project was finished, Baynard had paid some $27,000 to improve North Brandywine Park and the adjacent streets. Within a year, he had also supplied the athletic field with a quarter-mile cinder track and a grandstand, storage facilities for equipment, and changing rooms suitable for athletes.[8]

Baynard was a principal participant in the zoo's founding. In 1904 he had the north fishpond fenced to create a home for "a number of varieties of ducks and geese" and through the Washington Heights Association (on whose board he served), he had two acres of parkland enclosed for two Virginia deer a benefactor had donated. In 1905 the Washington Heights Association changed its name to the Wilmington Free Zoological Association and devoted itself to the stewardship of the zoo. Over the years, Baynard supported work at the zoo through monetary contributions and, in 1922, through his gift of two deer.[9]

When Baynard died in 1925, after only three years as board president, the park commissioners honored him for his energy, enthusiasm, and generosity. Nearly every annual report during his board tenure mentioned funding that Baynard had supplied for improvements in the park. Although his impact as president was necessarily limited because of the short period he served, during his 25 years as a commissioner, he led by his example of financial support, vision, attention to detail, and dedicated stewardship.[10]

EDGAR L. HAYNES

Following Baynard's death, the Board of Park Commissioners elected Edgar L. Haynes (1860–1956) as the fourth president.[11] Born in 1860, he entered the world of business in the 1880s when he joined the business office of a local newspaper, the *Daily News*. He rose to become manager and part owner of the paper, but sold his share in 1920 to go into banking. Elected a director of Artisans' Savings Bank in 1919, he was subsequently elected the

bank's vice president. He also served on the boards of the Wilmington and Brandywine Cemetery and of the Wilmington Fountain Society.[12]

Haynes joined the Park Commission in 1911 and he remained on the board for 45 years, until his death in 1956 at the age of 95. Although he served on the Park Extension Committee, it was as president that Haynes had the greatest influence on the park system. The enduring project that marked his presidency was the creation of a rose garden in North Brandywine Park. Haynes had reportedly long dreamt of establishing such a garden and the circumstances of the Great Depression made the dream a reality. During 1933 and 1934, federal funds routed through the city helped pay unemployed laborers to work on the garden while the Board of Park Commissioners supplied the other materials required—earth for filling and leveling the site, posts for the simple fence around the garden, iron arches for the gateways. DuPont Company vice president Jasper E. Crane donated the original 670 plants.[13]

During Haynes' presidency, the country was convulsed first by the Great Depression and then by World War II; yet his leadership allowed the park system to flourish in the face of these challenges. In the 1930s, the park board collaborated with government agencies to put unemployed workers back to work. The rose garden project was possible because of funding from the Public Works Administration. Before the New Deal programs ended, Brandywine Park gained three pavilions, a stone bridge over Elliott's Run, toilets, and improved roads as well as the rose garden. Park usage increased during the Depression years as people sought to entertain themselves with activities that were free. They visited the parks in increasing numbers, a trend that continued into the 1940s as wartime gasoline and tire rationing made automobile travel difficult.

Described as a man with a deep "appreciation of the tremendous value of the parks and playgrounds to this and future generations."[14] Haynes himself was quick to credit previous commissioners who had "laid the foundation for a park system so well that it has been a pleasure to its successors to continue the work."[15] But his impact was considerable. When Haynes took office in 1925, the Wilmington park system encompassed 582 acres, and when he left office in 1950, it totaled 1,057 acres. He continued on the park board for another six years, serving as president emeritus until his death. His colleagues praised him for his "long and faithful service and his many contributions to the public welfare." They recalled with gratitude his "untiring efforts toward the improvement and operation of the Park System for the enduring benefit of all the people of Wilmington" and noted particularly the respect accorded him in the community.[16] His legacy to the parks was both in the improvements to the park system that he left behind and in the monetary bequest he made in trust for future park projects, $10,000 of which was restricted to use on Haynes Park, which had been 30th Street Park until 1950 when the commissioners renamed it in honor of their retiring president.[17]

M. DU PONT LEE

When Haynes resigned his presidency, the commissioners elected M. du Pont Lee (1885–1974) as the fifth president of the Board of Park Commissioners. Born in 1885 and trained as a mechanical engineer, Lee joined the DuPont Company soon after college graduation. After an initial two-year assignment in purchasing, he began to use his engineering training, first on company construction projects and then on design projects. His DuPont career was marked by notable work in the development of dyes, rayon, and cellophane. Lee was a director and then officer of a company subsidiary, and he finished out his business career in the position of general adviser to the company's chief engineer, an office he held from 1946 until his retirement in 1950.[18]

Even before his retirement, Lee was active in the community, helping to organize Alcoholics Anonymous in Wilmington in the mid-1940s. In 1948 he accepted an appointment to the Board of Park Commissioners and the commission members elected him president in 1950. When he retired from DuPont in 1950, he began a second career, one of philanthropy and community service. He headed the city's Civil Defense organization from 1950 to 1952; at the same time, he set up Consulting and Advisory Services, Inc., an organization that assisted small business operators with free advice from retired business people.[19] In the mid-1960s, he worked actively with Just One Break (JOB), a group that helped people with physical and mental disabilities find employment.[20]

Lee proved a great asset to the park board as an advocate on behalf of recreation and open space. Described in an editorial as having "all of the zeal of an old timer," he took seriously his role

Edgar L. Haynes, left, was president of the Board of Park Commissioners from 1925 to 1950 and then was named president emeritus, a title he held until his death. M. du Pont Lee, right, led the Board from 1950 until 1965. (Courtesy of the Delaware Public Archives, Dover, Delaware.)

as a steward of the city's parks. "He considered every square inch of parkland to be sacred," declared the editorial, "and he fought every move, even by school officials, to lay paws upon it."[21]

Lee had been board president for five years when the Board of Education proposed taking part of North Brandywine Park in order to erect a new elementary school. Lee's reply to the Board of Education articulated why parks were important and captured the passion that fired his leadership. Enumerating the "many requests for the use of our park lands for other than their intended purposes," he identified the threats that put the parks at risk. In recent months, he recounted, the board had been asked to pave Rodney Square for parking, to give up public land for use as a "private pushmobile slide," to allow streets to be extended through park areas, to run a multilane highway through North Brandywine Park parallel to 18th Street, and to straighten and double the size of South Park Drive from Market Street to the Art Museum. "I think," he concluded, "that if we concur (with) … these various suggestions, all of which have been seriously made, the Brandywine Park System will be almost completely eliminated." Parkland was "free and open," but that did not mean it was available for such uses.[22]

Although his defense against encroachment by the Board of Education was successful, his attempt to keep an interstate highway, I-95, from crossing Brandywine Park was not. He again eloquently defended the park as necessary open space and a key site for recreation, but when it was readily apparent that the highway would be built regardless of the board's opposition, he took the practical position of working with the State Highway Department to ensure both that land would be given to replace the area lost and that the park board would have a voice in the design of the highway bridge to be built across the park.[23]

In addition to fighting these battles, Lee also led the Board of Park Commissioners as they navigated the perilous racial issues that arose in the 1950s. Described as a man who was dedicated to the idea "of making recreation and enjoyment of the beauties of nature available to as many

persons as possible," he believed such benefits extended to all Wilmingtonians. This was never truer than in 1956, when the municipal swimming pools were integrated without incident. Lee maintained that it was a success because "the plans were not publicized first."[24]

Lee opposed the revised City Charter that meant the end of the Board of Park Commissioners, suggesting that it would "spell disaster for the city's wonderful parklands."[25] By the time the charter's provisions dissolved the Board of Park Commissioners in 1967, Lee had retired, resigning in 1965 because of ill health. His colleagues immediately elected him president emeritus, a title he held until his death in 1974.

Edwin F. Koester

When M. du Pont Lee resigned, the commission members elected as president Edwin F. Koester (1892–1978), the man who would preside over the last meetings of the Board of Park Commissioners. Koester had been an ex-officio member of the commission from 1918 to 1957 because of his position in city government as chief engineer of the Surveying Department.[26] As an ex-officio board member, he served on the Planting and Horticulture Committee and the Executive Committee, and in 1957 he accepted appointment to the board as a commissioner. Because his tenure as president was short, the accomplishments to his credit were necessarily limited. During his 18 months as the commission's head, he saw the commissioners through the final tasks associated with construction of the interstate highway across one end of the park, and he prepared for the transfer of responsibilities to the new Department of Parks and Recreation. Presiding over the last meeting of Board of Park Commissioners on June 14, 1967, he thanked the commissioners for their service, recognized all of the members who had served since 1883, and, on behalf of the departing commission, expressed the board's hope for "continued operation of the park system on a sound and sensible basis."[27]

CHANGING MANAGERS

By the mid-1960s, the Board of Park Commissioners was managing 1,057 acres of land throughout the city, had outfitted the 46 parks and playgrounds with equipment and amenities, and was providing a wide-ranging program of recreational activities. In 1967, however, a massive change occurred that the first commissioners probably could not have envisioned. A reform of the City Charter disbanded the Board of Park Commissioners and established a Department of Parks and Recreation with a paid staff.

The reform of the City Charter was not uniformly welcomed. Certainly the timing was unlucky. Within a year of the last meeting of the Board of Park Commissioners in June 1967, the city was shaken by excruciating civil unrest following the death of Dr. Martin Luther King Jr. For nine months, the Delaware Army National Guard occupied the city. The turmoil and unhappiness had a shattering impact on the community, leaving many residents disheartened and others bitter and resentful. By the middle of 1968, when the Department of Parks and Recreation produced its *Annual Report*, director William Kapa indicated, "the condition of the parks has probably reached one of its lowest points." The situation arose because of "vandalism, disrespect for public property, elimination of the Park Police" and an array of difficulties arising from inadequate funding for wages, supplies, and maintenance.[28]

A year later, circumstances changed again when the City of Wilmington and New Castle County signed a 40-year lease agreement under which the county assumed responsibility for managing Brandywine, Rockford, Alapocas, and Canby parks as well as Green Hill Golf Course. The lease took effect on July 1, 1970, with the full merger completed by July 1, 1971. The city retained ownership of the park areas coming under county management, and the county assumed personnel, capital, and operating costs.

After two decades, State Representative Joseph G. Di Pinto, dissatisfied with the care being given to the park, initiated discussions to shift management responsibilities for Brandywine Park from New Castle County to the Delaware Division of Parks and Recreation, a unit of the state's Department of Natural Resources and Environmental Control. In conversations with the division's director, Charles Salkin, he developed his argument: Wilmington had no state park, and the city's premier parks—Brandywine Park, Rockford Park, Kentmere Parkway, Alapocas Woods, and H. Fletcher Brown Park—would be a good collective candidate for state management. Because assuming management of an urban park would be a substantial new step for the division, Salkin was cautious, indicating that funding was key and that it had to be sufficient to cover an on-site administrative staff and a park law enforcement team. Through the assistance of Governor Thomas R. Carper's office, negotiations proceeded until, on a sunny April morning in 1998, a small crowd gathered on the meadow below Rockford Tower to watch the transfer of management. Brandywine Park, Rockford Park, Kentmere Parkway, Alapocas Woods, and H. Fletcher Brown Park had become the Wilmington State Parks.

MANAGING THE PARK'S LIFE

The commercial and professional experience of the first commissioners prepared them well for managing the park in a businesslike manner, weighing needs and projects against funds, husbanding their financial and personnel resources, and protecting the park's assets. The board got off to a good start by investigating how other cities established and operated their parks. They provided themselves with a good initial survey so that infrastructure could be properly planned and they attempted to mesh their plans with projects undertaken by other city departments, most notably the Water Department and the Street and Sewer Department.[29]

The park board had had to balance routine work against special projects. An array of constant, year-round work faced the park staff—maintenance of roads, footpaths, and park buildings and equipment; seasonal care of trees, shrubs, and lawns; snow removal; care of the swimming pool; and the myriad unique tasks that arose in spite of war or economic hard times.[30]

With the basic infrastructure of Brandywine Park established, the board considered park improvements. Theodore A. Leisen, superintendent from 1893 to 1903, filled his monthly reports with projects to be undertaken years into the future. In 1895, even as the park road system was under construction, he recommended building "a pavilion ... on the edge of the bluff near the northerly end of the Washington Street Bridge." The board saw the project through to completion with construction of the "Sugar Bowl" pavilion in 1902. In 1900 Leisen proposed a bridge across the Brandywine near the foot of Rattlesnake Run. His plan called for a concrete span with three 60-foot arches in the creek, 30-foot arches at each approach, a 20-foot roadway, and two 5-foot sidewalks. Although that particular bridge was not constructed, Leisen's design was not wasted. The Van Buren Street Bridge, built six years later, was remarkably similar: made of concrete, with three 58-foot arches in the creek, 28-foot arches at the approaches, a 9-foot arch on the south side for pedestrians, and roadway and sidewalks comparable to the earlier proposed structure.[31]

In their 1929 booklet *The Parks and Playgrounds of Wilmington, Delaware*, the commissioners published a list of future improvements—playgrounds, swimming pools, baseball diamonds, tennis courts, paths, and new lights in "undeveloped park land."[32] During the Depression, board representatives carried to meetings with the Mayor's Emergency Relief Commission lists of projects that could be done "under the Public Works Act"— paving roads, improving footpaths, installing drains, and constructing toilets. Even during World War II, the board thought ahead to peacetime and projects to be undertaken after the war.[33] The park board's annual reports from the mid-1950s onward list proposals for the future. The 1955–56 *Annual Report*, for example, projected improvements for the next 5, 10, and 15 years. The report anticipated increasingly heavy use of the parks but rather seriously misread trends when it imagined incorrectly that large numbers of people would come into the city from the suburbs to use the parks.[34]

For all the routine tasks that came their way, the commissioners also had their share of odd, one-of-kind issues. In 1909, for example, the state ornithologist advised the Executive Committee that "red squirrels destroy birds eggs and drive out grey squirrels which do not destroy eggs," and, based on this information, the commissioners directed the superintendent "to have (the red squirrels) killed wherever possible."[35] In 1935 they considered an earnest letter from a local man who, in a spirit of admirable entrepreneurship during the lean years of the Depression, offered birdhouses for sale. "I am the builder," he wrote, "of a fine collection of BIRD-HOUSES, which would help beautifie peoples RESIDENCES, PARKS, GARDENS, PLOTTS, TRACTS, and LAWNS." [*sic*] He offered 28 birdhouses of different designs and sizes, different from any built in Wilmington or in the state, and "painted with DuPont paint."[36]

The commissioners expressed their cartographic preference in 1936 when they passed a resolution that "in the future when plans are presented to this board and plans made by this department shall have an arrow indicating the north point."[37] They responded to complaints about men and boys swimming nude in the Brandywine and disturbing Sunday promenaders. They crafted a procedure for turning out park lights during World War II blackouts and dealt with cows and horses turned loose to graze on playgrounds.[38]

FUNDING—THE CHALLENGE THAT NEVER SEEMED TO GO AWAY

Although by 1910 the city had assembled all the acreage that was to make up Brandywine Park, the board continued to face funding challenges, struggling to secure needed support to purchase land for other parks and to improve Brandywine Park. Annually the board and park superintendent proposed a list of projects and their costs, appended an account of on-going expenses, and prepared a resolution that they sent to City Council, asking the councilmen to borrow the designated amounts by issuing and selling bonds. After the bonds were sold, the board went back to the council to ask for the money raised by the sales.

Budget allocations often fell short of the board's request. In 1896 lack of funds caused the superintendent to lay off men working on road construction.[39] The *Annual Report* described the situation:

> Many censorious criticisms have been directed against this department on account of the incomplete condition of the driveway; the failure to have the Barley Mill Dam built; the lack of foot walks, and the absence of other accommodations in general, which are looked for in a public pleasure ground. This criticism has come both from the Press and Public, probably without a proper appreciation of the existing conditions. There is but one way of obtaining these accommodations, namely: by furnishing this department with an appropriation commensurate with the work before it.[40]

In 1911 William Poole Bancroft complained to the Mayor's Advisory Board that funding would not last through the next few weeks. Although City Councilman James Kane assured him that "Council will not let the park board want for money," Bancroft had arranged with the Park Commission's bank "to temporarily overdraw the account," a stopgap measure until the arrival of an anticipated $20,000 at the start of the fiscal year on July 1, 1911.[41] A year later, Bancroft again expressed disappointment after the board requested $23,000 but received only $18,000. As a result, "he did not know how they would make ends meet."[42] The 1913 *Annual Report* noted that "owing to the lack of funds it has been necessary to cut the expenditures to a point below that necessary for proper maintenance," and many important tasks were left undone.[43]

The board did not have to rely solely on city appropriations, however. The commission also received income from rental payments and fees and from a variety of benefactors. The houses that the board acquired when it purchased land for the park generated monthly rental income ranging from $7 to $15 per dwelling. The first parcels of land acquired for Brandywine Park included 12 houses, some stone and some frame, that the board felt,

might provide "moderate revenue" until the land was needed for park purposes.[44] The rental properties, of course, brought with them management responsibilities as well. In 1894, when the board acquired land at the foot of Adams Street, it also acquired a two-story stone house at 1601 Adams Street. In 1902 the commission paid $34.50 for repairs to the house's porch and the next year expended $8 to have the dwelling's parlor papered. The commissioners continued to maintain and rent the house until they demolished it in 1928.[45] At other properties, the commissioners had fences built, rooms painted, roofs repaired, and cesspools cleaned.

In addition, the DuPont Company paid $30 per year for Griffith Farm, and the Wilmington and New Jersey Ferry Company's annual rent for use of the 4th Street Wharf Lot was $150. Several businesses made annual payments to the board for the rights-of-way that they used across parkland. The Hartmann and Fehrenbach Brewing Company paid $10 for the right-of-way for a drain that crossed part of Brandywine Park, and the Delaware and Atlantic Telephone Company paid $1 to run lines across parkland.[46]

The collection of fees at the swimming pool, the receipt of fees from entrepreneurs for the privilege of plying their trade on park property, and the sale of wood or materials from the park also generated modest revenues. Several entrepreneurs sought licenses to do business in the park. In 1887 and 1888, T. L. Robinson operated a refreshment stand and "daguerreotype salon," where he produced an early type of photographic image. James H. Powell was permitted to operate a "photograph tent" at the foot of Adams Street in 1892 and 1893, though he apparently offered only pictures and no food or drink.[47]

In 1894 Henry S. Black and Company operated a "refreshment pavilion," a 16- by 30-foot structure near the dam in South Brandywine Park. Black's agreement with the board gave him the exclusive right to sell cigars, ice cream, soda water, and "general refreshments" along the south bank of the river. For this privilege, he paid $10 per month plus

3 percent of his gross receipts. He opened for business on June 1, 1894, but his first month was not as prosperous as he had hoped. His payment for June was $14.73—$10 rent plus $4.73 (the 3 percent of gross earnings). By the first of August, Black asked to be relieved of paying the 3 percent because business was so poor.[48]

Although interest in operating businesses in the park continued, by 1911 the commissioners took an unofficial stand against such endeavors, a position that they elevated to policy in 1922.[49] One of the rare exceptions to this rule occurred in the mid-1950s when Nilon Brothers reached an agreement with the board to operate a concession at the zoo. A key factor in the operation was that it earned sufficient profit to help pay off the debt associated with the creation of the Children's Zoo.[50]

In the 1960s, there was a brief flirtation with professional sports in Brandywine Park. In 1962 the Delaware Semi-Pro Baseball League installed lights on one of the diamonds in North Brandywine Park for a night game and charged a nominal fee. In the 1960s, the North American Football League negotiated to rent Baynard Stadium. The board initially declined the league's request to use the stadium because there was already a full calendar of

Parks Department and local school events. In April 1965, however, the board approved professional football in the stadium "for this season only," pending the mayor's approval. During the 1965–66 football season, the Wilmington Comets, part of the North American Football League, played in Baynard Stadium, and the following season, the Wilmington Clippers, associated with the Atlantic Coast Football League, used the stadium for their home game. The Clippers disbanded in September 1967 after two exhibition games and two league games because poor attendance numbers made it impossible for the owners to cover their costs.[51]

There were a few odd commercial proposals that received little serious consideration. In 1904 the board declined to allow L. H. Swartz to install a shooting gallery in the park and three years later, refused the applications of the Wilmington Amusement Company and the White City Amusement Company, each wanting to establish an amusement park in North Brandywine Park. The answer was also "no" to the representatives of the Wilmington Real Estate Board who suggested the board "operate a Tourist Camp in the neighborhood of Union Park Gardens or North Brandywine Park." In the 1950s, General Motors and the Electrical Appliance Dealers of Delaware both asked to use a portion of the park for commercial exhibits; the board turned them down.[52]

As the success of the park system gained public notice, private benefactors came forward to fund aspects of park operations. Board members themselves were among the most generous donors. William Poole Bancroft often underwrote projects where funds were short and Samuel H. Baynard's personal gifts helped shape North Brandywine Park. The Washington Heights Association, later the Wilmington Free Zoological Association, provided regular support for zoo improvements and operations.[53] Similarly, after William H. Todd donated a war memorial in North Brandywine Park, he followed up his gift with additional financial support for landscaping and maintenance.[54]

In 1927 the Board of Park Commissioners received a $20,000 bequest (the start of an endowment fund) under the will of May du Pont Saulsbury. Interest from the fund was to be disbursed periodically "for the permanent improvement of Brandywine and Rockford Parks."[55] In 1935 board president Edgar L. Haynes conferred with the city solicitor about establishing a park trust fund to manage the Saulsbury bequest and any future endowment gifts. By the end of 1935, the Wilmington Park Trust Fund Commission was a reality, and the principal bequest from Mrs. Saulsbury, plus another benefactor's $1,500 bequest, were transferred into the new commission's care. The following summer the board received its first disbursement, $215 of accrued interest from the gifts.

The park board also benefited from donors whose gifts freed the commissioners from expenses they would otherwise have borne. The Wilmington Fountain Society (organized in 1870) stands out as such a benefactor. From the early years of the 20th century, the Fountain Society supplied the park with water fountains for people, stone troughs for horses, and birdbaths, providing "a great amount of comfort to man and the dumb animals." The group's work in Brandywine Park began in 1904 when they installed the Mather fountain on South Park Drive west of Van Buren.[56] A watering trough for horses, the fountain proved unsatisfactory because of its design and insufficient water flow. The society eventually removed it and replaced it with a round granite fountain relocated from Market and 16th streets.

The granite fountain that the Fountain Society moved from Market Street to South Park Drive was a gift to the city in 1909. Donated by the National Humane Alliance to provide water for thirsty horses, it was installed through the cooperative efforts of the Wilmington Fountain Society, the Board of Park Commissioners, and the Street and Sewer Department.[57] By the late 1920s, however, increased reliance on automobiles and a corresponding decrease in the use of horses made it less essential. In addition, when plans were made for the new Market Street Bridge in 1928, the fountain stood in the path of the new traffic pattern, so the Fountain Society offered to remove it to a new location. After considering relocating it to the picnic grove in Rockford Park, the society and the Board of Park Commissioners settled on the current location on South Park Drive.[58] In the 1930s, the board improved the area around the fountain, creating a rock garden in the craggy cliff behind it. In the early years of the 21st century, state parks personnel addressed its neglected condition with substantial restoration work.

In the years following its first gifts to the park, the Fountain Society regularly installed drinking fountains and birdbaths wherever they seemed to be needed. In 1924 they placed a drinking fountain at the corner of Adams Street and South Park Drive, a fixture that was updated in 1940 and still occupied the site as late as 1956. They installed "pedestal type" fountains at the Rowan Street tennis courts, Baynard Stadium, and at the corner of 18th and Van Buren streets in 1925. By the end of the 1930s, the society had installed fountains at Rattlesnake Run, the Van Buren Street tennis courts, the zoo, the recently built picnic pavilion on the hilltop above the raceway in South Brandywine Park, near Elliott's Run, and along the path in South Brandywine Park.[59]

As horses became scarcer on Wilmington's streets, the park board provided space for the Fountain Society to store troughs that were no longer needed, and in 1924 park board member Edgar L. Haynes joined the board of the Fountain Society, rising to vice president of the group in 1933. In the mid-1960s, the Wilmington Fountain Society decided to cease operations. Its board offered to the Board of Park Commissioners the organization's assets, which totaled $65,000. In September 1966, the Wilmington Park Trust Fund Commission accepted the assets "to be held in trust by the commission for purposes set forth in the Society's charter."[60] The Fountain Society and the Park Trust Fund Commission agreed that the funds would be restricted to use for fountains and that "the capital funds are not to be spent but that income is to be used for the upkeep of the fountains." Any excess could be used as the commissioners desired.[61] The Park Trust Fund Commission continues to meet quarterly and disburses funds for grounds care and beautification for several city parks. Recently, the trust fund commissioners provided support to the Friends of Wilmington Parks for restoration of the Jasper Crane Rose Garden.

GRAPPLING WITH CHALLENGES, WRESTLING WITH ISSUES

When the Board of Park Commissioners came into being, Wilmington was a racially segregated community, and the commissioners were called to address racial concerns from time to time. In 1913 Wilmington's City Council forwarded to the board a request from Councilman John O. Hopkins, who asked that the municipal swimming pools, at the time numbering three and all used exclusively by white Wilmingtonians, "be open at least one day a week to the colored citizens." The board's response was a resolution asking City Council to provide the funding needed to build a swimming pool for the city's black residents.[62] The funding was forthcoming, and on June 27, 1914, over 1,700 people attended the ceremonies when the pool at 16th and Poplar streets was "opened with appropriate exercises." The Odd Fellows' Band supplied music, there were speeches from political leaders, and a new American flag was raised over the bathhouse.[63]

Black Wilmingtonians continued to press the board for better and more extensive recreational services for their community. The board, always chronically short of funding, responded as well as it could to the requests. The pattern of annual requests and board responses continued largely unchanged for several years, with efforts falling short of what many thought was needed. The board's own report in 1929 described the state of recreational facilities for the black community as "inadequate" and identified potential future sites for playgrounds and parks.[64] A 1938–39 recreation survey recommended construction on unused schoolyards of playgrounds for both white and black children.[65] Through the 1940s, the two races operated in separate, roughly parallel spheres, with playgrounds and swimming pools designated for each group, although by the end of the decade, the board granted permits for the Boy Scouts "to hold a Camporee for Negro Scouts in Bringhurst Woods" and for scouting activities at Canby Park.[66]

Board members seemed to accept the status quo regarding segregation, but on at least one occasion the commissioners made clear their unwillingness to accept the racism that some Delawareans embraced. In the early 1920s, the Ku Klux Klan made a strong reappearance in many parts of the country, and in 1921, the Klan launched an organizing campaign in Delaware. Between 1923 and 1926, newspapers reported at least six Klan rallies attracting between 1,000 and 2,000 people each.[67] In June 1926, the Board of Park Commissioners received a request to use North Brandywine Park for a meeting "in the interest of the Ku Klux Klan." When the man asking permission attended a board meeting to make his request in person, the commissioners advised him that, "as a quorum was not present action was deferred," and the man was asked to "present an application signed by members of his Committee."[68] There is no record of an application ever being filed. Interestingly, the lack of a quorum did not prevent the board from granting permission to another local group at the same meeting for a festival at Kirkwood Park. The Board of Park Commissioners could not stop the Ku Klux Klan, but they could keep the Klan out of the city's parks.

Interstate 95, constructed in the mid-1960s, included the I-95 Bridge spanning the Brandywine through the park. (Postcard from author's collection.)

After the 1954 school desegregation decision of *Brown v. Board of Education*, the commission worked toward a quiet transition from the segregation of parks and facilities to integration of the properties and programs under its control. Wilmington's schools were integrated without incident in the autumn of 1955. In the summer of 1956, municipal swimming pools were also integrated, again without incident. In a letter to the local press, board president M. du Pont Lee publicly thanked city residents and park personnel for their "handling of the city swimming pool integration policy." He later speculated that the process went smoothly because plans were not publicized before the change was instituted.[69]

Another central issue that confronted the Board of Park Commissioners was the challenge of protecting Brandywine Park's land from being lost to nonpark uses. In 1955 the Board of Education argued that it needed to use parkland for a new school and the Park Commissioners declined. Park Board president Lee, in an articulate letter to the Board of Education, detailed why parks existed, identified the many risks facing the parks, and reiterated the Park Commission's responsibility to protect them for the good of the community.[70] The controversy ended up in court and, in the end, the Court of Chancery ruled in favor

of the Board of Park Commissioners and issued an order banning the sale of parkland for a school site.

As the Board of Park Commissioners was saying "no" to the Board of Education, advocates of another, much larger project began an assault on Brandywine Park. In March 1957, the commission attended the first meeting about a "proposed expressway through the western part of the city." During discussions of the project, Lee again defended the parks and repeated the board's vision of its duty to preserve the park resources, including open space. In the 1956–57 *Annual Report*, Director of Parks and Recreation John B. Quinn characterized the threats to the parks as "this 'land-grab' disease" that was "already prevalent in many municipalities throughout the country today." He described efforts to use parks "for schools, armories, super-highways, public housing, developments, etc." and noted that highway planners take the line of least resistance, across land dedicated to the public.[71] In spite of the board's determination and the passion of the director of Parks and Recreation, the project prevailed: I-95 (and a bridge across the end of the park) opened in 1967.[72]

Another small portion of the park also succumbed to an alternative use at the end of the 1950s. In 1929 the Board of Water Commissioners had proposed building a pumping station in South Brandywine Park, but the request languished until 1958 when the board gave approval for such a facility in North Brandywine Park. Completed in 1959, the Water Commissioners named the pumping station after W. Compton Wills, chief engineer of the Water Department.[73]

Even as the I-95 project was under way, the State Highway Department put forward another road building project across Brandywine Park. In early 1965, the highway planners proposed a highway following the "scenic route" along the north bank of the Brandywine, from the Market Street Bridge through the park and along the stream to the Pennsylvania line. The board emphatically opposed the project, sending its objections to the Highway Department with copies to the mayor and governor.[74] The board prevailed in its effort to keep a new thoroughfare out of the park, but, in the face of the newly completed pumping station and the ongoing interstate highway work, the success probably felt like a very small victory indeed.

OUTREACH NEAR AND FAR

The Board of Park Commissioners sought a good relationship with residents in neighborhoods near the park. Early in Brandywine Park's history, the people living in newly developed Washington Heights occasionally asked permission to hold community events on the triangle of land bounded by Washington and 18th streets and the Boulevard—"Washington Triangle" to those who lived nearby.[75] The Washington Heights Association's 4th of July celebration in 1908 attracted 10,000 "enthusiastic Americans" to the triangle, where they enjoyed patriotic speeches, music, a flag raising, and "a magnificent display of fireworks."[76]

If they could, the commissioners granted the requests that came their way. They agreed to let neighbors plant flowers along the retaining wall on Monkey Hill and gave permission for another group to erect a flagpole on park property at Van Buren and Lovering. They allowed students from Warner Junior High School to take a park boulder "to be used as a memorial to the boys from Warner School who lost their lives in World War II" and supported neighborhood seasonal celebrations and events.[77]

The board saw a need for positive outreach to the park's commercial neighbors as well. In 1894 workers at Jessup and Moore's Augustine Mill complained about the steps approaching the pedestrian footbridge across the Brandywine. The board instructed the superintendent to put the area "in good condition" and keep it that way.[78] In 1913 the Wilmington and Brandywine Cemetery was building a chapel, and the board agreed to allow the cemetery company to dump excavated dirt from the construction project in the park. The commissioners worked cooperatively with the Jessup and Moore Paper Company and the Taylor quarry in 1917 and 1918 when North Park Drive needed repairs. For several years in the late 1940s and early 1950s, it allowed the Chamber of Commerce to use a portion of North Brandywine Park each November as the site for inflating the giant balloons used in the organization's annual Christmas parade.[79]

Members of the board collaborated with other boards in the city as well. In 1898, for example, when a set of steps next to the Washington Street Bridge was proposed to connect Washington Street with Park Drive below, the Board of Park Commissioners, the Board of Education, and the Street and Sewer Department shared the cost equally, each agency paying $311.60.[80] Beginning in 1907, the president of the park board participated in meetings of the City Executive Board (renamed the Mayor's Advisory Board in 1909). Created in 1907 by a City Charter amendment, the group included the presidents or chairs of the commissions that oversaw aspects of the city's operations—Street and Sewer, Water, Police, Education, and Health—plus the mayor and two members of the City Council.

The meetings were the ideal setting for the leaders to exchange information, share concerns, solicit pledges of mutual assistance, and forge collaborative relationships. When the park board wanted to pave Monkey Hill for the first time, park board president Samuel H. Baynard used a Mayor's Advisory Board meeting to ask Frank Pierson of the Street and Sewer Department if his department "could let the park board have some of the Belgian blocks ... which are being removed from some of the streets," and he was assured that there were plenty available. Before the year was over, the Street and Sewer Department delivered the needed paving materials.[81]

During the 1920s and 1930s, economic hardships allowed for meaningful outreach. In the years immediately after World War I, many of Wilmington's industries operated at less than full capacity, and large numbers of workers lost their jobs.[82] The Mayor's Advisory Board discussed the need to find jobs for unemployed Wilmingtonians. In October 1921, the men discussed steps taken "in connection with the unemployment situation," and at the end of the year, the mayor "requested each member [of the Mayor's Advisory Board] to bear in mind the Emergency Relief Fund."[83] The following spring, the park board reported that the park staff was making "all possible use" of workers sent to them, and by the end of 1922, the workers paid from the Mayor's Emergency Relief Fund provided sufficient labor to complete a number of projects that "would have been impossible to ever obtain an appropriation to do."[84]

After the 1929 stock market crash, unemployment loomed even larger on the economic horizon, and the Board of Park Commissioners found itself collaborating with federal relief agencies on several projects. As early as November 1930, the board provided work "as a relief to unemployment" for 45 men, and through the 1930s, Brandywine Park was one of the sites where workers from the Public Works Administration, the Works Progress Administration, the Civil Works Administration, and the National Youth Administration labored at one time or another.[85] As a result of their efforts, the park welcomed the addition of the Jasper Crane Rose Garden, three pavilions, and a stone fireplace in a picnic area. Workers under these programs graded roads and paths, laid pipes to improve drainage near the Josephine Fountain, repaired the roofs of the Brandywine Pool and one of the park pavilions, and helped construct park comfort stations.[86]

The board maintained a long, collaborative relationship with Recreation, Promotion and Service, Inc., a local nonprofit organization that, beginning in 1950, sponsored the "Old Timers' Picnic" every year in Brandywine Park. The picnic, an event for people of retirement age, featured music, dancing, games, and

contests.[87] The picnics continued after New Castle County assumed management of Brandywine Park, although they moved to other county park locations. Indeed, the event (now called the "Platinum Picnic") is still held annually under county auspices. During the 1950s, Recreation, Promotion and Service, Inc., sponsored summer concerts in North Brandywine Park near the Josephine Fountain, and in September 1961 the group staged the first Brandywine Arts Festival. It was a one-day juried clothesline art show that attracted 300 artists and included an ox roast as part of the day's activities.[88]

The board maintained useful memberships in national organizations devoted to park interests, and board members and the park superintendent attended numerous professional meetings that gave them the chance to see the Wilmington park system in relation to other urban parks. In 1897 board representatives attended the Park Commissioners and Park Engineers Convention in Louisville, Kentucky, a trip that also allowed them to see parks in Cincinnati and Indianapolis. The park superintendent regularly participated in meetings of the American Civic Association, the City Planning Conference, and the American Association of Park Superintendents. At the mayor's suggestion, Park Superintendent Edward R. Mack attended the 1917 Pittsburgh convention of the American Association for Promoting Public Baths to see what information he could gather to benefit the operation of the park swimming pool.[89]

The park superintendent and park personnel kept abreast of developments in park operations elsewhere through a variety of publications. In the late 1890s and early 1900s, the superintendents purchased books on landscape gardening and subscribed to *Park and Cemetery*, a monthly magazine devoted to management issues of public grounds. In 1909 Superintendent Mack added *Good Roads* magazine to his resources and in 1914, as playgrounds became increasingly important, *Playground Magazine*.[90]

Communication flowed in both directions as various journals showed an interest in Wilmington park developments. In May 1897, *Park and Cemetery* magazine wrote to

Superintendent Leisen asking for photographs of "your park" for publication.[91] Leisen apparently wrote articles about Wilmington's parks for various journals because he received requests for copies of his writings. In May 1898, a writer contacted Leisen about a "report" by the superintendent that he had "noticed in the Engineering News." Later in 1898, Fred R. Charles, assistant city engineer for Richmond, Indiana, wrote asking for "a copy of a recent report on the subject of 'Parks.'" Around the same time, *Garden & Forest—A Journal of Horticulture, Landscape Art & Forestry* wrote asking for Leisen's "Parks of Wilmington."[92] In 1909 the American Association of Park Superintendents invited the commission to contribute pictures of Wilmington's parks to the association's exhibit at the Seattle Exposition.[93] Although Wilmington's parks were not unique, the good management and care they received made them worthy of notice in the larger world.

The Board of Park Commissioners' *Annual Report*, first published in 1895, was another important means of outreach, both at the local level and to the larger community of park professionals elsewhere. The superintendent received a remarkable number of requests for the report. Of the 500 copies printed annually, the superintendent sent many to distant locations in response to requests from potential suppliers, such as bulb companies, garden and farm equipment companies, civil engineering firms, tree nurseries, and landscape architects. Park commissions, engineering departments, and libraries in other cities also requested the document. In 1899, for example, organizations, businesses, and government agencies in approximately two dozen cities wrote for copies of the *Annual Report*.[94] The reputation of the city's parks in general and its premier Brandywine Park in particular had begun to spread beyond Wilmington.

Beginning in 1950, the Board of Park Commissioners collaborated with a local nonprofit organization, to sponsor the "Old Timers' Picnic." This image of the event from the early 1950s shows picnickers gathered near the Josephine Fountain. (Courtesy of the Historical Society of Delaware.)

CONTINUITY AND CHANGE

The issues facing the Board of Park Commissioners changed with time, from matters associated with establishing a park and setting up management routines to the challenges of maintaining and improving an existing park. Once the commissioners had crafted organizational procedures and set a general operating schedule, most changes became adjustments within that framework. Maintenance tasks persisted, although they were undertaken with different tools and machines. Funding became more reliable, as the city government regularly appropriated funds to meet park expenses. Regular outreach yielded an appreciative city population well aware of Brandywine Park's assets.

Although changes in society produced certain unforeseen challenges, the Board of Park Commissioners remained faithful to its mission of providing parks for all of Wilmington's residents. The board sustained a clear focus that allowed the commissioners to protect Brandywine Park from most threats and to provide the leadership needed to take the greatest advantage of the opportunities that arose.

This view of a busy Monkey Hill, circa 1950, shows springtime
visitors to the park, a member of the park police force managing
traffic, and a railway crossing sign on the railroad spur that
conducted trains through the park to the paper mill that stood
where the Brandywine Park Condominiums now stand.
(Courtesy of the Historical Society of Delaware.)

Chapter 4

The Fabric of the Park

Although prior to the 1880s, local residents used the new park site for informal recreation, once it was officially under Park Commission control, it needed to be made safe, attractive, and accessible. It needed, in other words, roads, paths, and walls as well as certain amenities, including "comfort stations," pavilions, benches, and gardens.

Land Survey

Because the land purchased in 1886 was largely undeveloped with only a few small dwellings, the Board of Park Commissioners first needed a survey of the land and some maps based on the survey. In October 1887, J. C. Olmsted, of Frederick Law Olmsted's firm, sent to the board guidelines for preparing a suitable survey. Less than a month later, with the benefit of the Olmsted advice, the park board hired Samuel Canby to undertake the project.[1]

Canby, a Delaware native, had worked as an assistant city engineer and supervised the construction of the Cool Spring Reservoir in 1877. After a stay in Mexico doing railroad survey work, he returned to Wilmington as the Baltimore & Ohio Railroad's supervising engineer when the company constructed their bridge across the Brandywine between 1883 and 1885. After completing work on the bridge project, Canby accepted the park survey assignment, but it appears that he also found time to work on a railroad project in Colombia, South America, before tackling Brandywine Park. Interestingly, Theodore A. Leisen was also in Colombia working on railroad projects during that period, which raises the question of whether Leisen and Canby met and whether that acquaintance attracted Leisen to Wilmington.[2]

Canby got off to a slow start with the park survey. In 1889 the board approved hiring "men to finish the survey of the North Brandywine Park under the superintendence of Samu'l Canby." Early in 1890, the board asked the Executive Committee to finish the survey of South Brandywine Park "as speedily as possible" and authorized the president "to have the drawings placed in Mr. Olmsted's hands ... with the least possible delay."[3]

By March 1890, Board President William Marriott Canby carried the initial survey drawings to Boston "and placed them in the hands of Messrs. Olmsted, who agreed to locate the roadway through the South Park in three weeks."[4] With any anxiety over completion of the survey apparently forgotten, in 1890 the commissioners appointed Canby as the engineer responsible for supervising construction within the park.[5] He continued in that position through

The Board of Park Commissioners recognized the need to provide easy park access. South Park Drive, shown here in 1897 was the first roadway of any length laid out through the park. (Courtesy of the Historical Society of Delaware.)

1893, after which he left Wilmington for the Pacific Northwest, where he died in 1897.

ROADWAYS

It made all the sense in the world for the board to want roads built into the new park, but the commissioners also wanted to create a roadway system that differed from the rectilinear grid of the urban streets immediately adjacent to the park. They wanted park roads that followed the land's contours and took fullest advantage of the beautiful Brandywine Valley.

The board gave first attention to the road on the south side of the river because by 1894 the city owned an uninterrupted right-of-way from Market Street to the upstream end of the park above the pedestrian bridge. The commissioners already had detailed advice from the Olmsted firm about the proposed road's location. In 1889 Frederick Law Olmsted & Company recommended that the entire south drive run "*above* the long South Race instead of upon the site of the old, short South Race." In the firm's estimation, the suggested route (parallel to the race with the race between the road and the river) held a number of advantages. It required less disruption to the environment, unlike the route running closer to the river, which would require destruction of more trees and natural growth. In addition, the route close to the river was to be built over the course of an abandoned millrace and would be more expensive because of the cost of filling the race. The recommended route had easier grades and the additional advantage of easier "policing, lighting, watering, cleaning and repairing" because of its direct links to the city's regular street system.[6]

In April 1890, the firm provided a preliminary plan and profiles of the proposed drive "along the south shore of the Brandywine, from Market Street to Scott Street." The firm's letter reiterated the recommendation that the entire drive lie south of the race, noting that it would "preserv(e) for the use of the people the charming walk along the banks of the river with the picturesque, tree-clad slopes." However, recognizing that the commissioners might still prefer to build part of the drive north of the race, the firm provided an alternative plan showing the roadway crossing the race at the foot of Jefferson Street.[7] In the end, the board kept its original idea of having the park drive run below the race for part of its route and then above the race for the rest of the route, crossing the race at West Street rather than at Jefferson.

Even with finalized road profiles and plans, the commissioners moved slowly. In 1892 and 1893, some roadwork was completed. Early in 1894, Park Superintendent Theodore A. Leisen urged action, arguing that a nearby

Board of Education construction project made it "imperative" that the drive between West Street and Adams Street "be completed without delay."[8] Over the next six years, contractors graded and paved the route from Market Street to Clayton Street. By 1901 the Board of Park Commissioners' *Annual Report* described South Park Drive as "entirely macadamized" from Market Street to the end of Brandywine Park and noted that the macadam road continued, as Kentmere Parkway, all the way to Rockford Park.[9] As planned, the road fit the land's topography and natural appearance, ensuring that the park offered a welcome contrast to the nearby city streets.

The completion of South Park Drive in 1901 was fortuitous because the following year the board took control of the Elliott tract on the north side of the Brandywine. Finally having ownership of the land between Elliott's Run and the B&O Railroad allowed the commissioners to build a comparable park drive on the north side of the river, providing access from Market Street to the upstream end of the park.

Work had already been done (in a piecemeal fashion) along this stretch of parkland. Between 1895 and 1898, the board also graded, drained, and cindered Glen Avenue to approximately what is now the foot of Monkey Hill, although that roadway had yet to be created.[10] In 1900 the board proposed extending North Park Drive along a route uphill from the end of Glen Avenue on a diagonal course to connect with 18th Street. The proposed extension would then pass below the B&O Railroad Bridge and link up with a road above the paper mill.

The commission never built the diagonal drive. When the board developed the plan, the point where the proposed road headed uphill was the end of the park's land, but with city acquisition of the Elliott tract in 1902, it was possible to improve North Park Drive parallel to the river as had been done with South Park Drive. By the end of 1904, the new park drive was graded to within 100 feet of Elliott's Run; in 1905 a culvert was added that extended the roadway over the run; and by the end of 1906, the graded road

reached "a loop near the Baltimore and Ohio Railroad," an extension that "opens up what is known as Elliott's Woods, which is admirably adapted for picnic purposes."[11]

Monkey Hill in North Brandywine Park was a new thoroughfare that the commissioners added to the park as an extension of Van Buren Street, linking the Van Buren Street Bridge with 18th Street. The Board of Park Commissioners participated in the bridge's construction in 1906–7, sharing the project's cost with the Board of Water Commissioners.[12] The bridge was also an aqueduct, with a 48-inch water main running its length. It gave the park commissioners the link they wanted between the two sides of the park and the water commissioners the water main they needed between two city reservoirs.

Monkey Hill was first graded in 1907–8 and curbed and guttered in 1909.[13] After complaints about the condition of "Van Buren Road," the Board of Park Commissioners negotiated with the Street and Sewer Department to obtain Belgian block that had been removed from other city streets that were being resurfaced.[14] The Street and Sewer Department delivered the recycled paving blocks in the fall of 1922 and paved the road the following spring. At the Street and Sewer Department's suggestion, the park board named the road "Buffalo Drive" because it ran past the zoo's buffalo enclosure.[15] With subsequent construction of the Monkey House nearby, the road became Monkey Hill. When concern was expressed that the road was dangerous due to leaves or wet conditions, the board president asked the Street and Sewer Department to consider resurfacing "Van Buren Street . . . from the north approach of Van Buren Street Bridge to 18th Street (Monkey Hill)."[16] His 1955 request went unfulfilled, and as a result, one of the few examples of Belgian block paving in the city was preserved.

The Board of Park Commissioners also graded and paved some of the streets bordering on or running through the park. Between 1898 and 1908, the commissioners worked with the Street and Sewer Department to put Lovering Avenue, at the south edge of the park, into usable condition.[17] On the north side of the Brandywine, the board helped improve both 16th Street and 18th Street between 1901 and 1914. During this period, 18th Street, the park's northern boundary, was a special project of Samuel H. Baynard, who paid for substantial road improvements along the street.[18]

The Boulevard (renamed Baynard Boulevard in 1925 after the death of Samuel H. Baynard, the area's developer) also fell under the park board's authority. In 1891 the North Side Improvement Company laid out and sold building lots on the land that lies along what is now Baynard Boulevard. Two years later, the Levy Court built the Washington Street Bridge, connecting the city with the newly developed area, which the company named "Washington Heights."[19] The Board of Park Commissioners agreed to let the North Side Improvement Company lay a road between the bridge and the building sites north of the park, and the company agreed both "to bring the said avenue to established grades" and to do work that "shall be satisfactory to the Park Commission."[20]

After the Washington Street Bridge was completed but before the developer had improved the boulevard, people began driving over the parkland along the proposed boulevard route. The board erected a fence at the end of the bridge and posted a guard to prevent further travel where paving was to be done. In August 1893, the Levy Court told the commissioners "to remove the Guard and all other obstructions to public travel along the route of the Avenue or Boulevard connected with Washington Bridge."[21] In its reply, the board reminded the Levy Court of the commissioners' responsibility for the parks and for any improvements, including roads, in the parks. The commissioners noted that the Levy Court had no "supervisory authority" over the park board and pointed out that "the Park Commissioners never entered into any agreement with the Levy Court respecting the Boulevard." Their agreement was with the North Side Improvement Company, and because the development company had not fulfilled its side of the bargain, "the public have acquired as yet no right in that

land as a highway inasmuch as it is neither a county road nor a public highway of the city." The land would remain "dedicated to the uses of a park" until the boulevard was properly improved. "When the proposed boulevard is laid out and opened," the commissioners declared, "and its bed from the bridge to Eighteenth Street graded and paved so as to comply with the condition annexed to our consent to its passing over the park lands, then a right of way will be acquired by the public."[22]

The North Side Improvement Company began work on the boulevard, but late in 1895, the company "declined to carry out their agreement to grade and pave the boulevard from Washington Bridge, through the park land," claiming "they had done more than their share of improvements to the Boulevard and could not do any more." The project could not be left unfinished, however, so the park board persuaded the Street and Sewer Department to accept responsibility for the roadbed of the boulevard between the bridge and 18th Street, thus taking on the job of grading and paving the new street and installing concrete gutters, "providing this Board will pay one half the expense of putting in gutters and grates." The park board agreed to pay half (up to $400), and the road was completed in 1896.[23]

By 1913 the basic roadwork throughout the park was done, and any future work involved improving existing roads and addressing issues raised by the increased use of automobiles. Safety was a constant worry, and as automobile use increased during the early years of the 20th century, the commissioners became increasingly concerned.[24] By the 1920s, the Delaware Safety Council began to ask for safety precautions on park roads. When the Washington Memorial Bridge was under construction in 1920, the Safety Council pointed out the hazard created by pieces of equipment and piles of crushed stone on the road and asked the board to erect a sign reading "Danger. Under Repair. Drive Slowly. Sound Horn."[25]

The 1929 *Annual Report* noted the board's concern for "better protection along the steep banks of the park drive." The commissioners erected a series of "concrete

This 1926 picture shows frame shelters near the dam in South Brandywine Park.
In 1939 a masonry pavilion that still stands along the pathway replaced the earlier pavilions.
(Courtesy of the Historical Society of Delaware.)

PATHWAYS

At the end of the 19th century, foot traffic was as vital as wheeled traffic and certainly more common among city residents, who walked to most destinations. Wilmington's public transportation system began in 1864 with a horse-trolley line along Delaware Avenue. In 1888 the city's first electric streetcar made its way up Market Street through Brandywine Village to the city line, but most Wilmingtonians walked, or occasionally cycled, on their daily rounds.

In the 1890s, the park road system was in the earliest stages of development; footpaths that predated the park already allowed easy access for park users. Wilmington residents using the area for informal recreation and Jessup and Moore employees walking to and from work wore pathways along the river and across the parkland. By the middle of the 1890s, the commission allocated a portion of each annual budget to the creation of new paths and included in each annual report information on paths completed and those planned for the year ahead.

The earliest walkways were simple earthen paths worn into the grass, and the first "paved" pathways probably had gravel surfaces. In 1896 Park Superintendent Leisen and board members J. Newlin Gawthorp and Dennis J. Menton, in anticipation of "paving" some park paths, traveled to Ocean Grove, New Jersey, to "examine tar (and pitch) pavements as laid down there."[29] Although the board paved some paths with brick and others with tar or "bituminous macadam" (a form of asphalt with stone), for several decades beginning in 1910, the commissioners had most of the paths surfaced with cinders, a material eventually replaced with more durable asphalt or concrete.

posts of an attractive design with wire cables" at dangerous points along park roadways and set the speed limit along South Park Drive at 20 miles per hour.[26] Over the next four years, the commission installed along both park drives sets of concrete guard posts with heavy wire cable threaded between them, safety barriers that remained in use into the mid-1960s.[27] Six of the concrete posts survive along North Park Drive near the dam, although the cable that once connected them is gone.

It was not until the September 1964 board meeting that the commissioners gave official names to the park's roads. They named South Park Drive and North Park Drive along the Brandywine as well as Stadium Drive (south and east from 18th Street at Baynard Stadium to North Park Drive), Franklin Drive (south from 18th and Franklin to Stadium Drive), and Kentmere Drive (north from Lovering Avenue and DuPont Street to Union Street).[28]

WALLS

The Board of Park Commissioners constructed walls in the park from the 1890s until approximately 1920. The walls, built of readily available local stone chosen to complement the landscape, followed the contours of the land, ensuring that the park's appearance was a refreshing change from the hard, straight lines of the surrounding city streets. The stone came from the park itself, excavated during park road building work and set aside to be reused later for wall construction.

Between 1896 and 1899, the commissioners built the wall along South Park Drive between Market and West streets. Constructed along the route of an abandoned mill-race and constructed from materials excavated when the drive was built, the wall buttressed the steep bank from the water's edge below upward to support the roadway. It became a popular promenade where visitors strolled and enjoyed the view of the river. Superintendent Leisen included in his design for the wall a circular overlook near the foot of West Street because it took advantage of the park topography and afforded "a fine vista up the creek."[30] Leisen's incorporation of such an overlook was typical of the Victorian taste for such vantage points in natural settings.[31]

As the South Park Drive wall was being completed, work began on a wall along the cliff top at the north end of the Washington Street Bridge. After an effort to "clean up and beautify the rocky bluff" above Glen Avenue, Leisen recommended building a stone wall at the cliff's edge.[32] Completed in 1901, the construction of the wall along the cliff became the first step in a project to build a pavilion on the promontory overlooking the Brandywine from the north side.[33]

The stone retaining wall along nearly 400 feet of Lovering Avenue both supports the roadway and marks the park's edge. In 1903 and 1904, the Board of Park Commissioners graded Lovering Avenue and, with stone excavated during the road project, began the wall starting near the foot of Franklin Street. As work continued on the wall between Harrison and Hancock streets, the rock saved during grading work proved insufficient. The board opened a quarry in the bank below Lovering Avenue and South Park Drive and quarried stone to complete the wall and to build the stone steps leading down from Lovering to South Park Drive.[34]

LIGHTING

By happy coincidence, the creation of Brandywine Park occurred just as new technologies became available to make the park hospitable and pleasant. In 1888 the board authorized the Executive Committee to put up "suitable lights where required," and within a year the committee had approval to purchase four iron lampposts at $7 each in preparation for providing gas light for park visitors.[35] In 1894 Superintendent Leisen asked the board to install electric lights in Brandywine Park, arguing that "even a few would enable visitors to enjoy the summer evenings there." The board allowed installation of "not more than eight electric lights (between) Clayton St. and the pavilion," apparently referring to a structure built the previous year at the Rattlesnake Run entrance to the park.[36] Lights along South Park Drive, first recommended in 1900, were in place by 1911. While gaslights provided the earliest illumination along the drive, electric fixtures soon prevailed, and electric lights illuminated the Van Buren Street Bridge, the traffic island at the north end of the bridge, and park pathways.[37]

Not unexpectedly, the board received requests for additional lighting. The Washington Heights Association wanted lights at the zoo, and the workers at the Jessup and Moore Paper Company wanted lights along the path between South Park Drive and Lovering Avenue.[38] The commissioners themselves quickly saw the merit of providing good lighting in a variety of park locations and supplied illumination to park toilets (1908), pavilions (1912), picnic areas (1922), and tennis courts (1934).[39] As Leisen had imagined, adding lighting allowed greater numbers of park visitors greater enjoyment of their park.

Comfort Houses

Early in the process of transforming the newly purchased land into a park, the board began constructing "comfort houses" (public toilets) at strategic locations. As early as May 1888, the Executive Committee reported progress on a building "for Public Comfort." By 1896 Brandywine Park was equipped with four recently remodeled comfort houses, one on each side of the river for men and one on each side for women.[40]

Over the years, the board had comfort houses removed, renovated, replaced, and new ones added. In 1904, for example, the Executive Committee had the "old comfort house in S. Brandywine Park at Franklin St." dismantled because it had become "obnoxious."[41] The following year, the board accepted from the Water Department responsibility for two comfort houses, one at Market and 16th streets and a second at Jefferson Street.[42] The board's 1905 *Annual Report* indicates that during 1905, the commissioners paid $379.50 to have water closets built.[43]

An accurate accounting of facilities is difficult because some were moved and others adapted for alternative uses. In 1905, when the new water closets were constructed in North Brandywine Park, the board gave the old comfort house to the Zoological Association for use as a monkey house. In the 1930s, after the commission built a new public toilet near the stadium, the superintendent moved parts of the old comfort station to another city park to serve as a picnic shelter. The 1937 toilet near the stadium was also adaptively reused, serving from the 1970s as an office and currently operating as the park rangers' headquarters. Occasionally facilities were moved, as in 1914 when the comfort house that was just west of Monkey Hill was relocated to a site near Elliott's Run. Records do not reflect where along the run it was placed or when it was dismantled.[44]

During the Great Depression, work relief programs also made possible the construction of new sanitary facilities in Brandywine Park. Late in 1930, the Park Commission called for bids on a new comfort station built of brick and stone and having a "European style slate roof" in South Brandywine Park. The winning contractor, with a bid of $1,508, began work immediately. By the following spring, the company had completed the stone building that stands at the foot of Rattlesnake Run.[45] In 1931 similar specifications were provided in a call for bids for a comfort station in North Brandywine Park; within a year, workers had constructed another of the stone buildings to serve visitors to the zoo. In 1937 workers erected the final comfort station built under the work relief programs, the stone toilet near Baynard Stadium. Begun in the autumn of 1936, it was ready for use the following spring.[46]

All three were built to similar specifications with the same basic characteristics: each is a rectangular stone building with hipped roof. The specifications required use of native stone and slate to preserve the rugged, rustic look of the park's natural setting even while the buildings provided a necessary amenity. The earliest building constructed, the toilet at the foot of Rattlesnake Run, is the smallest of the three, and each successive building was slightly larger than the one before. Their increased size indicates the board's awareness of the growing use being made of the park, as the financial hardships of the 1930s made free recreational opportunities more and more attractive.[47] The buildings were slight enlarged as the years progressed because the park board realized that heavy usage made larger facilities desirable.[48]

In addition to constructing new sanitary facilities, the commission concerned itself constantly with improvements to existing buildings and equipment, installing electric lights and fitting them "with modern fixtures."[49] In 1928 the Levy Court built a new bridge across the Brandywine at Market Street, a project that required the removal of the old comfort station there. The Board of Park Commissioners urged the Levy Court to build a new public toilet in connection with the bridge.[50] The replacement comfort station was built into the bridge itself, located below street level in the southwestern bridge abutment and entered via a stairway leading downward from the sidewalk to the facilities. It remained in operation until the 1960s.

PAVILIONS

If providing comfort stations was a practical necessity, building park pavilions gave the Board of Park Commissioners an opportunity to supply park visitors with pleasant places sheltered from sun or rain and to offer vantage points from which to observe the passing scene. Such amenities were expected in a 19th-century park. The number and variety of pavilions constructed over the years testify to the popularity of the park, which made providing shelters a priority.

The board constructed the first pavilions in Brandywine Park in the early 1890s. In 1893 the park engineer erected a 30 foot by 60 foot pavilion on "low ground" near the Rattlesnake Run entrance to the park, and a year later he built a "refreshment pavilion" in the same vicinity.[51] It is unclear how permanent these structures were intended to be—the 1893 pavilion cost $787 and the 1894 structure $232, which suggests that the earlier, more costly pavilion may have endured longer than a season or two, particularly because board records from 1909 mention the demolition of a pavilion in this area.[52]

Other pavilions that the park board built during this era did not last because they were "rustic" structures built of less sturdy materials, primarily wood; the structures that have survived are masonry. "Twig" settees and chairs in cast iron were common features in many Victorian gardens as were unpretentious garden pavilions and summerhouses. Park planners carried "rustic furnishings" into city parks, treating the parks as large gardens and building rustic shelters there. For many city residents, the parks were the only "gardens" to which they had access for refreshment.

In 1895 the Board of Park Commissioners constructed, at a cost of $545, a "rustic pavilion" in the North Brandywine Park picnic grounds. Other than its dimensions, 30 feet by 45 feet, we know only that it was deemed "thoroughly satisfactory."[53] In February 1897, Superintendent Leisen drew up plans for the "small rustic Summer House," and by the end of the year, it had been constructed of cedar "at a point overlooking the race and the creek" and

fitted with seats to provide "a pleasant resting place and shelter."[54] Nicknamed the "Bird Cage," it remained, with some repairs, into the early 1960s. The foundation on which the little pavilion stood survives and, while the exact locations of other rustic pavilions in the park can only be guessed, the "footprint" of this one provides an example of the Victorian taste for scenic vistas in natural settings.

In 1895 Leisen recommended that the board build a pavilion as an "observatory" that would afford "a picturesque outlook up the Brandywine." He imagined it above the river near the northern end of the recently completed Washington Street Bridge.[55] In 1899 work got under way on a wall along the cliff top at the recommended location, and by the summer of 1901, the board solicited bids from contractors and selected Simmons & Brother to build the new pavilion.[56]

According to their 1901 *Annual Report*, the Park Commissioners expected the "concrete-steel pavilion" built on a granite base to be finished by Memorial Day 1902.[57] On April 13, 1902, Wilmington's *Sunday Morning Star* announced that "The iron work for the new pavilion to be built in Brandywine Park is almost ready for delivery." The Edgemoor Branch of the American Bridge Company produced the ironwork; the 10 Ionic columns supporting the roof were cast iron, from "Pattern No. 4871," probably a standard item in the company's catalogue and reasonably easy to produce. To complete the pavilion, workers clad all the ironwork in concrete. In 1904 the board had seats installed around the interior circle of the pavilion.[58] Eventually called the "Sugar Bowl" because of its lid-like domed roof, the structure served for several decades as a meeting place, site for concerts and church services, and venue for community and patriotic programs. Over the years, the park board periodically repaired the pavilion, but by 1949, the structure was in such dangerous condition that the commissioners removed the distinctive roof, and the pavilion was reduced to the level of the railings.[59] Sadly, the next few years were no kinder, and a decade later, further demolition was required. The 1958–59 *Annual Report* noted

[Top] The "Sugar Bowl" pavilion got its name from its domed roof that some observers thought looked like the lid on a sugar bowl. Completed in 1902, the stone and concrete pavilion provided "a picturesque outlook up the Brandywine." (Courtesy of the Historical Society of Delaware.) [Right] In 1949 the domed roof, judged to be dangerous, was removed. A decade later the railing was replaced by a chain link fence. (Courtesy of the Delaware Public Archives, Dover, Delaware.)

that the "cracked and crumbling concrete railing" had been removed and replaced with a three-foot chain link fence.[60]

In 1911 the Board of Park Commissioners built a large rectangular picnic pavilion "in the opening near the picnic woods" in North Brandywine Park, not far from the site where the Baynard Athletic Grounds would soon be established. Constructed with concrete pillars and floor, its "shingle" roof, probably cedar, had copper cresting.[61] A low concrete wall encircled the open interior space. In 1938 young Wilmingtonians, working on a National Youth Administration (NYA) project, built a substantial brick fireplace into one corner of the shelter.[62]

The NYA work was one of several park projects during the Great Depression. Most of the New Deal projects in Brandywine Park came under the umbrella of the Works Progress Administration (WPA), established in 1935. The WPA program in Delaware eventually employed 5,000 people and extended the length of the state, from boardwalk renovations in Rehoboth and Lewes to improvements at Wilmington's marine terminal. Delaware's WPA workers sewed, translated books into Braille, and painted fireplugs. They operated nursery schools, recorded information about historic buildings, and ran a recreation program that included a basketball league that, at its height during the 1938–39 season, averaged 250 games per month and attracted 159,931 spectators.[63]

In Brandywine Park, WPA workers in 1938 built the stone pavilion just off South Park Drive "on the bluff near the old quarry" overlooking the Brandywine. The shelter's massive stone fireplace bears a date stone reading "1938."

Behind the fireplace, there were two small rooms, originally used as a guard's room and a room for storing wood, although plans called for them eventually to be equipped as toilets.[64] The pavilion had been restored in the mid-1990s for use in educational programs, but in January 1997, fire destroyed the shelter's timber framing and roof. In 2002–3 a collaborative effort by the Division of Parks and Recreation, the Friends of Wilmington Parks, and generous private donors restored the heavy timber framing and slate roof.

The second WPA pavilion stands along the path in South Brandywine Park near the dam. Square rather than rectangular like the other shelters, this smaller structure, like the 1911 shelter in North Brandywine Park, has reinforced concrete pillars to support a hipped roof, and there are low concrete walls around the perimeter of the floor. Early post-cards show frame pavilions near this site, and board minutes from June 1938 reported that foundations were "being laid for a picnic pavilion to replace the old one near the creek, built in 1893, which is in bad repair."[65] Completed in April 1939, the pavilion provided a "resting place with a view of the river."[66] Although high winds damaged the structure in 1999, this pavilion too has been recently restored, with timber framing and slate roof replaced in 2000.

Near the end of the program's operation in the park, the WPA built the picnic pavilion at the foot of Monkey Hill. Begun in late 1940 and completed in June 1941, it too featured a massive fireplace and had stone piers and heavy timber framing that supported a slate roof.[67] In the 1980s, a fire seriously damaged the pavilion, and it stood for several years as nothing more than a stone shell. In 1999 and 2000, in a joint effort, Delaware's Division of Parks and Recreation, the Junior League of Wilmington, and the Friends of Wilmington Parks restored the pavilion.

Pavilion construction may go through cycles, but it apparently never stops completely. In 1973, wooden pavilions were built on the site of the old swimming pool at Adams Street and South Park Drive, and in the early 1990s, a small shelter near the zoo was installed in a frequently visited section of the park.

THEODORE A. LEISEN

In its first five years of managing Brandywine Park (1886–1891), the Board of Park Commissioners supplied the new park with a few benches, four iron lampposts for gaslights, and a "public comfort." In the next decade (1891–1901), however, they made substantially more progress, improving roads and paths, building walls, installing lights, and erecting pavilions and comfort stations. As the park board pushed its program forward, one of the visionaries participating in laying the park's basic foundation was Theodore A. Leisen, chief park engineer and superintendent.

When 27-year-old Leisen, a civil engineer, started his city employment in 1891, he was a draftsman in the Engineering and Surveying Department. By 1893 he was park engineer for the Board of Park Commissioners. Chief engineer two years later, he eventually served as both park engineer and superintendent. In 1903 the Board of Water Commissioners appointed him as their chief engineer, a post he held for the next five years. Ongoing cooperation between the water and park commissioners kept him involved in aspects of park projects.

In 1895 Leisen recommended construction of "a large pavilion and observatory" in then-new Rockford Park. The "massive structure" was to be of local stone so that it would have an "antique appearance."[68] The Board of Water Commissioners needed a new water tower, and the park board wanted an observatory. The two boards merged their projects and produced Rockford Tower, a single structure serving both purposes.

In 1906 the city's expanding water system required a new water main to connect two reservoirs, Cool Spring, completed in 1877, and a new reservoir, later named Porter Reservoir, to be constructed on Concord Pike north of the city. The two reservoirs were located so that the main connecting them had to pass through Brandywine Park. At the same time, the Park Commissioners wanted a bridge across the river to link both sides of the park. The interests of the Water Commissioners and the Park Commissioners again coincided. The Van Buren Street Bridge satisfied both needs—as a bridge and, with a water main running its length, as an aqueduct. Completed in 1907, the bridge was both functional and, as Leisen intended, "ornamental in design."[69]

Leisen understood the challenges of transforming unimproved acreage into parkland. Undaunted by chronically tight budgets, he gave constant attention to providing amenities expected in "a pleasure ground." He took advantage of "scenic vistas" that park topography offered, building a scenic overlook in the utilitarian retaining wall along the south side of the Brandywine and selecting the "Sugar Bowl" pavilion site because of its "picturesque outlook up the Brandywine."[70]

PLANTINGS AND HORTICULTURE

The Board of Park Commissioners gave attention to the horticultural features that colored visitors' experience of

Brandywine Park. The board had already planted 50 evergreens in North Brandywine Park when, in January 1895, Leisen recommended that the commissioners plan for an additional 1,000 trees. "We would probably wish to set out as early as possible all the trees that will be necessary," he wrote.[71] A year later, the board planted 110 trees, a combination of pin oaks and Norway maples, along the Boulevard, Washington Street, and 18th Street. The commissioners demonstrated their interest in horticultural matters in 1897 when they agreed to meet at 7:15 p.m. on a November morning to examine the site near Market Street and "to go over ground and select trees to be planted." In 1899 the board ordered 1,090 shrubs and trees to distribute among the five park properties for which they were then responsible.[72]

During the early years of Brandywine Park's development, the commissioners had the superintendent purchase loads of manure in order to feed the new plantings.

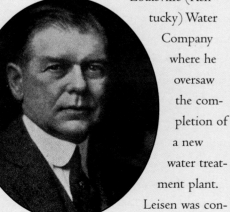

THEODORE A. LEISEN

Born in Philadelphia in 1864, Leisen worked for six years on railroad construction in Colombia before coming to Wilmington in 1891. In 1908 he left Wilmington to be chief engineer and superintendent at the Louisville (Kentucky) Water Company where he oversaw the completion of a new water treatment plant. Leisen was con-

sulting engineer when Frankfort, Kentucky, built its water system. He relocated to Detroit in 1914, where he supervised construction of what was then the world's largest water filtration plant. During World War I, he was Major Leisen, camp utilities officer at Camp Custer in Michigan, and in 1923 he left Detroit to become the general manager of Omaha's Municipal Utilities District. There he designed a substantial Service Building for the company (1926) and the company's Downtown Headquarters Building (1927). Leisen retired in 1939 at the age of 74 and returned to Detroit, where he died in 1944. In 1993 the Nebraska Section of the American Water Works Associa-

tion established the Col. Theodore A. Leisen Memorial and Training Endowment Fund to encourage water industry professionals to add to their training and to encourage graduate students to consider the water industry as a field of work.

Wilmington was a fortunate beneficiary of Leisen's attention and talent. He enhanced the city parks' open space with elegant and useful structures, and his efforts enlarged and improved the city's water system. A century later, Wilmingtonians continue to benefit from his steady combination of experienced practicality, engaging vision, and passionate tenacity.

(Courtesy of Douglas County Historical Society, Omaha, Nebraska.)

In February 1898, Superintendent Leisen paid the Gilpin Avenue Club stables 40 cents per load for 14 loads of manure. By 1900 he had negotiated the price down to 25 cents a load from another supplier, but the most advantageous arrangement was one he reached in 1903 with the Street and Sewer Department: to have "the best of the street sweepings from the paved streets delivered to the park lawns."[73]

In the 20th century, primary emphasis remained on trees and shrubs. In 1900 the board purchased nearly 3,000 shrubs and trees for the city's parks, with a fair share being allocated to Brandywine Park. Meant to enhance and develop bare acres into attractive park settings, the plants were also occasionally used to screen the park from its neighbors.[74] In 1919 a New York nursery offered to sell to the commission small trees "dug up from the battlefields" of France, suggesting them as appropriate as "memorial trees" to honor those who died in World War I, an offer the commissioners apparently did not accept.[75]

The community noticed when park specimens did not thrive. A letter to a local newspaper in 1944 strongly recommended that the trees in Brandywine Park be thinned because they were "so closely grown." In the late 1940s, disease struck the pin oak trees along Baynard Boulevard, causing concern to the board and an outcry from local residents, one of whom wrote to the board about the trees' condition and expressed the hope "that the board will be able to do something to stop this disease and preserve the remaining trees."[76] In the end, many of the trees died, and newly appointed commissioner M. du Pont Lee collected private funds to pay for their replacement. Lee's passion for preserving the tree-filled park encouraged the Executive Committee to adopt the policy that "whenever and wherever a growing tree is destroyed on park lands," another tree would be planted to replace it.[77] It was a policy the board invoked when the commissioners insisted that, with the construction of I-95, the State Highway Department plant trees to replace those removed for the highway project.[78]

The most substantial horticultural impacts on

Brandywine Park came as a result of donors whose gifts transformed the park. In 1929 the Board of Park Commissioners and a leading local attorney, J. Ernest Smith, embarked on a joint project that provided the park with one of its best known and most loved plantings, the Japanese cherry trees. Early in 1929, the board announced that "an interested citizen has offered to donate a plantation of Japanese Cherries." In November, the board president reported that the trees had been ordered and "donated by a distinguished citizen" whose identity was revealed a month later. By early December, the trees, of two varieties that bloomed at different times, were in the ground.[79]

Smith and his wife, Josephine Tatnall Smith, lived near the park and enjoyed strolling in the area where the trees were planted. Mrs. Smith was reported to have remarked to her husband that the site would be lovely if there were Japanese cherry trees there.[80] By the time the trees were planted, however, Mrs. Smith was already in declining health. Although she may have seen them flower in the spring of 1930, she never lived to see them well established and blooming in profusion. She died in January 1931 at the age of 76.[81] In subsequent years, the flowering trees brought large numbers of people to the park each spring, and after the installation of the Josephine Fountain in the midst of the trees in 1933, the area was illuminated by electric lights each spring when the trees were in bloom.[82]

The second major planting project, the Jasper Crane Rose Garden, followed on the heels of the cherry trees and arose out of a fortunate intersection of circumstances. Laid out in 1933, the garden was a Public Works Administration (PWA) project. Established in 1933, the PWA underwrote public projects that put laborers idled by the Depression back to work and provided improvements for cities across the country.[83]

A rose garden in the park had long been the dream of Board President Edgar L. Haynes. The establishment of the PWA was the means to make the dream a reality. Before determining the garden's design, Haynes and other park commissioners studied public rose gardens in several other

eastern cities.[84] They also sought the help of
J. Horace McFarland, founder and first
president of the American Rose Society.
McFarland had the advantage of living
relatively close by, in Harrisburg,
Pennsylvania. By the time he was invited to
participate in the garden planning process,
he had already produced several books on
gardening and rose cultivation, and he was
the editor of the *American Rose Annual*.[85]

While the federal government funded
the labor, the city (through the Board of Park
Commissioners) supplied the other necessary
materials—soil, fencing, even buffalo manure
from the herd at the zoo. Jasper E. Crane
donated the roses: 670 plants of 58 different
varieties. He selected plants that he had
cultivated successfully in his own garden, and
the designers arranged the beds so that 400
more roses could be planted "when funds are
available."[86]

Crane, a DuPont Company vice president
who joined the company in 1915, was elected a
company director in 1927, rose to a vice presidency by
1929, and retired in 1946. A civic-minded man, Crane was
a director of the YMCA and Red Cross, chaired the state's
Temporary Emergency Relief Committee in the 1930s, and
headed Delaware's Finnish Relief Campaign in 1940. His
own garden was characterized as "a showplace," and his
enthusiasm for gardening led him to contribute the roses
for the Brandywine Park garden.[87]

The rose garden enjoyed huge success. In 1935 the
American Rose Annual predicted that it would be "one of the
loveliest rose-gardens in the country," and in 1946 the same
publication declared the garden "splendidly kept," a place with
"an atmosphere of quality, dignity, interest and repose."[88]

During the 1950s, the garden was at its height, with
1,000 plants and 100 different varieties; each year it grew
with the addition of awardwinning new roses, varieties with

The Jasper Crane Rose Garden, built in 1933–34, was a project that combined efforts of the city and federal governments and private citizens. DuPont Company executive Jasper Crane donated the first roses, 670 plants of 58 varieties. This circa 1950 picture shows the garden with 1,000 plants of 100 varieties. (Courtesy of the Historical Society of Delaware.)

names like "Sutter's Gold," "Capastrano," "Mission Bell,"
"Vogue," and "Helen Traubel."[89] The garden had come to be
called the Jasper Crane Rose Garden, and interest continued
through the 1960s, with nurseries making regular donations
of plants, often of new varieties. Between 1951 and 1963,
for example, Armstrong Rose Nurseries of California
donated a total of 141 plants, and during the same time the
Conard-Pyle Company of nearby West Grove provided 56
plants. Other donors provided an additional 28 rose
bushes.[90]

As time passed and park resources were directed
elsewhere, the garden suffered. During the 1990s, the
Friends Society of Brandywine Park (predecessor of the
Friends of Wilmington Parks) cared for the garden but
faced the dual challenges of unhealthy plants and no
irrigation system. Then in 2000, a descendant of Jasper

Crane donated $5,000 for restoration work on the garden and the City of Wilmington matched the grant, making it possible for the Friends of Wilmington Parks to launch a restoration project that included replacing the aging rose bushes, all of which had been planted in the 1950s and 1960s. During the course of the project, workers discovered that the modest metal fence surrounding the garden had been constructed of plumbing pipes and joints, a reminder of the hard times during which the garden was created and of the practicality of the men who planted it. At the conclusion of the restoration in 2001, the Friends were able to celebrate a new addition to the array of roses in the garden with the introduction of a newly hybridized rose appropriately named "Jasper Crane." Nationally recognized rose hybridizer J. Benjamin Williams donated the "Jasper Crane" rose to honor his personal friendship with Crane and as an indication of his dedication to public gardens.[91]

Flowers were late in coming to the park, although in April 1939 the board gave permission to a group of neighborhood women to plant flowers along the wall next to Monkey Hill. In the spring of 1940, the board received $25 for an iris planting near the zoo, and two years later the commissioners reported the creation of "an iris and chrysanthemum garden near the Zoo." The irises apparently flourished because by 1950 the commission had received donations for the "Iris Gardens," receiving a gift of 800 German iris in 1952 that were planted in two 26-foot beds on either side of the path leading to the Josephine Fountain and in similar beds along the path to the Todd Memorial.[92]

The cherry trees, the Jasper Crane Rose Garden, and other horticultural gifts given with such generosity all expressed a public spirit and civic pride. These sentiments motivated Wilmingtonians at a time when the park was evolving from its early, unfinished state to become a focal point for the city, a place of beauty where residents and visitors alike could find the refreshment and renewal that the founding commission had envisioned.

THE LITTLE CHURCH IN THE PARK

The Board of Park Commissioners with the Wilmington Fountain Society and with the agencies providing relief from unemployment during the Great Depression. Both relationships shaped the park's character by providing fountains, pavilions, comfort stations, roads, paths, and at least one bridge. Another collaboration had a similarly transforming impact on the park. In 1917 the board held a special meeting with the Society of Colonial Dames and the Society of Colonial Wars. The two groups asked the commissioners for permission to move "the old Presbyterian Church … onto the park land east of West Street and south of the South long race." Given the Dames' pledge to care for the building once it was moved, the Board of Park Commissioners gave its approval.[93]

The building in question—the small, brick, gambrel-roofed church on the corner of West Street and South Park Drive—originally stood in the 900 block of Market Street. It was built in 1740 as the spiritual home to a congregation of Scots-Irish Presbyterians. The congregation recorded the church's construction date by spelling out "1740" in darker bricks (still visible today) in one exterior wall. The number of worshippers waxed and waned over the years, but by 1840, their number was sufficiently large to warrant a new church.

With the dedication of a new, larger church, also on Market Street, the congregation used the old church for Sabbath School and meetings and eventually rented it to the Historical Society of Delaware. By 1895 the Historical Society was renting meeting space to the National Society of the Colonial Dames of America in the State of Delaware for $2 per year.[94]

In April 1916, the First Presbyterian Church sold the land on which the little church, now vacant, stood. The Wilmington Institute Free Library had purchased the land and planned to erect a grand new building facing what would soon become Rodney Square. The sale of the land cast doubt on the future of the 1740 building. In May a delegation from the Colonial Dames met with the

from the first bridge and then built the replacement suspension bridge a few more feet downstream, creating the current trio of bridges at the upstream end of the park. By the end of 1910, the railroad had begun to route its traffic across the new span.

The old railroad bridge, now sitting idle, became the topic of speculation among a variety of interested parties debating whether the span should be given to New Castle County. In December 1912, the B&O Railroad executed a deed conveying ownership to the county.[9] The bridge abutted the park, and although there were no immediate plans for its use, the park superintendent undertook preliminary plans for grading the approaches to the bridge. By 1915 the Board of Park Commissioners' Executive Committee and representatives of the Levy Court met to discuss plans to remodel the bridge, now designated the Augustine Bridge, because of its proximity to Jessup and Moore's Augustine Mill.[10]

As the decade dwindled, attention turned downstream to Washington Street, where the 1893 Washington Street Bridge was slated for replacement. The old bridge was to be replaced, and there was general concern regarding how traffic would be handled with a major river crossing closed for an extended period. The Augustine Bridge offered an answer, and by the summer of 1920, three partners collaborated to adapt it to vehicular traffic: The Levy Court replaced the railroad tracks with a concrete deck while the Street and Sewer Department paved the bridge approaches and the Park Commission improved the bridge abutments.[11] On August 9, 1920, as soon as the conversion from rail to vehicular use was complete, the Washington Street Bridge closed to traffic.[12]

The "new" Augustine Bridge initially linked the streets on the south side of the Brandywine only to an

The Van Buren Street Bridge, built in 1906–07, was also an aqueduct, carrying a 48-inch water main that linked two reservoirs. The trail in the distance is the path that became Monkey Hill.

(Postcard from author's collection.)

extension of 18th Street that looped around the north edge of the Brandywine Park, near the playing fields recently improved by Samuel Baynard. Although a route to Concord Pike had been surveyed as early as 1912, it was not until 1933 that the Levy Court built a road, Augustine Cut-Off, to link the converted bridge to Concord Pike. The bridge then became known as the Augustine Cut-Off Bridge.[13]

VAN BUREN STREET BRIDGE

In the early 20th century, Wilmington's growing population placed increasing demands on the local water system, and the construction of a reservoir north of the city on Concord Pike was expected to help meet these expanding needs. To link the new Porter Reservoir with the existing Cool Spring Reservoir, the Board of Water Commissioners needed to build a new water main, and because of the locations of the two reservoirs, the main had to follow a route through Brandywine Park.

The Water Commissioners' need for the new main coincided with the Board of Park Commissioners' desire for a new bridge to link the two halves of Brandywine Park. In particular, the zoo, which had opened in North Brandywine

Park in 1904, had proven a popular attraction, and the park board was eager to offer Wilmingtonians easy access to all parts of the park, including the zoo.

The two boards agreed to collaborate on a bridge that would also carry the water main, with the Board of Water Commissioners bearing two-thirds of the project's cost and the Board of Park Commissioners assuming the remaining one-third.[14] In May 1906, the Wilmington Board of Water Commissioners solicited bids for construction of a bridge that would cross the Brandywine at the foot of Van Buren Street. Not only would the intended span offer to both pedestrians and the horse-drawn vehicles of the day access to the north part of Brandywine Park, but it would also support the needed 48-inch water main.

The proposed bridge was to be of reinforced concrete and have a 16-foot roadway bordered by a 4-foot sidewalk on either side. The contract specifications required three main arches, each 56 feet wide; four side arches, each 28 feet wide; and one 9-foot arch over the sidewalk on the south side of the river. Theodore A. Leisen, now the chief engineer of the Water Department, was responsible for drawing up the specifications and getting the project launched. Referring to the bridge design, he declared, "It will be ornamental in design and should prove a valuable acquisition to the parks and to the vast number of people who frequent them."[15] On June 11, 1906, the water commissioners awarded the contract to the John A. Kelly Company of Philadelphia. Kelly's $36,000 bid was the lowest; the only Wilmington bidder, A. S. Reed and Brother, submitted a proposal that exceeded Kelly's by $17,000.[16]

Within a month, the company began erecting a trestle across the creek, but an early August flood destroyed the structure. In addition to flooding, delays in delivery of steel work and a legal squabble over water rights slowed construction. In 1906 there was still a millrace on the north side of the river, comparable to the surviving south millrace. The Lea Milling Company, whose flourmills were located where Superfine Lane condominiums now stand, owned the right to the water in the north race. The Lea interests,

fearful of having their water rights compromised, threatened to seek an injunction to stop construction of the bridge unless their concerns were addressed. As a result, the Board of Water Commissioners changed the original design, widening the arch across the north race from 28 to 33 feet. The process of making this accommodation cost not only time but also added $1,251 to the price of the bridge.[17]

All of these factors so slowed work on the bridge that it could not be completed before cold weather arrived in the autumn of 1906 and halted the concrete work. The structure was finished the following year, providing the city with both a handsome bridge and a substantial aqueduct.

When the bridge was completed in 1907, there were 330 registered automobiles in the state of Delaware. By 1910 the number had increased to 940 and in 1920 stood at 14,600.[18] The bridge's engineering did not hold up particularly well under ever-increasing loads of traffic, and by December 1909, the water main began to leak. Attempts to repair the problem were only temporarily successful and over the next several decades the leaking was a chronic headache for the successive commissions and departments responsible for the bridge. The water seeping into the concrete fabric of the bridge caused such serious deterioration that in 1996 the Delaware Department of Transportation, which assumed responsibility for the bridge in 1965, determined that it was necessary to rebuild the span. Prior to removing the old structure, the crew made casts of all the original decorative details. Then they demolished the structure down to the arches, which they preserved. After removing the offending water main, they reconstructed the span, replicating almost exactly the appearance of the original bridge and preserving one of the park's scenic images, the graceful Van Buren Street Bridge spanning the Brandywine.[19]

WASHINGTON MEMORIAL BRIDGE

In 1891 Wilmington businessman Samuel Baynard and several of his colleagues joined forces as the North Side Improvement Company. They purchased 60 acres of land on the north side of the Brandywine, subdivided it into

[Top] *The circa 1905 image of the Washington Street Bridge, the Sugar Bowl, and the Boulevard (later called Baynard Boulevard) stretching into the distance shows Washington Heights, a sparsely populated new residential neighborhood just north of Brandywine Park. (Postcard from author's collection.)*

[Bottom] *Two decades later, the Boulevard has become a fashionable street of substantial well-kept homes set in the midst of lush lawns. (Postcard from author's collection.)*

Seasonal Beauty

Spring means that the cherry trees around the
Josephine Fountain are billowing with blossoms
and summer brings the Jasper Crane
rose into glorious bloom.
(Courtesy of the Friends of Wilmington Parks.)

Golden autumn is reflected in the long liquid
mirror of the millrace and winter, rarely as white
as this early-20th-century view, strips away the
leaves to show the basic contours of Brandywine
Park. *(Photograph courtesy of Don Eros;
postcard from author's collection.)*

Bridges on the Brandywine

SOUTH RACE JEFFERSON ST.,
1515 · Brandywine, Wilmington, Del.

[Top] *The three bridges, a metal truss bridge, a stone arched span, and a suspension bridge, stand in close proximity at the upstream end of Brandywine Park.*
(Postcard from author's collection.)

Visitors used bridges both formal and informal to cross the millrace.
(Postcard from author's collection.)

The Van Buren Street Bridge, built soon after the zoo opened in North Brandywine Park, provided visitors with easy access to attractions on both sides of the river-the zoo on the north side and the Brandywine pool on the south side.
(Postcard from author's collection.)

The Washington Memorial Bridge rose on elegant arches above both the river and South Park Drive.
(Postcard from author's collection.)

The Market Street Bridge is the sixth to cross the Brandywine in this vicinity, providing a gateway into the city from the north.
(Photograph by author.)

The park walk near the Swinging Bridge

was along a rocky path lush with greenery.

(Postcard from author's collection.)

The lake at the zoo was home to waterfowl in

summer and a site for ice skating in the win[...]

(Postcard from the author's collection.)

The park's neighbors in nearby Washington

Heights headed up efforts to establish

a zoo in Brandywine Park. This circa 191[...]

postcard shows the path leading into the zo[...]

and toward the rustically designed

"Washington Heights Deerpark."

(Postcard from author's collection.)

Water seems always at hand in Brandywine Park.
The old tree leaned over the millrace for over 200
years until wind toppled it in 1999.
(Postcard from author's collection.)

The park drive between Washington Street
and Market Street offers a scenic view of the
Brandywine. (Postcard from author's collection.)

The river and race run close to one another
near the dam, but are increasingly farther
apart as they move downstream.
(Postcard from author's collection.)

This view, known as Canby Vista, overlooking the Brandywine

upstream above Brandywine Park was a favorite of William

Marriott Canby. It is easy to understand his love of the river

and the park he helped create along its banks.

(Postcard from author's collection.)

By 1918, however, the bridge was suffering from the increased volume and weight of traffic. A consulting engineer reported that only "lighter type" trolley cars should be allowed to use the bridge, and the Levy Court restricted the speed of vehicles crossing the bridge to six miles an hour. It was clear that a new bridge was needed, and in March 1919, only months after the end of World War I, the State General Assembly approved the establishment of the Washington Street Bridge Commission, charged with overseeing construction of a new span. When the commissioners drew up the standards for the bridge design, they specified the new span should have "a memorial character" to honor Delawareans who had given their lives during America's brief participation in the war. The commission also settled on the Washington Memorial Bridge as the name for the new bridge.[21]

The commission closed the Washington Street Bridge on August 9, 1920, had it dismantled, and started construction on August 21. While the bridge was going up, the Bridge Commission's executive director faced the challenge of gathering a complete list of the Delawareans who died in the war, names to be inscribed on a memorial plaque on the bridge. Once he had collected what appeared to be a complete list, he sent it to all the newspapers in the state so that people could provide corrections.[22]

Construction on the bridge went smoothly, and the new span opened to trolley traffic on December 7, 1921, and to vehicular traffic two weeks later, on December 23. The local press heralded the "magnificent" bridge as "a fine gateway to the city for all traffic from the north."[23] Anticipating the bridge's dedication, the Bridge Commission was determined to provide a fitting ceremony for such a memorial. Invitations to the dedication went out to veterans of the Civil War and Spanish-American War and to Gold Star

Local officials named the new span the Washington Memorial Bridge, a tribute to the Delawareans who died in World War I and to George Washington's connection to the Brandywine and to Wilmington. (Postcard from author's collection.)

The Washington Street Bridge, built in 1893, provided access to a new neighborhood north of the river. It was demolished in 1920 to make room for the Washington Memorial Bridge. (Postcard from author's collection.)

building lots, and began marketing sites for new homes in a development called "Washington Heights." Two years later, at the behest of Baynard and his partners, who subscribed $7,500 toward construction costs, the Levy Court erected a metal truss bridge across the Brandywine where the current reinforced concrete bridge stands.[20] The 1893 Washington Street Bridge provided the access necessary for Baynard's real estate venture to succeed, and residents began buying lots along the development's primary street, The Boulevard.

DEDICATION OF
WASHINGTON MEMORIAL BRIDGE

[Left] An honor guard by Troop 23, Boy Scouts of
America, stands at attention before a pylon on which
was mounted, veiled behind an American flag,
a memorial plaque listing the Delawareans
who died in World War I.
(Courtesy of Wilmington Public Library.)

[Right] When the flag was drawn aside, the
memorial plaque was unveiled, revealing the
names. (Courtesy of Wilmington Public Library.)

[Bottom] The festivities marking the
dedication of the Washington Memorial
Bridge included a parade and pageant with
over 800 participants. These "Flower
Fairies" threw flowers from the bridge into
the Brandywine to show their desire "to
decorate the graves of the fallen
Delawareans who did not
return from France."
(Courtesy of Wilmington Public Library.)

Mothers, women who had lost a son during World War I. The Bridge Commission's dedication festivities, held on Memorial Day 1922, included a parade, pageant with 800 participants, and speeches.[24]

As an ornament on the Wilmington landscape, the bridge used sculpture and poetry both to commemorate Delawareans who died in the World War I and to recognize George Washington's connection to the Brandywine River and to Wilmington. Eagles atop globes captured the sense of victory that the end of the war brought. The obelisk shape of the four tall pylons linked 20th-century America to ancient Egypt, where such obelisks were erected at temple portals. Four bronze plaques listed not only names of people, battles, and wars but also included images and poetry. Bridge Commission member John Rossell noted in his address at the dedication that the commissioners had chosen a quote from Alfred Lord Tennyson's "Charge of the Light Brigade" to honor soldiers who were "unafraid and resolute, unmindful of shot and shell" as they fought for their country.[25] To those gathered at the dedication, the bridge must have represented both honor for the past and hope for the future, and it remains an example of the human impulse to record publicly the contributions of individuals to society.

Market Street Bridge

The current Market Street Bridge, built in 1929, is the sixth bridge to cross the Brandywine at this location. The first bridge, dating from 1764, was a suspension bridge supported by chains, as was the second, built when the first became "somewhat dilapidated." In 1822 a flood swept away the second bridge, and the Levy Court replaced it with a wooden covered bridge. In 1839 a flood destroyed the first covered bridge, and the Levy Court built another wooden covered bridge.[26]

In 1887 the Levy Court replaced the covered bridge with a metal truss span that could accommodate the Wilmington City Railway Company's electric trolleys, which were taking the place of horse-drawn streetcars. In 1888, a year after the bridge's construction, the company ran its first electrified trolleys across the Market Street Bridge, through Brandywine Village, and up Philadelphia Pike as far as the city line.[27]

The metal truss bridge, which had a speed limit of eight miles an hour, served the city for four decades, but by the 1920s, city leaders characterized the span as "somewhat rickety (and) inadequate to modern traffic."[28] It was time for another Market Street Bridge. When residents of the nearby neighborhood saw plans for the new bridge, they anticipated it as a "decided improvement" that would both provide an attractive entrance to their community and demonstrate the city's progressive character.[29]

While the Washington Memorial Bridge was under construction, the Bridge Commission designated a detour around the construction work, but the Market Street Bridge

The Market Street Bridge, built in 1928-29, replaced the "rickety" Market Street Bridge that had been erected in 1887. Workers built the new bridge in sections, completing the upstream lanes first and then the lanes on the downstream side. Traffic continued to flow at this crucial crossing, even as construction was underway. (Courtesy of IA Holdings Corporation.)

was one of the primary gateways into the city, too essential a crossing to be completely closed. Thus when the Levy Court began construction in 1928, it followed a work plan that allowed construction on the new bridge while traffic still crossed the Brandywine on the old bridge. The contractor's crew erected the new span in two sections. They built the western, upstream half of the bridge first, with traffic continuing to cross via the old metal truss bridge. Once the western half of the new bridge was completed, traffic began to use that part of the bridge, and work began on the eastern half of the new bridge. Finally, the old bridge was demolished.[30]

The nearby Washington Memorial Bridge rose above the Brandywine on soaring, weight-bearing arches. The Market Street Bridge, however, was too near the water to be constructed similarly so the bridge's designers used a cantilever design with a shallow, decorative arch that provided the desired "attractive lines."[31] The Levy Court's plans for the 1929 bridge required a slight realignment of traffic on the south approach to the bridge, displacing the 1909 National Humane Alliance fountain from the inter-section of Market and 16th streets. Until the Delaware Department of Transportation (DelDOT) renovated the bridge in 2002, steel railroad tracks crossed the north approach to the bridge. They were part of the Philadelphia, Baltimore, and Washington Railroad spur that ran to the Jessup and Moore Paper Company. When a train passed along the tracks, safety barriers on either side of the bridge dropped and held back traffic. DelDOT removed the rails during its bridge refurbishment project.

When the Levy Court built the Market Street Bridge, horses were being seen less often on Wilmington's streets, the flour mills of Brandywine Village were in their last days, and railroad cars held up traffic on the bridge only rarely. Although those elements now are gone, aspects of life in the late 1920s survive. The bridge is still an important link across the river, the adjacent community still wants an attractive gateway into their neighborhood, and Wilmington's Bus Route 1 still follows the same path up

Philadelphia Pike that the Route 1 trolleys traveled in 1888.

I-95 Bridge

When Congress passed the Federal-Aid Highway Act in 1956, the legislators imagined a highway network linking all parts of the country. Delaware's part in that web would be tiny, less than 24 miles, but it had an impact on Brandywine Park. In February 1957, the local press published plans for the route through Wilmington, and the State Highway Department hosted public meetings to present information about the proposed six-lane freeway. It was soon clear that there was substantial public opposition to the route through the city.

In March 1957, the park commissioners attended their first special meeting about the "proposed expressway through the western part of the city." After some discussion, Board President M. du Pont Lee defended the parks and open space and articulated the board's sense of its duty to preserve those assets. In April 1957, Lee briefed the Executive Committee about "the events which took place at the public hearing" concerning the proposed expressway.[32]

In the weeks and months that followed, Lee appeared at open meetings held to discuss the highway and expressed the board's strong opposition to parkland being used by the State Highway Department. In the 1956–57 *Annual Report*, Director of Parks and Recreation John B. Quinn remarked on the pressures exerted on Brandywine Park, and on parks in general, because of the automobile's growing dominance and the propensity of highway planners to appropriate public lands without recognizing the parks' "priceless recreational value, their beauty, their use for intangible purposes which can never be measured in a practical sense."[33]

Opponents filed a court case to prevent the highway's construction, but the effort, which delayed the project for two years, was unsuccessful. Construction began in January 1959. Lee and the commissioners then determined to do what they could to minimize the adverse impact it had on the park. Early in the process, the board met with State Highway Department representatives who indicated a willingness "to cooperate with the Board of Park Commissioners" so that the bridge crossing the park would have "an architectural design of good taste so as to maintain the aesthetic beauty of the Brandywine Park."[34] The Highway Department provided sketches of design options and presented scale models of possible bridges, soliciting the board's input when it selected the final bridge design. At the same time, the board elicited from the Highway Department an agreement that the department would plant a new tree for every tree "sacrificed" during construction in the park.[35] The agreement also required the Highway Department to compensate the city park system with new park land to replace land taken by the highway bridge. The board's 1960–61 *Annual Report* advised that the commissioners were "following closely the planning for the highway, with the view of keeping to a minimum the destruction of trees and of preserving the natural beauty of the parks."[36] The park commissioners determined that land in the area of Cool Spring Reservoir would be suitable to replace the land lost in Brandywine Park, reasoning that it would "provide park and recreation facilities in this large, heavily populated sector," where such amenities were in short supply.[37]

Over the next six years, the process of building the highway and constructing the bridge along the western edge of Brandywine Park proceeded. As the Board of Park Commissioners watched closely. The commissioners set clear rules controlling the construction crew's access to the work site, restrictions intended to protect park structures and to preserve the park's peace and quiet as much as possible.[38] At one point, the park director reported that the Highway Department had "assured him that Stadium Drive would not be closed until a road replacing it was built." The board recommended that the captain of the park police "keep an eye on the work to see that the road is not closed."[39] The bridge and highway opened in 1967.

THOSE OTHER BRIDGES

The Board of Park Commissioners was responsible for several small bridges within the park, some

This small stone bridge, circa 1909, spanned Elliott's Run in North Brandywine Park, providing necessary access across the small stream within the park. (Courtesy of the Historical Society of Delaware.)

accommodating vehicles and others pedestrians. One of the earliest was the bridge that carried South Park Drive over the South Long Race at West Street. Because the board decided to run South Park Drive south of the raceway for part of its route and north of the race for the balance of the route, the commissioners had to erect a bridge to carry the roadway across the race. By July 1898, work on the drive had progressed to the crucial crossing, and construction began on the bridge abutments, built with substantial granite columns anchoring the corners of the bridge, which crossed the race at an angle. The Edge Moor Bridge Company built the steel girder bridge with a simple railing ornamented with scrolled metal details. Ever the advocate of stone as a building material for the park, Park Superintendent Leisen declared that "masonry arches would have been in better keeping with the surroundings," but the funds available were only enough to pay for the less expensive steel bridge.[40]

The second major bridge within the park carried Lovering Avenue over Rattlesnake Run. Originally designated the Clayton Street Bridge because it spanned what amounted to a continuation of Clayton Street downward from Delaware Avenue toward the river, the structure is a single-arch stone bridge that replaced a wood or wood-and-metal span that dated from the early 1890s. The earlier bridge required frequent repairs that Leisen characterized as "temporary."[41] By 1900 the plank floor was "in very bad condition," and the following year, the Board of Park Commissioners collaborated with the Street and Sewer Department on the construction of a new stone bridge to replace the unsatisfactory earlier one. The bridge was completed in 1902.[42]

The commissioners also erected a small vehicular bridge to carry North Park Drive over Elliott's Run soon after the Elliott tract became part of the park. In 1904 the superintendent reported that a new bridge had been installed there, using old girders from the Clayton Street Bridge that had been replaced two years earlier. Within five years, a new, more substantial bridge crossed the run, this one built with square stone piers and rustic logs for railings.[43] In the years that followed, the park commissioners erected replacement bridges as North Park Drive was improved and widened. The current span, a plain concrete deck with limited stone ornamentation, appears to date from the latter part of the 20th century.

In addition to providing for vehicular traffic, the park board appreciated that it needed to provide and maintain footbridges to allow park visitors to cross the millraces. In 1896, for example, the park superintendent prepared plans for iron footbridges for this purpose. The Edge Moor Bridge Company eventually manufactured three "lattice" bridges at a cost of $140 each. They were installed at Jefferson and Adams streets and 300 feet above Van Buren Street.[44] Over the years, these bridges provided constant work for park crews who scraped and painted

them, replaced their wooden floors with concrete, and finally replaced them altogether with the wooden structures that now serve park visitors. Not only did the WPA workers grade roads and footpaths, but they also built the stone pedestrian bridge over Elliott's Run in 1937.[45] Constructed with the same care expended on other WPA projects in the park, the stone arched bridge is a handsome complement to the modest concrete vehicular bridge immediately adjacent to it.

CONCLUSION

In addition to their practical worth and their beauty, the bridges that span the Brandywine River, the millrace, and the park runs collectively also record the long sweep of history from the late 19th to the 21st century. In the most basic terms, it is a story of automobiles replacing horses and cars and trains proliferating and thereby playing an increasingly important role in American life. Bridge construction reflected technology's changes, as metal truss designs gave way to concrete and concrete soon was combined with steel.

Read like documents, each bridge tells a bit of the city's story. The Swinging Bridge is a reminder of the days when workers walked to their jobs and the Brandywine was an industrial, not recreational, river. The B&O Railroad Bridge and Augustine Cut-Off Bridge capture that period of change when first railroads and then automobiles played successive key roles in the nation's transportation system. The Van Buren Street Bridge and its leaky water main reflect the city's steady growth in the early 20th century and the needs that had to be addressed because of that growth while the Washington Memorial Bridge shows Wilmingtonians' recognition of the city's connectedness to the larger world, a link that could not be denied after World War I. While each contribution may be modest, as part of Wilmington's overall history, each little story adds depth and richness to our understanding of the past.

Chapter 6

Memorials in the Park

P ublic spaces, including or perhaps particularly parks, have long been used as sites for commemorative markers and statues. Delaware patriot Caesar Rodney gallops perpetually along the side of Rodney Square, 15th-century explorer Christopher Columbus keeps vigil on Pennsylvania Avenue, and assassinated President James A. Garfield oversees the intersection of 23rd Street and Concord Avenue. Brandywine Park too is a public space with numerous memorials. The park landscape reflects the impulse to honor those who made noteworthy contributions to society and connects visitors with the city's and the nation's past.

While it is far from common, it is not totally unheard of for monuments or statues to be moved from one site to another. The statue of President Garfield has occupied its Concord Avenue site since 1918, but when it was new in 1895, it stood at Washington Street and Delaware Avenue. The bronze effigy of Adm. Samuel Francis du Pont at the 19th Street entrance to Rockford Park originally anchored the center of Du Pont Circle in Washington, D.C. Although Du Pont Circle kept the name it acquired with the statue's installation in 1884, in 1918 a fountain replaced it, and the memorial was moved to Wilmington. By 1920 the admiral had a new home in Rockford Park. Interestingly, nearly half the monuments that visitors pass regularly in Brandywine Park started out at another location. The Bringhurst Fountain, the Churchman memorial, and the McKinley memorial all experienced some degree of dislocation between first installation and current placement. Knowing they have moved, however, does not diminish what their stories can reveal about the times that produced them.

The Bringhurst Fountain

The tall ornamented pillar that stands regally adjacent to the Jasper Crane Rose Garden has known something of a peripatetic existence for so solid a piece of sculpture. The gray and red Aberdeen granite shaft with its solid granite base and ornamental urn make up the Bringhurst Fountain. It first stood on the point of land where Pennsylvania and Delaware avenues converge, now an ivy-clad triangular park occupied by Charles Parks's sculpture of a tall youth flanked by two dogs.

In 1872 a prominent Wilmington couple, Mr. and Mrs. J. Taylor Gause, donated the site for a memorial to Ferris Bringhurst, founder of the Wilmington Fountain Society.[1] Two years earlier, in May 1870, Bringhurst had called together a group of concerned Wilmingtonians to organize a charity for the purpose of supplying water for residents and

[Left] *This granite fountain honors Ferris Bringhurst, founder of the Wilmington Fountain Society. Erected in 1872, it stood at the junction of Pennsylvania and Delaware avenues. Removed in the 1960s when the site was renovated, it was stored for two decades before going on display again in the Rose Garden in 1988. (Postcard from author's collection.)*

[Top] *In 2004, the Friends of Wilmington Parks built a terrace adjacent to the Rose Garden overlooking the Brandywine. After conservation work on the Bringhurst Fountain was completed, the Friends moved the memorial to the middle of the new terrace. (Courtesy of Don Eros.)*

their horses and dogs. In its first year, the society placed four fountains and two water troughs on the streets of the city.[2]

A year after he founded the Wilmington Fountain Society, Bringhurst was killed in a laboratory accident at his family's pharmaceutical company, and his death led the society to pay tribute to his leadership and kindness. The memorial was a fountain inscribed on one side "To the Memory of Ferris Bringhurst, First President of the Wilmington Fountain Society" and on the other "Kindness to God's Creatures is a Service Acceptable to Him."

It began operating on July 1, 1872. Early 20th-century postcards show the fountain furnished with a drinking cup secured near the water spigot by a chain. An iron fence surrounded three of the fountain's four sides. The decorative sculptural details included elements typical of the Victorian age in which it was created: the classic urn on the top of the shaft denoted death, and carved cat-tails and water lilies reflected the Fountain Society's association with water.

In the mid-1960s, a local philanthropist purchased the land where the fountain stood, intending to improve the site as a park, but the out-of-fashion fountain did not fit the redevelopment plan. W. W. ("Chick") Laird rescued the Victorian monument and offered to store it, which he did for nearly two decades. In the late 1970s, the Delaware Avenue Community Association proposed restoring the memorial to public view, considering, among other sites, the Park Plaza Condominiums then under construction. Finally on August 4, 1988, the mayor, staff members from the city's Parks and Recreation Department, and representatives of the neighborhood association gathered in the rose garden to rededicate the Bringhurst Fountain in its new home.[4]

In 2004, as an extension of their earlier work to restore the Jasper Crane Rose Garden, the Friends of Wilmington Parks initiated a project to create a new setting for the fountain, to restore a birdbath to the center of the rose beds, and to provide park visitors with a vista overlooking the river. The Friends constructed a stone plaza with walls for sitting and ramps allowing access to the path below, moved the fountain to a central point on the plaza, and provided the memorial with much needed conservation and restoration.

The Churchman Memorial

As with the Bringhurst Fountain, the Churchman memorial "drinking fountain," erected in memory of Clarke Churchman, also moved from its original location, although the move was a matter of but a few feet. Perhaps the most poignant memorial in the park, the small granite horse trough, which was dedicated in 1904 and sited where 16th Street meets the Washington Memorial Bridge, commemorates the death of 24-year-old Lt. Clarke Churchman, the only Delawarean killed in the Spanish-American War.

Churchman had sought an appointment to West Point and a military career, but his efforts and those of his socially prominent mother to win him admission to the academy had ended in disappointment. In 1893 Mrs. Churchman went to Chicago to serve her state as hostess at the Delaware Building of the World's Columbian Exposition (the Chicago World's Fair). She earned a reputation as a gracious and helpful hostess to all who visited the state pavilion. In October 1893, Delaware Congressman John W. Causey, with a delegation of other Representatives, visited the fair. While there, they became acquainted with Mrs. Churchman and at the end of their visit, the men asked Mrs. Churchman how they could thank her for her kindnesses. She made no secret of her dream for her son, and Causey promised to name him to a cadetship at West Point. Clarke began his West Point studies in the autumn of 1894.[5]

On February 15, 1898, the battleship U. S. S. *Maine* blew up in Havana Harbor, killing 260 and setting off the Spanish-American War. For that reason, West Point held graduation early so that the class of 1898, with Churchman

Clarke Churchman (1873–1898), a member of the West Point class of 1898, was honored in 1904 as the only Delawarean to die in the Spanish-American War. (Courtesy of the United States Military Academy at West Point.)

and his classmates, could be commissioned as officers and begin their active service. Clarke, now a second lieutenant, was assigned to the 12th Infantry in support of the Rough Riders at San Juan Hill. According to the local press, on July 1, 1898, Clarke was using his field glasses to determine the range "so that his men might adjust the sights of the rifles" when he was shot. He died the next day. After being buried on July 2 on the Cuban battlefield, his body was returned to America in December 1898 and re-interred at West Point.[6]

In 1904 the Blue Hens' Chickens, a society of young people descended from patriots who fought in the American Revolution, erected at Washington Street and the Boulevard a "horse fountain" in memory of Clarke Churchman. The group invited the state's patriotic societies, Wilmington officials, and all the city's schoolchildren to the dedication on April 26, 1904. After unveiling the fountain, the donors turned it over to the Wilmington Fountain Society, which had agreed to care for it. Receiving it on behalf of the Fountain Society, local attorney Josiah Marvel thanked the donors for their thoughtfulness in erecting "so useful a memorial."[7]

When the Board of Park Commissioners approved the installation of the nearby Todd Memorial in 1925, the Churchman fountain had to be moved. With the cooperation of the Wilmington Fountain Society, they reinstalled the little horse trough, with its basin for dogs and spigot for people, to the corner on the south side of 16th Street at the end of the Washington Street Bridge.[8]

McKINLEY MEMORIAL

Like the Bringhurst and Churchman fountains, the memorial to the assassinated President William McKinley originally occupied a different site in the park. When installed during the summer of 1908, the bas-relief sculpture stood on the south side of the Brandywine near the intersection of Van Buren Street and South Park Drive.

McKinley had carried Delaware in the elections of 1896 and 1900, defeating William Jennings Bryan both times. A Civil War veteran and a man of considerable charm, President McKinley had barely started his second term when, in September 1901, while at the Pan-American Exposition in Buffalo, he was assassinated by an anarchist. Deep national mourning marked his death; one Wilmington publication described his "kindness and gentleness of disposition, sweetness of nature and goodness of heart" as an example for future presidents and concluded that "There were no better men than William McKinley; there are few as good."[9]

An early idea for a McKinley memorial entailed constructing an arch at one of the entrances to Brandywine Park. The final design was a more restrained monument with sculpted depictions of McKinley.[10] The memorial's two bas-relief panels are set in granite: the smaller panel, a round medallion, shows the mature McKinley in profile; the larger, rectangular panel shows McKinley as a 19-year-old sergeant with the Ohio Volunteers, carrying coffee and rations to soldiers on the Antietam battlefield in September 1862. The New York sculptor who created both images, James Edward Kelly, was well known for his work depicting military personages and events. In 1895 he had met Maj. Gen. James Harrison Wilson, later chair of Wilmington's McKinley Memorial Committee, when Wilson attended the dedication of a Kelly statue at Gettysburg.[11] In 1902, when Wilson proposed to the park board a project to honor "our murdered president," the commissioners pledged a 10 percent match for funds raised by Wilson's committee. Wilmingtonians contributed $3,500, which the Park Commission complemented with $350. After paying $3,700 for the memorial, the committee earmarked the balance for maintenance of the monument and the installation site.[12]

When the McKinley Memorial was installed, the local press declared it "a decided improvement to that section of the park."[13] It stood at the south end of the recently completed Van Buren Street Bridge, and on September 17, 1908, the anniversary of the Battle of Antietam, Mayor Horace Wilson, Park Commissioner Samuel H. Baynard, and General Wilson unveiled the monument in a remarkably informal ceremony. Only the three men attended; the members of the McKinley Memorial Committee, who had worked long and hard to raise the funds for the monument, learned of the event when they read about it in the evening papers. They insisted that the unveiling had not been official.[14]

In the 1960s, when the construction of the I-95 Bridge across the western end of the park went directly above the McKinley monument, the State Highway Department agreed to relocate the memorial. The Board of Park Commissioners, after considering a move upstream, determined that the similarly rocky hillside at the foot of West Street was preferable, so the statue moved to its current location in 1963.[15]

Todd Memorial

Often called simply the "War Memorial" for many years after its installation, the Todd Memorial still occupies its original site in the park, just north of the Washington Memorial Bridge in a triangle of parkland bounded by Washington Street, 18th Street, and Baynard Boulevard. On Armistice Day (November 11, 1925), more than 9,000 people gathered there to see the memorial unveiled. Warm weather and cloudless skies helped ensure a good turnout for the ceremony to commemorate the sacrifice of the Delaware soldiers and sailors who had died in World War I.[16]

In 1925 Wilmington native William H. Todd donated a memorial to Delaware's World War I dead, a sculpture that combines a 35-foot granite shaft and a bronze statue of Winged Victory. (Postcard from author's collection.)

William H. Todd, the monument's donor, was born in Wilmington in 1867, though by 1925, Brooklyn, New York, was his home. At an early age, he worked during school vacations as a rivet boy in the Pusey and Jones Shipyard boiler shop. By age 16, he had a full-time job with the shipbuilder and gradually worked his way up to assistant foreman. After moving to New York in 1893, he rose through the ranks at the Brooklyn Navy Yard until, by 1916, he headed Todd Shipyards Corporation. He operated his business on a cooperative, profit-sharing system, protecting and rewarding the employee-stockholders through successive corporate reorganizations. At the time of Todd's death in 1932, the company owned shipyards in Brooklyn; New Orleans; Mobile, Alabama; Tacoma, Washington; and Portland, Oregon.[17]

Todd donated a bronze sculpture, "Winged Victory," created by Augustus Lukeman. Mounted on a rectangular granite pier bearing the words "Erected in Honor of the Soldiers and Sailors of Delaware Who Served in the World War, 1917–1918, A Gift of William H. Todd in Memory of His Father and Mother/1925," it is set in a circular plaza in front of a 35-foot granite shaft. Cast at the Roman Bronze Works of Brooklyn, the winged figure is a woman in classical dress, arms raised and a branch in her left hand. Stylized arrows bound by bands decorate the granite shaft

near the top and an urn-shaped sculpture surmounts it. At the foot of the plaza, on a granite base, a bronze plaque lists the names of the Delawareans "Who Died in the Service of their Country 1917–1919."[18] Speakers at the dedication ceremony included New York Governor Alfred E. Smith and Delaware Senator Thomas F. Bayard. A large contingent from New York attended the unveiling as an honor to Todd, by then a prominent New Yorker.

In June 1921, Todd had given a similar World War I memorial to his adopted hometown, Brooklyn. Also sculpted by Augustus Lukeman and cast by the Roman Bronze Works, it was erected in Prospect Park. It too features a winged female figure, but instead of a representation of victory, it depicts an angel of death, an angelic figure with huge wings who seems to be supporting or perhaps "gathering in" a weary soldier. While the mood of the Wilmington memorial is victorious, the Brooklyn monument is somber. The memorial list names the borough's dead and honors "the men and women of Brooklyn who died in the world war" and "gave their lives for liberty and universal peace, honor, duty, country."[19]

The Todd Memorial in Brandywine Park is a noteworthy link to the larger world of American sculpture.

J. Ernest Smith, prominent Wilmington attorney, donated over 100 flowering cherry trees in 1929 and, after the 1931 death of his wife Josephine Tatnall Smith, he gave the Josephine Fountain as a memorial placed amidst the trees. Dedicated in 1933, the fountain and trees (shown in this circa 1954 picture) were so popular a destination that during the spring in the 1930s the area was lighted so visitors could enjoy the blossoms at dusk. (Courtesy of the Historical Society of Delaware.)

Lukeman, the sculptor, studied with famed American sculptors Daniel Chester French and Launt Thompson. French and Lukeman collaborated on the 1917 Lafayette Monument (also in Prospect Park) and worked together again on the Brooklyn war memorial that Todd donated in 1921, Lukeman sculpting the figure and French preparing the bronze plaques. Launt Thompson, Lukeman's other principal teacher, created the statue of Adm. Samuel Francis du Pont in Rockford Park. All three artists enjoyed wide renown and produced a vast number of commemorative sculptures throughout the country.[20]

JOSEPHINE FOUNTAIN

In 1933 prominent Wilmington attorney J. Ernest Smith donated the Josephine Fountain as a memorial to his late wife, Josephine Tatnall Smith, who often strolled along the river through Brandywine Park and inspired his donation of 114 cherry trees to the park. After Mrs. Smith died in 1931, he honored her life by placing the elegant marble memorial fountain amidst the grove of flowering trees. Dedicated in April 1933, the fountain and its surrounding trees were designated the Josephine Gardens.[21]

Architect Edward Canby May and sculptor John Brockhouse, who designed the memorial, modeled it after a 16th-century Italian fountain that Niccolo Tribolo designed for the Medici family.[22] At the top, the figure of a draped woman holding a cornucopia stands above a series of pedestals and basins of smooth, unpolished stone. Carved cupids, grotesque masks, lions' heads, winged cherubs, goats' heads, mermaids, and dolphins decorate the piers and basins. The fountain is set on a large octagonal base. A nearby bronze plaque identifies the fountain as a memorial to Josephine Tatnall Smith. In the 1930s, thousands of visitors came to see the fountain and the blossoming cherry trees each spring. For several years during this period, the Wilmington Fountain Society underwrote the cost of having the area illuminated with electric lights in the evenings while the trees were in bloom.

J. Ernest Smith donated a small endowment for the care of the fountain, but over the years, neglect left the entire work in poor repair. The basins had crumbled in some places and were broken in others, and the plumbing system no longer functioned. The New Castle County Department of Parks and Recreation removed the sculpture in stages and stored it to prevent further deterioration until, by the late 1980s, only the base remained. The Department of Parks and Recreation restored the fountain in 1997–98, replacing missing features with cast stone, and rededicated it in April 1998.

VIETNAM MEMORIAL

In the early 1980s, local citizens sought to create a memorial to the Delawareans who died in the Vietnam War, an undertaking that was plagued by controversy, both over a suitable site for the memorial and over the project's cost.

Some proponents favored the area that was being developed near the Amtrak Station, a location, they felt, where large numbers of people would see the memorial. That suggestion proved unacceptable because the development plans were not complete and supporters of the Vietnam Memorial were eager for the project to proceed. Other civic groups argued for placing the memorial in H. Fletcher Brown Park. Initially, the New Castle County Council approved that site until it became clear that it would cost an additional $44,000 to modify the park to accommodate the memorial design. The county had already allocated $190,000 for the project and refused any changes that increased the price tag.

In February 1983, after investigations of alternative sites and public hearings, County Council designated

The Vietnam Memorial, dedicated in 1983, honors Delaware's sons and daughters claimed by the conflict in southeast Asia. (Courtesy of the Friends of Wilmington Parks.)

Brandywine Park as the location for the memorial.[23] The monument combines Charles Parks's sculpture of one soldier carrying the body of a fellow soldier on a "hillock" paved with stone blocks. Around the base is an array of medallions listing different branches of the military and eight rectangular plaques honoring the Delawareans who died or were missing in Vietnam.

A group of some 1,000 people gathered on November 11, 1983, to see the memorial dedicated. A parachute draped the sculpture until it was unveiled; at the ceremony, 10 participants read aloud the names of the Delawareans listed on the plaques, beginning with the name of Army Captain James H. Johnson Jr., who died on October 3, 1963, and ending with the name of Colonel Paul Meder, the last Delawarean to die in Vietnam, December 21, 1972.

AFRICAN-AMERICAN MEDAL OF HONOR RECIPIENTS MEMORIAL

In the late 1990s, local artist Charles Parks created in bronze another military memorial with two figures: a Civil War soldier and a 20th-century parachutist, representing the long service African-Americans have offered America. Wilmingtonian and army veteran Wilson K. Smith had long hoped to create a memorial to African-American Medal of Honor recipients. Smith's goal was to have the monument placed inside the Pentagon, but military officials considered it "too tall" for that location.[24]

As was the case with the Vietnam Memorial, the proposed monument generated discussions and some disagreement. The first challenge of the project was finding a suitable location. Originally, the City Council approved a site at 18th and Van Buren streets, but the steepness of the terrain presented difficulties. A suggestion of 18th and Monroe streets prompted public opposition from park advocates who argued against placing the memorial where it would interrupt the open stretch of green meadow along 18th Street and raised questions about how much open space a park can lose before its function as a park is compromised. Different interested

The African-American Medal of Honor Recipients Memorial lists 105 African-Americans who have received the Medal of Honor in conflicts from the Civil War through Vietnam. (Courtesy of the Friends of Wilmington Parks.)

parties suggested a wide range of locations around Brandywine Park, but in the end the mayor and City Council decided on 18th Street and Baynard Boulevard. The proposal raised a second, painful difference of opinion that remained unresolved, the question of the appropriateness of using public space for a monument that honors members of a single race to the exclusion of all others.

Dedicated in September 1999, the sculpture of the two soldiers stands on an octagonal base set in a circular, paved plaza. The plaques around the base of the memorial recount the stories of African-Americans who received the Medal of Honor for service in conflicts from the Civil War through Vietnam. After it was dedicated, the African-American Medal of Honor Association added its own plaque to the site, recognizing the Wilmington City Council and officials for contributing to the completion of the monument.

CONCLUSION

Through their gifts, a variety of individuals and groups have provided a rich array of memorials in the park. Each adds, in its own way, a narrative that deepens our understanding of the story of Wilmington and the history of America. The Bringhurst Fountain provides insight into the lives of well-to-do Victorians whose recognition of a public need prompted action of an immediate and personal sort. The Wilmington Fountain Society gave the Bringhurst Fountain to the city, and several individuals within the society also donated horse troughs or water fountains that were placed in city neighborhoods. Josephine Fountain, the gift of a loving

husband in memory of his wife, was a private donation, a reminder of a time when wealthy individuals made contributions for projects they largely controlled, a contrast to today's general practice of donors supporting established "causes" with their contributions.

The most common and long-standing practice is, of course, to use public space to honor political leaders and military endeavors. Several of Brandywine Park's memorials fall into that category, each offering a different link to the past. The McKinley Memorial, the only one to honor a political leader, is a simple, almost classical work, highlighting a change in memorial traditions. In recent times it has become customary to honor political leaders not with statues but by naming highways, bridges, and airports after them.

The Churchman Fountain, the Washington Memorial Bridge, the Todd Memorial, the Vietnam Memorial, and the African-American Medal of Honor Recipients Memorial all connect the viewer to America's military history. The Churchman memorial offers an opportunity to consider the extent to which the Spanish-American War marked the start of America's journey "outward," since it was that particular war that made the Philippines an American territory. The Washington Memorial Bridge and the Todd Memorial are both reminders of the country's involvement in World War I. Although Americans were in Europe for only a year, the period ended any illusions Americans might have had about being isolated from the rest of the world and therefore safe.

The Vietnam Memorial is a touching monument to the Delawareans who were lost in the conflict, and it calls to mind the painful ruptures that the war caused in American society, in Wilmington as well as elsewhere. The memorial to the African-American Medal of Honor recipients, the most recently installed, honors a deserving group of soldiers and sailors while it offers a reminder of the issues that society continues to confront.

Chapter 7

Fun & Games, Strolling & Sitting

Parks provided spaces where city dwellers could engage in all sorts of recreational activities, from vigorous active exercise to passive leisurely pastimes. Park planners intended the parks to be used in both ways, feeling that the refreshment of leisure, whether active or quiet, would prove restorative.

Many existing park properties devoted areas to playgrounds, playing fields, and swimming pools. Beginning in the late 19th century, advocates associated with the "recreation movement" encouraged city park departments to include many more forms of active recreation. The first recreation supervisor hired by the Wilmington Board of Park Commissioners, Jennie M. Weaver, articulated the generally held attitude toward the benefits of park recreation: "Recreation," she noted, "in one form or another is necessary at all times for all men, women and children, and as a city provides opportunities for the same so in turn will its citizens be better, happier and healthier."[1]

The Board of Park Commissioners understood the benefits of both active and passive recreation, and in Brandywine Park the two types of "distractions" developed simultaneously. As the park and activities within it developed, the commissioners addressed effectively the ongoing need to balance active and passive uses so that there was ample space provided for both pursuits. They endeavored as well to extend access to the park to as wide a range of users as possible.

Park Users

A vast number of individuals and groups sought permission to use portions of the park for a wide range of activities. During the summer of 1914, the captain of the park police kept a record of what groups used the parks. His list included Sunday schools, fife and drum corps, churches, the Girls Friendly Society, Sunday Breakfast Mission, Christian Missionary Alliance, Mutual Benefit Association, the Boy Scouts, and the Daughters of Pocahontas, a women's fraternal organization.[2]

Throughout the 20th century, civic groups frequently asked permission to use portions of the park for organized activities. Some wanted space for members to gather for picnics, parties, and entertainment and others wanted to stage fund-raising events or offer public programs. The character of the requests changed with time, as society and tastes changed, and the number of requests increased after World War I.

Fishponds, established in North Brandywine Park in 1891, were a popular site for eager anglers. The start of the zoo involved fencing one of the ponds for the display of waterfowl. (Courtesy of the Historical Society of Delaware.)

During the 1920s, for example, the Delaware Anglers and Gunners Association sponsored several fly casting tournaments in the Washington Triangle, the area bounded by Washington Street, 18th Street and Baynard Boulevard.[3] In the same period, the Wilmington Chautauqua Association used the park at least six summers as the setting for a week's worth of musical programs, dramatic readings, and lectures on a variety of topics.[4]

Park usage varied with the times, and this was especially apparent in 1930s Wilmington. Straitened financial circumstances caused families to seek free recreation in the city's parks, finding relaxation and refreshment in the open spaces and on the playing fields. In 1933 Park Superintendent Edward R. Mack noted that the restricted working hours associated with the Depression meant more people had more leisure time that needed to be filled. Plans were under way, he announced, "to extend the (park) system until it affords a real playground for the leisure hours of humanity."[5]

Wilmington families enjoyed free programs that a variety of sponsors offered in Brandywine Park. Beginning in the mid-1930s and continuing into the early 1940s, several organizations and agencies, including the WPA, provided summer concerts in the open air near the Todd War Memorial, with the park board supplying lights and chairs for the events. Discontinued during World War II, the concerts failed to see much of a revival in the 1950s, as movies and television offered alternative entertainment.[6]

Brandywine Park, with its varied terrain and range of athletic options, was, as the *Morning News* noted in 1940, "a park for the whole family." Recounting the park's establishment, the paper described its woods as "an alluring walking spot for romantic lovers and for plain nature lovers" and provided a catalogue of "42 recreational facilities," including those at Baynard Stadium, playing fields, picnic grounds and fireplaces, tennis and badminton courts, the swimming pool, and "last but not least, the one and only zoo."[7] In the 1940s, the circumstances associated with World War II caused many families to look to Brandywine Park for recreation as gasoline and tire shortages curtailed automobile travel and families sought entertainment close to home. The Board of Park Commissioners observed in 1944, "The restrictions in the use of automobiles have resulted in a greater use of picnic grounds in Brandywine and other intown [*sic*] parks. To accommodate this increase, additional picnic tables and fireplaces have been built."[8] Easter 1945 brought crowds to the park for the Easter parade. "Brandywine Park came back to its own last Sunday," reported the *Sunday Star*, "a perfect Easter, with thousands, including many in Uncle Sam's uniforms, wandering about and enjoying the natural beauty to the limit ... Before the gas shortage and travel restrictions, the old favorite of youth, Brandywine Park and its adjacent areas, was sadly neglected by citizens who always saw greener pastures and fairer parks elsewhere. They need never have stirred—they have one of the most beautiful natural parks right here at their doorsteps."[9]

During the 1950s, fund-raising events came into

vogue. Several fraternal organizations hosted peach and strawberry festivals near the Todd Memorial, and on at least one occasion, the Warner Junior High School PTA sold refreshments during a park event. Briefly during the 1930s, local theaters held Easter egg hunts in Brandywine Park, but during the 1950s, such events enjoyed great popularity. Each year, several sponsoring groups offered Wilmington children the chance to search the park's spring landscape for treasures.[10] In the 1960s, local rod and gun clubs invited youngsters to participate in "fishing rodeos" along the banks of the Brandywine, a popular diversion that attracted 300 to 400 hopeful young anglers on a regular basis.[11]

Brandywine Park was a consistently popular site for camp and Scouting programs. From the mid-1940s to the mid-1950s, the Wilmington YMHA (Young Men's Hebrew Association) and YWHA (Young Women's Hebrew Association) regularly used the park for summer day camps. For an even longer period, from 1919 through the 1950s, Boy Scouts and Girl Scouts also took advantage of the space and natural character of Brandywine Park. They earned merit badges as they built fires and practiced outdoor cooking, held day camps, learned canoe safety, and occasionally camped overnight.[12]

Throughout the years, patriotic functions were a regular part of Brandywine Park life. In 1919 the Delaware Branch of the American Legion observed Armistice Day by ending their parade in North Brandywine Park in the open space along 18th Street. After the 1925 dedication of the Todd Memorial, the monument was a site favored for patriotic observances, and the logical place for World War I veterans to mark Armistice Day. As late as the 1960s, the veterans group still gathered there, assisted by the Park Department, which supplied American and Delaware flags, chairs, and an amplification system.[13]

Because much of the park's 178 acres is open space, it has also been used by a variety of military groups. In 1926 the board granted the National Guard permission to erect a recruiting tent at the entrance to North Brandywine Park near the Market Street Bridge. Personnel from Fort du Pont came to the park for drill exercises in the late 1920s, and the Civilian Defense Council held "a gas demonstration" in Baynard Stadium in 1943. During World War II, the War Finance Committee attracted attention to the Fifth War Loan Drive by anchoring a barrage balloon in North Brandywine Park near Baynard Boulevard. In 1950 the Delaware National Guard's 261st Anti-Aircraft Artillery Brigade displayed equipment in North Brandywine Park on Armed Forces Day.[14]

Before the end of the 19th century, various religious groups sought permission to use park space. The board's initial interaction with religious denominations started with the commission denying the Seventh Day Adventists permission to camp out in Brandywine Park in 1897 and in 1902 refusing to allow the Christian Scientists to put up literature distribution boxes in the park, claiming that public parks "cannot be used for the dissemination of the doctrines of any particular political or religious creed."[15] In the long run, however, the commissioners were generally willing to allow the city's churches to use the park. Beginning in 1912, for example, the Board of Park Commissioners allowed Sunday evening services in North Brandywine Park. The gatherings, first sponsored by the Presbyterian Union and later by the Wilmington Council of Churches, were a regular feature of park life during July and August for two decades.[16]

In 1914 the board, interested in increasing park use by all kinds of groups, sent letters "to Sunday Schools and Churches calling attention to the picnic facilities," and the commissioners were rewarded for their efforts when "a considerable number made use of the parks."[17] In addition to the Sunday evening summer programs, churches used the park for picnics, for concerts, for Easter sunrise services, and as the site for a Christmas crèche for several years; on a couple of occasions, congregations performed baptisms in the Brandywine Pool. In 1926 the Holy Name Society celebrated a "field mass," and the Episcopal bishop held "missionary services" in North Brandywine Park.[18] In the 1930s, the Sisterhood of the Congregation Chesed Shel

Emeth also used the park for a picnic and, in the 1950s, for the annual children's picnic associated with the temple's Hebrew School.[19]

In addition to these seemingly routine events, there were other, not-so-frequent events in the park that demonstrated the breadth of its usage. In 1914 the Delaware Equal Suffrage Association planted a pin oak in North Brandywine Park to mark the members' determination to win the vote. The following year, the board permitted the group to perform a play in the park, to sell "light refreshments," to take up a collection, and to charge for seats, but the commissioners gave their permission "on condition that there be no suffrage propaganda or display of suffrage banners."[20] The park was the site of at least one protest against the war in Vietnam, union rallies on Labor Day in 1915 and 1941, four dog shows, and a number of events that brought together drum and bugle corps for music and competition.

There were also those strange, one-time-only applications that surely must have caused both consternation and amusement among the commissioners. In November 1927, Mr. Beacom, perhaps of Goldey-Beacom College, was given permission "to have a typewriter delivered by parachute in North Brandywine Park." There is no indication why Mr. Beacom felt the need to do this. Two decades later, the board denied a request from the Junior Chamber of Commerce to hold "a preliminary Turtle race in Rodney Square," although the group was allowed to stage their event in North Brandywine Park near 18th and Van Buren streets. There is no record of the winner's name.[21]

The words of park users over the years make it clear how important the work of the Board of Park Commissioners was to the community. In the spring of 1915, Edward R. Mack, park superintendent, received a letter from the pastor of the Union A. M. E. Church asking to use Eden Park for a day in July and another day in August. Although the letter does not concern Brandywine Park, the tone of the request articulated what having access to a community park meant. "We appreciate your favor of the past," the clergyman wrote, "And as we are too few in number to do big things—an outing there for the [Sunday] school and the Society will help to make the vacation period sunshine instead of sorrow and disappointment." Mack granted both requests.[22]

In the late 1930s, the board's minutes occasionally reported the extent of park usage. In July 1938, for example, the listing of "permits so far this season" for all the city's parks included 3,869 permits issued for use of the tennis courts, 1,226 for softball games, 679 for baseball games, 216 for picnics with fires, and 22 for large picnics. But there were also permits for day camps, a sunrise service, an Easter egg hunt, a baptism, a strawberry festival, and a field day. There seems little doubt that Brandywine Park and the city park system were indeed essential to the Wilmingtonians who used them so extensively.

ACTIVE RECREATION

Although Brandywine Park had no supervised playground program, it still offered a wide range of opportunities for active recreation. Ice skating and baseball were two sports activities that received substantial attention during the park's early years. Superintendent Theodore A. Leisen's notes record a number of winters cold enough for skating on the Brandywine and, after 1904, on the fish-ponds at the zoo. In January 1896, the Phoenix Fire Company flooded the surface of the river ice near the foot of Adams Street to provide good skating. A year later nearly a month of low temperatures allowed skaters to be on the ice. On January 13, 1897, Leisen recorded, the temperature was 13°F at 7 a.m. and rose to 24°F by early afternoon, when there was "a large crowd skating in Brandywine."[23] Although skating continued to engage the interest of park users for several more years, the necessary cold conditions did not persist to an extent that allowed it to be a yearly activity.

By the mid-1890s, the superintendent was at work on plans for a "baseball ground" in North Brandywine Park, and he also gave consideration to making room for cricket as well. Establishment of suitable ball diamonds progressed

[Left] Ice skating has been a popular winter activity

on the Brandywine, both in 1913...

...and in 1940.

(Courtesy of the Historical Society of Delaware.)

until, in the early years of the 20th century, there was a diamond in North Brandywine Park for men and "grown boys" and one in South Brandywine Park for small boys.[24] The Board of Park Commissioners noted baseball's popularity in the 1919 *Annual Report*, remarking that "with the return of the young men from service," there were times that the park's facilities were "too few to accommodate the teams that desire to play."[25] Baseball's popularity has persisted to the present with each summer's Little League program filling the bleachers anew with enthusiastic fans.

Tennis is another activity that has enjoyed long and consistent popularity among park users. The sport rose to great popularity in the late 19th century, and in 1909 the Board of Park Commissioners instructed the superintendent to build a tennis court at the foot of Adams Street. Actual construction was accomplished in stages, at what seems an achingly slow pace from the vantage point of the 21st century. In 1912 and 1913, the superintendent reported that earth was being taken to the proposed site and used to fill the low area between the race and the river. Although players used tennis courts "on the turf near Eighteenth Street and the Boulevard" in 1914, it was not until 1915 that the board could report that there were two tennis courts opposite the Wilmington and Brandywine Cemetery and that two more were under construction at Rowan Street

and Shallcross Avenue. Within two years the Rowan Street courts were completed; by 1922 they had been enlarged to a total of six courts.[26]

People played other sports and engaged in other activities, but it was baseball and tennis that received the most consistent attention from the commissioners. They were also the two sports that caused the most trouble in regard to leisure activities on Sundays. In 1927 lobbyists both for and against opening the tennis courts on Sunday petitioned the board for a decision regarding whether sports playing on Sunday would be allowed in Brandywine Park. Faced with a request for tennis courts to be open on Sunday, the board noted that, ever since the Park Commission was formed, its policy had been "to prohibit the playing in the parks on Sunday of any of the various games of amusement and pleasure." Based on that past practice, the commissioners passed a resolution, with seven ayes and two nays, to continue the prohibition. Requests continued, and in 1931 the board adopted two rules relating to tennis. The first set the times of play for different groups, allowing players "who are not employed during the day" to be refused permits after 5 p.m. so that working people had preference for the hours after the end of the workday. The second rule amended the regulation against Sunday games so that it to read: "The playing of athletic games except tennis on Sunday is prohibited."[27] Church leaders continued to object to opening the swimming pools and tennis courts on Sunday, but within four years, the board had also eased the rule on Sunday baseball games, modifying the ban against athletic games by setting a time limit; now tennis could be played at any hour on Sunday and "athletic games (were) prohibited before 2 p.m. standard Time."[28]

The board established few regulations specifically aimed at recreation, although an Executive Committee decision in 1899 did limit bicycling to "the path west of Adams St up to 9 am, at a speed not exceeding 5 miles per hour" and prohibited "the ringing of bells."[29] As the 20th century progressed, the commissioners also felt the need to control sports involving projectiles, in 1935 prohibiting golf, in 1951 banning BB guns, and in 1954 warning that "indiscriminate use of our parks … for the purpose of shooting arrows from a bow would not be tolerated."[30]

If there was one area of concentrated active recreation in Brandywine Park, it was around Baynard Stadium and along 18th Street. After the city graded 18th Street in 1912, leaving a high bank of earth along the edge of the street, Samuel H. Baynard underwrote the cost of having the earth redistributed over an area west of Franklin Street. The site had previously been such that there was room for only one baseball diamond; the 40,000 cubic yards of earth that was moved to the area provided a foundation for three diamonds and a football field, the start of the complex of facilities that the board designated the Baynard Athletic Grounds in 1913.[31]

Although there were no regular summer playground programs for youngsters in Brandywine Park, the park occasionally hosted special events such as this 1950 horseshoe tournament. (Courtesy of the Historical Society of Delaware.)

After World War I, Baynard continued making improvements to the Athletic Grounds, adding a quarter-mile cinder track and football field and a "stone and concrete grandstand." He purchased five cottages near the sports facility and converted them to provide storage and dressing rooms for the athletes. On June 24, 1922, the stadium and field of the Baynard Athletic Grounds were officially opened with "suitable exercises and by an Athletic and Gymnastic" program.[32]

When schools applied for permission to stage activities in Brandywine Park, they generally used Baynard Stadium, although other groups also hosted events there. The facility accommodated field days, soccer games, field hockey classes, dog shows, football games, bicycle races, horseshoe tournaments, and, in 1926, the Board of Education's "May Day Exercises." The stadium was also the site of a "Charles Lindbergh celebration" when the aviator visited the city in 1927 and the place where President George W. Bush's helicopter landed during his 2001 visit to Wilmington.[33]

In the mid-1950s, focus shifted to the Brandywine River for one weekend a year when the Buck Ridge Ski Club from Pennsylvania staged a "canoe slalom competition" for one or two days each April. The initial event in 1955

[Top] *Baynard Stadium provided facilities for high school athletes to compete in a variety of track and field events, such as this 1951 relay. There were also football games, field days, bicycle races, and several dog shows in the stadium. (Courtesy of the Historical Society of Delaware.)*

[Bottom] *The Brandywine Pool opened in 1898, the city's first swimming pool. Operating six days a week (closed on Sunday), the pool was open to men and women on different days of the week, a practice that continued into the 1940s. (Courtesy of the Historical Society of Delaware.)*

attracted 50 canoeists. By the end of the decade, the Wilmington Trail Club co-sponsored the outing, which attracted from 100 to 150 participants each year. The 1963–64 *Annual Report* described the stretch of the Brandywine between Market and Washington streets as "one of the better and more challenging courses in the United States." The annual slalom event continued into the mid-1960s.[34]

The city's first swimming pool, 50 by 100 feet, opened in 1898 in Brandywine Park, at the foot of Adams Street between South Park Drive and Wawaset Street. Originally, the board had planned to place the pool between the race and the river near the foot of Adams Street, but when the Water Department offered to supply water for the pool without charge, the commissioners opted for the Wawaset Street location. In the early days of operation, the water in the pool was changed on Mondays and Thursdays.[35]

Operating from the first Monday in June until September 30, the pool initially ran on a schedule that allowed men and boys to swim five days each week and women and girls one day. The pool served an average of 250 patrons per day during its first year. Apparently disregarding women's restricted access to the pool, the park commissioners observed in 1899 that "the small number of women who avail themselves of the opportunity [to swim] scarcely warrants reserving one-sixth of the time for their use." By 1905 women were allowed to swim in the pool two days each week, but the practice of separate days for men and women persisted into the 1940s.[36]

All of the city pools were subject to special scrutiny in the 1940s when the threat of polio caused great concern. Between August 1 and August 12, 1944, nine cases of polio were reported in the city. Wilmington's health commissioner requested that the city's swimming pools be closed "as a precautionary measure to prevent the spreading of infantile paralysis," and the board complied with the request, as it did again in 1947 and 1948.[37]

By 1925, with the opening of the Price Run Pool, there were five municipal swimming pools, and the Brandywine Pool was small by comparison to the later facilities.[38] It remained in use until 1942; then it sat unused until the late 1950s, when the commission finally demolished the bathhouse and filled in the pool.[39] Even before the pool was erased from the park landscape, the commission used the adjacent area to create a "playground for 'tots'" in the mid-1950s, just east of where the bathhouse stood. Subsequently the Park Department erected a picnic pavilion and installed shuffleboard courts where children once splashed and swam.[40]

PASSIVE RECREATION

In their 1895 *Annual Report*, park board members reflected on the benefits of passive recreation as well as active, recognizing that time spent among the trees of an urban parkland could lift some of the burdens of modern life. In the simplest terms, park greenery was meant to provide relief and refreshment to city dwellers wearied by the hard surfaces, noise, air pollution, and crowded environment that surrounded them on a daily basis. Nature had the capacity to heal and restore spiritual and physical vitality. As Frederick Law Olmsted had stated in his 1883 letter to the commissioners, when large numbers of people live in close proximity and are confined indoors in their work, "it does them good to be brought occasionally under the influence of natural scenery."[41]

Certainly all of the effort put into providing paths, pavilions, and benches in Brandywine Park encouraged city residents to visit the park and enjoy at least passive recreation there, walking among the trees, sitting along the

river or in a shady glen listening to the water or the birds, or lingering with a book under the protection of a rustic pavilion's roof. By the early years of the 20th century, the commissioners recognized the popularity of the park as a place for families to gather for picnics. They began to install picnic tables in various groves around the park and, in 1911, to build a substantial picnic pavilion in North Brandywine Park.

The Board of Park Commissioners also realized that the parks were an appropriate setting for music. In 1899 Park Superintendent Theodore A. Leisen recommended that parks sponsor open-air summer concerts. "As a rule both here and elsewhere," he suggested, "music attracts a large and appreciative audience; the assembled crowds are usually orderly, and the moral effect is beneficial. If the funds are available nothing would do more to popularize the Parks than a regular series of concerts."[42] It is unclear the extent to which the commission found funding for the suggested

The Brandywine and the Van Buren Street Bridge have been enduringly popular with local artists such as this painter working in the early 1950s in South Brandywine Park. (Courtesy of Nancy Schanes.)

musical programs, but there certainly were individuals interested in having music in the parks. In 1907 Edgar M. Hoopes, proprietor of the *Wilmington Morning News*, asked permission "for the use of the parks for concerts using the Columbia concert phonograph," and the board accepted his offer. In May 1912, Bethany Band played a special concert in North Brandywine Park, and four years later, during the summer of 1916, a "public spirited citizen" paid for daily concerts by the First Regiment Band, with a portable band-stand making it possible for the concerts to be in a different location each evening. In 1919 the Community Chorus pro-vided open-air concerts through the summer and fall, per-forming from a stand erected on the meadow behind the zoo. The Todd Memorial became a popular location for orchestra and band concerts during the 1930s and 1940s and was the site for an All-City Band Concert in July 1954. In the mid-1950s, summer concerts in the Josephine Gardens attracted audiences of 1,000 each week.[43]

Art remains a popular form of passive recreation in the park, both for artists who enjoy the opportunity to use the Brandywine and its beauty as a subject and for admirers who flock to Brandywine Park for the Brandywine Arts Festival each September. The students of Howard Pyle and later the Wilmington Society of Fine Arts staged annual art exhibitions beginning in 1913. The catalogues of their

shows reveal a steady interest in the Brandywine River, and many shows included one or more paintings featuring the river. The tradition continues today with artist Edward Loper and his students, who are often seen on spring and summer days, working at their easels in the midst of the park.

The Brandywine Arts Festival began in 1960 as a one-day juried clothesline art show in Josephine Gardens. In 1962 the exhibit attracted 300 artists, including painters, sculptors, and photographers. Sponsored by Recreation, Promotion and Service, Inc., the event also offered ox sandwiches from a 674-pound ox that was roasted in the park. Now attracting 250 artists annually and lasting two days, the festival draws several thousand attendees and has become a major event on Brandywine Park's calendar.

CONCLUSION

Recreation can consist of active endeavors—playing games, running, swimming—or it can be passive—relaxing in the greenery of an urban park as the burdens of modern life are lifted. Brandywine Park offers a long history of both sorts of recreation. Recreational park use has changed in many ways over the past century, with shorts and tee shirts replacing flannel trousers on the tennis courts, Boy Scouts no longer camp in North Brandywine Park, and only the occasional kayak is sighted on the Brandywine. At least one of the tennis courts is now a basketball court, and a playground and shuffleboard court stand where the swimming pool once provided a cool splash for young Wilmingtonians. But a visit on any warm summer weekend will still find families gathered for picnics and informal games, enjoying the respite from life's burdens that the park's green meadows, shady trees, tumbling water, and quiet spaces offer.

The Brandywine Arts Festival began in 1961 as a one-day juried clothesline show. This 1965 image of the festival shows paintings and drawings on display but none of the crafts that later became part of the event. (Courtesy of the Historical Society of Delaware.)

In 2000–2001, the Zoo installed a new entrance with impressive gates and a new gift shop for which the architects won a design award. (Courtesy of Homsey Architects.)

Chapter 8

THE ZOO

The zoo exists almost as a separate entity within Brandywine Park, a park feature that has enjoyed enormous popularity and attracted many visitors. Indeed, many Wilmingtonians identify Brandywine Park as the place where the zoo is located.

In the zoo's early days, visitors came, curious to see both indigenous animals—deer, squirrels, ducks—and more exotic creatures—monkeys, bears, alligators. The last quarter of the 19th century was an important period for the establishment of zoos in America, a movement that followed the example set by English and European cities. By the 1870s, London, Paris, and Berlin all featured "zoological gardens" that attracted large numbers of visitors. In the United States, Central Park's Zoological Garden was first planned in the 1850s and soon became the undertaking of the American Zoological and Botanical Society; the facility opened in the early 1860s. The Zoological Society of Philadelphia, formed in 1859, opened its zoological garden in 1874. Similarly, the Cleveland Zoo opened in 1882, the National Zoological Garden in Washington in 1889–90, and the Bronx Zoo in 1895. It was not surprising that interested Wilmingtonians proposed a similar "zoological garden" for Brandywine Park.

FOUNDING THE ZOO, GATHERING THE ANIMALS

Although the Wilmington Zoo dates from the early 1900s, Dr. Evan G. Shortlidge focused attention on that particular section of the then-new Brandywine Park in the early 1890s. Shortlidge lived in nearby Brandywine Village and earlier sat on the Wilmington Board of Education for 40 years (18 as board president). He was the city's mayor for one term (1893–95), was a member of Wilmington's Board of Health, and was United States Fish Commissioner for Delaware. As fish commissioner, he directed the work of a fish hatchery at the city's water pumping station at 16th and Market streets. Beginning in 1882, the hatchery provided shad that were used to stock the Delaware River. In 1891 Shortlidge laid out a series of "five fish hatching ponds" in North Brandywine Park where yellow perch and black bass were propagated. It was onto one of these fishponds that the first birds—swans—were introduced in 1904, marking the start of the zoo.[1]

In 1904 Dr. James H. Morgan, who helped launch the zoo project by offering to donate the swans for the fishponds, contributed a variety of waterfowl, including ducks and swans. Morgan also provided his sketched plans for placing animals in the park, and by the end of the year, squirrel cages, a duck house, and a deer house had been constructed and

[Left] The Sugar Bowl marked the entrance to the zoo, which was down the slope behind the pavilion. The pathway, equipped with rustic railings, meandered past exhibits arranged in tiers down the hillside. (Postcard from author's collection.)

The bear pit, circa 1915, was a popular exhibit for many years. (Courtesy of the Historical Society of Delaware.)

hard-surfaced paths laid in the section of the park that would grow into the zoo. Samuel H. Baynard, who joined the Board of Park Commissioners in 1900, underwrote the cost of fencing the fishpond, where "a number of varieties of ducks and geese" were installed. The first year of the zoo's operation was described as "a very successful effort." By the end of the year, the zoo was home to two Virginia deer, three Belgian hares, a sea turtle, and a sea gull. Donors offered bears, prairie dogs, opossums, pheasants, wolves, wild cats, raccoons, guinea pigs, foxes, a dozen more hares, and a mountain lion, but all were declined because of lack of facilities and funds.[2]

The Washington Heights Association, on whose board Baynard served, played an important role in encouraging these initial efforts. In 1905 the association changed its name to the Wilmington Free Zoological Association and, for the next two decades, supported the zoo in a variety of ways.[3] As the Wilmington *Board of Trade Journal* reported in April 1905, "the association has pledged its time, talent and patriotism to keep a free zoological garden for the benefit of the general public."[4] The zoo enjoyed continued success, attracting crowds of visitors and financial support from around the city. By the end of 1905, there was a bear pit, winter quarters for the animals, and the Board of Park Commissioners donated an old comfort

house for conversion to use as a monkey house.

CHANGE AND GROWTH

Over the next two decades, change and growth were the hallmarks of the zoo. The Wilmington Free Zoological Association constructed pens and cages and extended the deer and elk runs. The population of the zoo grew and diversified, by 1923 expanding to include waterfowl, squirrels, deer, bears, monkeys, elk, buffalo, wolves, eagles, a raccoon, a ground hog, and a fox. The following year a Rocky Mountain goat, an angora goat, and two ringtail monkeys joined the menagerie.[5]

A newspaper account that marked the zoo's 25th anniversary in 1930 provided an enlarged list of zoo animals that included alligators, parrots, an anteater, and "Old Jerry," a monkey. The article identified by name the various bears in the zoo: Junie, a Maine black bear; Buster, an Alaskan brown bear; and Jim, a European brown bear. Jim had been a dancing bear in Atlantic City; when he got old and was no longer popular, his owner gave him to the zoo. When Jim was not asleep or eating, the newspaper reported, the old bear "stood on the outer edge of his pool and danced unceasingly to the delight of the visitors who swarm there each Sunday and holiday." There was also a fourth bear, Lindy, a honey bear from the Bahamas. Lindy was named after Charles Lindbergh, who visited Wilmington in 1927.[6]

The hardships of the Depression took their toll on zoos around the country. In October 1935, for example, the director of the Broad Ripple Zoo in Indianapolis contacted Brandywine Park's superintendent, advising him that the Indiana zoo was being discontinued and offering eight Nubian lions ranging in ages from six months to five years and eight alligators. The zoo was selling the big cats for the cost of crating and shipping and also offered 20 monkeys for sale "at your own price."[7] There is no indication that the Wilmington Zoo took advantage of the opportunity to add to its collection.

Operating the zoo included not only the day-in-day-out care of the animals but also circumstances in which special care was needed. In 1943, when the weather turned cold, the zoo's alligators had to be sent to warm quarters at the Philadelphia Zoo for the winter.[8] During World War II, as the entire nation dealt with rationing, Wilmingtonians learned that their zoo neighbors did too when the local press reported on the problems that wartime food restrictions created for feeding the animals. The bears were getting meat twice each week instead of every day, and the staff made up for the lack of meat by feeding the bears massive amounts of bread instead.[9]

In January 1955, the park superintendent sent three newborn bear cubs—Snowball, Igloo, and Icebox—to a local veterinarian for "proper care and feeding" for four to

six weeks to ensure their survival and eventual good health. December 1955 and January 1956 were unusually cold, and the lack of modern heating equipment in the zoo's buildings presented a challenge. Park crews spent long hours obtaining firewood to keep the animal houses warm, and a night shift "kept fires burning full force each cold evening to protect the animals and to prevent freezing of water pipes." Sadly, because of the excessive cold, the three bear cubs born on January 24, 1956, to Gertie, a black bear, did not survive. By January 26, the three infants who had been named Shivers, Chills, and Shakes had all died.[10]

Over the years, the zoo has been home to a great variety of animals. The list of zoo residents has included the gamut of creatures, from the exotic—tigers, cougars, leopards, bobcats, snakes, lizards, and llamas—to the indigenous—rabbits, opossums, otters, ferrets, and turtles. Most recently, in 1998, the zoo added a habitat to house a pair of Andean condors.

Support, Financial and Otherwise

Over its century of operation, the zoo has enjoyed support from several sources and in a variety of forms. The Wilmington Free Zoological Association not only made regular financial contributions to the zoo's operations but also acted as an advocate on behalf of the zoo. Beginning in 1908, the Wilmington City Council included the zoo in its annual budget, initially turning over to the Board of Park Commissioners $1,000 per year that was to be transferred to the zoo association. The amount increased in 1922 to $3,000.[11] Samuel H. Baynard donated not only funding but also, on at least one occasion, animals to the zoo. In the 1950s when the "Bunnyland" exhibit was under construction, donors contributed funding for rabbit hutches and landscaping.[12]

Benefactors' gifts of actual animals also enlarged the zoo population. In 1921 Baynard donated two white deer, T. Coleman du Pont presented 11 elk, and Senator L. Heisler Ball arranged for the donation of a buffalo from the Wichita National Forest. The acquisition of an elk herd elicited support from the local Elks lodge, which pledged $200 "to help meet expenses" associated with adding the animals to the zoo.[13] The board had the fence of the old deeryard repaired, and the herd moved into its new quarters. The following year, in response to an offer from the U. S. District Forester in Cache, Oklahoma, Baynard underwrote the cost of catching, crating, and delivering a bull buffalo from Oklahoma to the zoo.[14] In 1943 Mr. and Mrs. Hugh Ryan donated "Alley Oop," a three-foot, eight-year-old alligator because the creature had tried "to bite chunks of Mr. Ryan."[15] During the early 1950s, benefactors gave five monkeys and pairs of pigeons, but the zoo had to decline offers of a chinchilla, three other monkeys, and a kangaroo, because there was no room for them.

CHANGE IN MANAGEMENT

In 1926 the Wilmington Free Zoological Association turned over its assets and the zoo to the Board of Park Commissioners, which established a committee to oversee the zoo's operations.[16] In many regards, life went on as it always had, with buildings being improved and new cages constructed. The committee helped the caretakers respond to questions from concerned citizens or advocacy groups about the zoo's operation. Periodically, the Society for the Prevention of Cruelty to Animals expressed concern over the care of the animals and suggested improvements at the zoo, but such exchanges between the Zoo Committee and outside groups were few, and the committee heard commendations as often as criticisms. During the Depression, when the park board found tasks for unemployed workers in the park, the zoo benefited with graded and cindered paths, rebuilt cages, and other improvements.[17]

The Board of Park Commissioners recognized the limitations it faced in the zoo's operations. On the occasion of its 25th anniversary, the board reflected that it sought "to keep the zoo as small and as interesting as possible for three reasons: There are no available funds for the maintenance of a larger zoo, ... there is not sufficient ground to devote to an enlargement of the present zoo and

the climate of this city is not conducive to the well being of animals from tropical and frigid countries." At the time, the facilities included "a monkey house, two bear cages, a rabbit cage, a pit for prairie dogs, a pen for buffaloes and one white deer, and a duck pond."[18] The Zoo Committee gave attention to staff efforts to keep the facilities in good repair, to provide upgraded cages for the bears, to turn the old bear pit into a habitat for prairie dogs, to remove the elk yards and restore the area "to its natural condition," to prepare a new yard for buffalo and deer, and to build a new pen for the alligators and new cages for the woodchucks. They found ways to put old buildings to new uses and to raise the funds to build new cages as replacements for old ones.[19]

The Board of Park Commissioners made certain that the zoo enjoyed good relations with the press. In the summer of 1943, for example, when Wilmingtonians suffered from unusually hot weather, one local paper reported that the zoo's bears, Buster, a North American black bear, Yellowstone, a grizzly, and Lindy, the Himalayan sun bear, did not like leaving "their cool running-water bathing pools."[20] Three years later, Wilmingtonians learned that Lindy was making his seasonal move from winter quarters in the monkey house to an outside cage "open to the sun."[21]

Buffalo first came to the zoo in 1921. Originally Monkey Hill, which was paved in 1922, was called "Buffalo Drive" because it went past the buffalo enclosure. (Courtesy of the Historical Society of Delaware.)

BUNNYLAND AND THE CHILDREN'S ZOO

In 1954 there were two additions to the zoo's facilities. Bunnyland, just east of the Van Buren Street Bridge on the south side of the zoo, was a grassy area where rabbit hutches stood on tall legs. Each hutch held a different rabbit. Provided with flagstone steps and a gravel path, the special exhibit offered an improved opportunity for visitors to see and admire the rabbits. Bunnyland operated as a project at the main zoo and, not unexpectedly, garnered particular support from the Delaware Rabbit Breeders Association, which offered different species of "blue-blood rabbits" for the displays. Financial donations as well supported creation of the special exhibit, underwriting the construction of a dozen rabbit hutches.[22]

The second and larger addition, the Children's Zoo, opened in June 1954. Its 11 buildings were designed to bring familiar stories and Mother Goose characters to life. The buildings included Farmer Brown's Barn, Little Red School House, Noah's Ark, Wishing Well, Blessed Events House, Little Red Hen House, Three Little Pigs' House, and three circus wagon cages.[23] The Wilmington Lions Club

first proposed a children's zoo in 1951.[24] Park Board President M. du Pont Lee met with the Delaware Society for the Prevention of Cruelty to Animals (SPCA), and the organization responded with approval for the proposed plans. The Lions Club sponsored and then built the facility, with "the assistance of many of the city's citizens, organizations, and contractors who selflessly donated generously of their time, labor, and materials." Dedicated on June 29, 1954, and described as "a child's fairyland," the Children's Zoo attracted more than 46,000 visitors in its first year.[25]

With a "Zooperintendent" hired to manage operations, the "zoo within the zoo" was open only part of the year, spring to autumn. In 1956 the Children's Zoo opened on May 1 (rather than June 1, as had been the practice previously) so that groups of schoolchildren could visit before the end of the school year.[26] At the Children's Zoo animals were donated or loaned for the season, rather than kept year-round. Donated animals were then given to individuals who wanted them as pets, at times just for the winter, while the loaned animals went back to their owners at the end of the season in September. In the spring of 1957, for example, the list of over two dozen donated creatures included a number of birds (a white hen, a toucan, a cockatiel, two peacocks, two

p] In 1951, Wilmington children were able to see what was planned for the proposed Children's Zoo to be built at the Wilmington Zoo. (Courtesy of the Delaware Public Archives, Dover, Delaware.)

ottom] Plans for the Children's Zoo used well-known fairy tales as the zoo's theme and included the Three Little Pigs House, the Little Red Hen House, and Farmer Brown's Barn. (Courtesy of the Historical Society of Delaware.)

Opened in 1954, the Children's Zoo had more than 46,000 visitors during its first year and it became an important part of any child's visit to the park. (Courtesy of the Historical Society of Delaware.)

[Right] Humpty Dumpty contributed a colorful presence to the fairy tale theme of the Children's Zoo. (Postcard from author's collection.)

Chinese hens, and a cormorant) as well as two monkeys, a number of various rodents, an alligator, five skunks, a goat, two baby foxes, and a litter of puppies. The loaned animals included several farm animals—pigs, a pet goose, a lamb, calves, ducks, and chickens—plus an aquarium and four parakeets.[27]

In addition to annual donations of animals for the exhibits, the Children's Zoo generated other support for its particular efforts, including monetary gifts earmarked for improvements. One early benefactor paid for wooden doors to be installed on the Three Little Pigs cage and for work on the Pussy Cat and Owl cage.[28] The popularity of the Children's Zoo extended beyond Wilmington. In 1957, when NBC inquired about events or festivals that might be of interest to its *Wide, Wide World* audience, the park superintendent sent information and photographs of the

Children's Zoo.[29] The exhibits continued to attract children for many years, until the buildings were finally dismantled in the late 1970s. The storybook theme and design had become outdated, and a change in exhibit philosophy required a more educational focus to the displays. Because of the shift in approach as well as the need for larger, more suitable cages for the animals, the fairytale buildings were demolished, and accommodations better suited to the new exhibition goals took their place.

THE DIFFICULT 1950S AND 1960S

As the zoo reached its 50th anniversary in 1955, it became clear that the facilities for the animals were inadequate, and systems deficiencies prevented needed expansion. Although there were caretakers for the zoo's animals, there was no full-time manager. The Board of Park Commissioners remained in favor of operating the zoo, describing it as "a valuable asset to the community" that made Wilmington "a more enjoyable and worthwhile place in which to live."[30] But the inadequacy of the animals' quarters and the aging systems and buildings presented serious challenges. In 1956 the Wilmington Zoological Society incorporated as a new organization, replacing the Wilmington Free Zoological Association. The new group sought to work with the Board of Park Commissioners to create a master plan for the zoo and address the zoo's most serious facilities problems, in particular the antiquated and unsatisfactory heating system in the Monkey House.[31]

By the early 1960s, however, conditions had not improved sufficiently to offer much hope. In December 1962, the Delaware SPCA recommended that the zoo close and that the animals either be placed elsewhere or "humanely destroyed." A week later the Delaware Humane Association threatened legal action over conditions at the zoo, alleging violation of the state's laws against cruelty to animals. On January 10, 1963, the Board of Park Commissioners announced that the zoo, except for the Children's Zoo, would close, and the animals would be placed in suitable homes.[32] A year later, the Board of Park Commissioners began to discuss with the Wilmington Zoological Society, the Board of Education, and the New Castle County Parks and Recreation Commission how the zoo could be redeveloped and reopened. The parties agreed that the Children's Zoo would remain unchanged. At the same time, zoo staff were to make children of school age and younger the target audience for exhibits and programs at the main zoo, with animals selected for their "educational value and appeal to children."[33]

Redevelopment plans did not progress as expected, however, and the Children's Zoo also came under fire for its shortcomings. At a January 1966 meeting of the park board's Executive Committee, representatives of the Wilmington Zoological Society expressed disappointment over the apparent lack of interest in the Children's Zoo as

indicated by the city's failure to provide financial resources to maintain and improve facilities. The commissioners agreed but pointed out that they were faced with funding that allowed them no alternatives.[34] A year later, in January 1967, the society withdrew its support because of "dissatisfaction with inadequate physical plant and lack of qualified personnel at the Zoo." In spite of this pronouncement, the board pledged to continue operating the facility.[35]

Within months, Wilmington's revised City Charter dissolved the Board of Park Commissioners and, in July 1967, the city's Department of Parks and Recreation took over supervision of the zoo, a situation that prevailed for four years. In 1971 the Wilmington Zoo became the Brandywine Zoo when management of Brandywine Park shifted from the City of Wilmington to New Castle County. Zoo supporters formed the Delaware Zoological Association in 1979, the same year that a new tiger exhibit opened. The group worked with the zoo's staff to make plans and undertake improvements at the facility. The Monkey House, long closed to the public, was refurbished and reopened, and the zoo took on new vitality with the new partnership.

Change came again in 1998, with the transfer of management from the county to the state's Division of Parks and Recreation. That year, the condor exhibit opened, and the zoo got a new "front door" with an award-winning design that included an entranceway, shop, and educational facility.

The zoo staff and the Delaware Zoological Association continue to work together to promote an interest in Delaware wildlife, to encourage volunteers to help meet zoo needs, and to raise funds for improvements. In the early years of the 20th century, the Board of Park Commissioners, interested citizens, and the Wilmington Free Zoological Association undertook to provide Wilmington citizens with an entertaining outlet that also promised some degree of education. The tradition continues today, with the zoo offering extensive educational opportunities for patrons of all ages, from toddlers to adults.

There were park police on duty in Brandywine Park from

1888 until 1967 when the park force became part of

Wilmington's city police force. These officers, circa 1950, patrolled

parks throughout the city, including Brandywine Park.

(Courtesy of the Historical Society of Delaware.)

Chapter 9

The Park's People

Brandywine Park has benefited greatly from he people whose jobs were focused on keeping the park safe, attractive, and inviting. Directed by the Board of Park Commissioners, the park superintendents in turn oversaw the supervision of park personnel, including the park guards, recommended to the commissioners acquisition of equipment and supplies that made the park work easier and more efficient, and assisted the board in making decisions about improvements and changes to the park itself.

Park Superintendents

The Board of Park Commissioners hired Edward Tatnall as the first park superintendent in 1888, almost two years after they purchased the initial acres for the park. Within a month of that first land purchase, Tatnall had contacted the board to report a fire in the woods in North Brandywine Park. The blaze, caused by sparks from a locomotive, should be sufficient, he went on, to persuade the commissioners that they needed a superintendent to care for the park. "The fire last night," he wrote, "could have been stopped early if it had been any body's business to do it."[1] In spite of Tatnall's argument, over a year passed before the board agreed to hire a park superintendent, appointing Tatnall to the position in July 1888.

Tatnall supervised the first park guards, a crew of four, and initiated the practice of using them for work around the park as well as for keeping public order. Tatnall had been a florist before he became superintendent and lived near the park. In 1890 the board added to the park's professional staff by hiring Samuel Canby as park engineer to supervise the various construction projects that were under way. Three years later, however, the board's appropriation was so reduced that the commission had to cut expenses. Noting that "there is likely to be but little strictly engineering work at present," the commissioners elected to merge the jobs of superintendent and engineer into one. Both Tatnall and Canby were asked to resign, which they did. Tatnall, William Kimmey, and Theodore A. Leisen all applied for the newly enlarged position of park superintendent. The board selected Leisen, who already worked for the city Street and Sewer Department as an engineer, and assigned him responsibility for the parks.

It is difficult to imagine what the park would be like if Theodore A. Leisen had not applied his particular vision and discipline to the superintendent assignment. His recommendations to the board helped furnish the park with walls, roads, bridges, and vistas. In addition to the physical changes Leisen made to the park fabric, he also shaped the job of superintendent with his practices and procedures.

The diary that Leisen kept while superintendent records the details of his days and weeks, describing the weather conditions, noting who was working among the park personnel and what jobs they were doing, who was absent and why, and how the park was being used by visitors. The attention he paid to particular aspects of the park allowed him to make insightful and helpful recommendations to board members, who were never in the park as regularly and for as long as Leisen. In February 1897, he recorded that the Brandywine was six feet above the dam "& over walks near pavilion," information that lead the commissioners to raise the level of the ground by filling the area with earth, and making it less likely to flood. Later that month, he used his engineering skills to develop a plan for a new park on the east side of the city, providing him with the intimate knowledge that would facilitate the provision of amenities and ease the job of assigning workers to maintenance and landscape work later.

Leisen also produced early annual reports for the Board of Park Commissioners, each year writing an extensive, detailed report of his own work and recommendations, photographing elements in the park to be featured in the publication, gathering and organizing data for inclusion, and then reviewing and correcting the proofs as the report neared publication. He used his writing skills to produced articles that were published in widely circulated journals and, in general, was a tangible link between Wilmington's parks and the larger world, at least those parts of the larger world concerned with public parks.

The board eventually changed Leisen's title to chief engineer, and in 1900 he was elected secretary to the Board of Park Commissioners when the previous secretary resigned. This added $5 per month to his pay, increasing it from $135 per month for performing the duties of superintendent to $140 per month for being both superintendent

and secretary. He remained with the park board until June 1903, when he resigned to become chief engineer for the city's Water Department, a job he held until 1908, when he left Wilmington for Louisville, Kentucky.

Even as Leisen moved from park work to work for the Water Department, he served as a consulting engineer to the Board of Park Commissioners for a year, while Alexander J. Taylor took over the job of park engineer and superintendent. When Leisen's year as a consultant ended, the position of consulting engineer was abolished, and the salary of the park superintendent increased by the amount that had been paid to the consulting engineer. Taylor came to the Board of Park Commissioners from the Street and Sewer Department, where he had been a civil engineer. He joined the park board in December 1903 but resigned to return to the Street and Sewer Department in 1906.[2]

From the applicants to fill the vacancy created by Taylor's departure, the board hired Edward R. Mack, who started work in September 1906 at a salary of $110 per month. If he proved satisfactory, the commissioners pledged, they agreed to increase his pay by $10 per month each September 1 until he reached $140 per month.[3] Mack had moved to Wilmington in 1905 to work as an engineer for the Water Department. In 1918, when the secretary-treasurer to the Board of Park Commissioners resigned, the board members elected Mack to take his place, and he remained in that job for the rest of his career. Briefly during World War I, he volunteered for overseas duty with the YMCA, for which the board granted him a one-year leave of absence, but he withdrew his application within four months and returned to work in the parks.

In addition to his responsibilities as superintendent and secretary to the Board of Park Commissioners, Mack became the superintendent and secretary to the Wilmington Fountain Society in 1918. It was a convenient arrangement that facilitated the installation of fountains in Brandywine Park and smoothed the way for adjustments that periodically had to be made in the fountains' placement. When the Todd Memorial was under construction, for example, it was

Edward R. Mack, photographed here in 1930, served the Board of Park
Commissioners from 1906 until 1944 as park superintendent.
(Courtesy of the Historical Society of Delaware.)

necessary to change the location of the Churchman
Memorial. Originally installed at the corner of the
Boulevard and Washington Street, the 1904 horse fountain
now stood in the way of the sidewalk and steps that
constituted the approach to the Todd Memorial. The
president and secretary of the Fountain Society met with
the park commissioners, and together they selected a new
site on the south side of 16th Street, where the fountain
now stands.[4] Similarly, when the National Humane Alliance
fountain had to be moved when the new Market Street
Bridge was built in 1929, the Fountain Society and Board
of Park Commissioners agreed on a new location. Mack
played a key role in the negotiations.[5]

Mack's tenure lasted until he died at the age of 67 in
1944.[6] Under his leadership and supervision, park personnel
achieved noteworthy improvements in Brandywine Park and
the other city parks. Park acreage in the city rose from 280

acres in 1906 to 900 acres in 1944, Brandywine Park's road
system was completed, three new bridges spanned the
Brandywine, the Jasper Crane Rose Garden and the cherry
trees of the Josephine Gardens took root, and relief work in
both the 1920s and 1930s added to the fabric of the park.
Mack's widow, writing to the commissioners after his death,
quoted him as saying, "I have loved my work—every minute
of it—and have been privileged as few have to remain long
enough to see many of my dreams realized."[7] Six years after
Mack's death, the Board of Park Commissioners changed
the name of 6th Street Park to Edward R. Mack Park.[8]

To fill the vacancy created by Mack's death, the
commissioners elected William J. Dougherty as
superintendent of parks and secretary to the board in April
1944. He too was a long-term employee, starting work with
the park system in 1913, first in an engineering capacity
and after 1920, as park maintenance supervisor.[9] Like Mack
before him, Dougherty was elected superintendent of the
Wilmington Fountain Society and, after 1950, appointed
board secretary. Dougherty remained the park superintendent until his death at age 58 in February 1953.

Within a month of Dougherty's death, the board
appointed John B. Quinn to fill the park superintendent's
position. He moved into the job at $6,000 per year, which
was $1,000 more than Dougherty had been paid.
But Dougherty and his family had lived rent-free at 2001
Rockford Road, and the board elected to increase the
compensation to the superintendent and make up the
additional $1,000 per year by renting 2001 Rockford Road
for $85 per month. Quinn came to the board with academic
training in forestry and experience with the National Park
Service, the Delaware Department of Forestry, and the
Delaware Highway Department. By autumn 1954, Quinn's
title had changed to Director of Parks and Recreation, and
the park system employed 82 employees. Within three years,
his supervisory responsibility extended to: the Division of
Parks, the Division of Recreation, and the Division of
Public Safety and Protection.[10] The zoo attracted public
attention during Quinn's term with the opening of both

Bunnyland and the Children's Zoo. A director who energetically supported improvements in the department's recreation programs and facilities, Quinn also proved a passionate defender of the parks and their preservation. He wrote eloquently about the "land-grab" disease that threatened the parks in the late 1950s, as the proposed school adjacent to the park and the I-95 projects appeared on the horizon.[11] In September 1958, within months of preparing the *Annual Report* that defended park lands against "the insidious encroachment of the growing 'canker of public expediency' which generally usurps 'idle park lands,'" Quinn died of cancer at the age of 46. Six months later, the Board of Park Commissioners appointed Edward P. Laverty, who had been Quinn's superintendent of the Division of Parks, to the post of Director of Parks and Recreation.[12]

Laverty, who had been a general foreman when Dougherty was director, served as temporary superintendent following Dougherty's death, until the commissioners appointed Quinn. A native Wilmingtonian, Laverty had served the parks since the early 1940s, performing a variety of different duties. He assisted with the design of a number of the parks, working on the layouts and marking sports fields and courts. He played a significant role in the management of the Greenhill Golf Course when that facility came under city ownership and provided fiscal oversight to parks projects. From the mid-1950s, he was superintendent of parks, and his tenure as director of parks and recreation, which began in 1958, lasted until 1967. Then, with the election of a new mayor, Laverty returned to his position as superintendent of parks, and William L. Kapa was appointed the superior position of director. Laverty remained with the city parks until he retired in 1979.

Kapa, who held a bachelor's degree in recreation and had been program director for the Catholic Youth Organization, moved into public service as the Director of Parks and Recreation for the City of Wilmington in 1967. He was the first director to work without the direction of the Board of Park Commissioners, which was disbanded with the revised city charter. In 1971, when the city transferred management of the parks to New Castle County, management of Brandywine Park became the responsibility of Ralph S. Cryder, who had become director of the county's Department of Parks and Recreation in 1966. After Cryder's departure from the department in 1978, there were three more directors in quick succession until 1989, when William L. Kapa assumed the job for the county, once again taking charge of Brandywine Park. He remained in that position until he retired at the end of 1996. January 1997 marked a change in county administration, and under the new county executive, Joseph Freebery provided leadership on behalf of the county. His responsibilities for Brandywine Park ended in April 1998, when the State Division of Parks and Recreation assumed management of the Brandywine Park.

With the 1998 shift in management to the state, Ronald L. Crouch became the administrator of the Wilm-

Charlie Newlon (left) and Duane Green conducted a comprehensive survey of the trees in Brandywine Park for the Friends of Wilmington Parks in 1997. (Courtesy of the Friends of Wilmington Parks.)

ington State Parks collectively. The state's involvement brought to the park three key elements—funding, the security of rangers policing the park, and an on-site team of managers who were in the park on a daily basis. With Crouch and his team in place, Wilmingtonians saw positive changes in Brandywine Park. In their first year on the job, the state's park crews rid neglected woodlands of over 100 dangerous trees and cleared away undergrowth in areas that had enjoyed too little attention. They replaced broken benches, repaired neglected sidewalks, installed new grills and picnic tables, and, having declared the park a "carry in-carry out" park, deployed clean-up crews to keep the park tidy. Within a year of taking on Brandywine Park, a "wind event" that involved sustained high winds brought down nearly 100 mature trees in a small area along the millrace in South Brandywine Park, closing the pathway for several weeks and requiring a massive unexpected expenditure for clearing.

Not all projects went as planned. In 1997 consideration was given to addressing the erosion problem along Rattlesnake Run, an area that had also become woefully overgrown with undergrowth encroaching on the pathway and obscuring any grassy meadow that might once have covered the sides of the run. The initial work on cleaning up Rattlesnake Run ended abruptly when neighborhood residents, unaware of the long-range plans for restoring the area, objected to the removal of some of the mature trees. The work languished until the state assumed management of Brandywine Park and undertook to see it through to completion. Although delayed when a century-old brick sewer collapsed just above Rattlesnake Run, the restoration work was finally accomplished, and the final configuration of the land allowed for control of erosion, improvement of the quality of the runoff water before it reached the river, and a substantial improvement in the appearance of that particular entrance into Brandywine Park.

State staff members were in the park daily where they could keep an eye on park conditions and could address potential problems before they became serious. When Hurricane Floyd swept over the area in September 1999 and

The change to state management brought a welcome infusion of attention to Brandywine Park. State Parks employees tackled invasive plants that had choked and marred the landscape. (Courtesy of the Friends of Wilmington Parks.)

sent the Brandywine to 19 feet above flood level as it rampaged through the park, Crouch and his staff kept their eyes on the storm, assessing the impact of flooding and planning action to address damage as soon as the waters receded. The presence of division workers on their rounds and of park rangers around the park brought an increased sense of safety to Brandywine Park, which had been missing for some time. Not unexpectedly, these improved conditions brought visitors back to Brandywine Park, and it entered the new century with renewed prospects.

PARK PERSONNEL, GUARDS, AND THE RULES

Over the years, there have been a wide range of workers under the superintendent's supervision. In addition to laborers who performed all the jobs necessary first to build the park's features and then to maintain them, there were office personnel, a "keeper" at the Brandywine Bath

PARK REGULATIONS.

No person shall ride or drive upon any part of the Park except upon the roads intended for such purposes.

No person shall bring led horses within the limits of the Park nor turn any horses, cattle, goats, swine, dogs or other animals loose in the park.

No person shall indulge in any threatening, abusive, insulting, or indecent language, or commit any obscene or indecent act in the Park.

No person shall carry firearms, shoot birds, or other animals, nor throw stones or other missiles, or in any way disturb or annoy the birds or animals within the boundaries of the Park.

No person shall throw any dead animals or other offensive matter into the Park, nor foul any spring, brook, or other water within the boundaries of the Park.

No person shall cut, break or otherwise injure or deface any trees, shrubs, plants, turf, rock or any building, fence, bridge, or other structure within the Park.

No person shall erect, paint, paste or otherwise affix or distribute any signs, advertisements or circulars within the Park.

No person shall injure, deface, destroy, or remove any notices or regulations for the government of the Park.

Penalties, $5.00 to $10.00

From the earliest days of Brandywine Park, rules governed public behavior. These regulations date from 1887.

House (swimming pool), and a hierarchy of groundskeepers (grass foreman, chief gardener, and gardeners first and second class). During the 1920s and again in the 1930s, economic hard times brought crews of unemployed men to work in the park under work relief programs. The mayor's Emergency Relief Fund Committee, organized in 1921 and supported by public donations, paid workers through the Associated Charities and sent them to various work locations, including Brandywine Park, where they assisted regular work crews with projects. At a Mayor's Advisory Board meeting in 1922, Park Board President Samuel H. Baynard reported that their help had allowed work to be completed that would otherwise not have been possible. During the Great Depression, several unemployment relief programs—Works Progress Administration (WPA), Public

Works Administration (PWA), National Youth Administration (NYA), and (Civil Works Administration)—assigned workers to Brandywine Park, where they worked on a wide range of maintenance and construction projects.

During the first half of the 20th century, the length of time workers served the interests of the city's parks was impressive. Superintendents Edward R. Mack and William J. Dougherty worked in the parks for 37 and 40 years respectively. Helen M. Scott, hired in 1925 as a stenographer assisting the superintendent, continued to work for the commission for 30 years. When John Cummings died in 1937, he had been a park gardener for 34 years.

The park guards were among the most visible individuals associated with the smooth operation of Brandywine Park. When the Board of Park Commissioners bought the first land for Brandywine Park in 1886, they knew they needed a means of maintaining public order. Indeed, one city councilman voted against spending money to purchase land for parks because he claimed that "if a park is established 25 or 30 police officers will be required to keep the people from running away with the rocks and bushes and that the park will have to be lighted by at least 50 lamps, which will not cost less than $21.75 each."[13]

The councilman may have felt justified in his opinion because, before the land along the Brandywine River became a park, local residents referred to the area as "Brandywine Glen," and it had "rather an unsavory reputation." The Board of Park Commissioners was not deterred, however. In 1887 the commissioners, declaring their intent to "break up all evidences of disorder and rowdyism," established regulations to govern proper park behavior and the following year, hired four uniformed police officers to enforce the new rules.[14]

A captain, responsible for "the preservation of order in and the protection of all parts of the parks," supervised the force and kept records of occurrences in the growing number of city parks and playgrounds. The regulations governing the park guards were numerous and detailed. The officers' primary duty was "by vigilance, careful attention, and frequent patrol, to preserve order and prevent damage."

The men were to be civil and respectful to one another, and when they met on duty, "must not stand long together, nor walk in company." They were supplied with "guard boxes" for shelter but were not to remain there "except in severe or inclement weather." In their efforts to control misbehavior, they were not to arrest individuals "for a trivial offence when it is probable that a reprimand would be likely to prevent a repetition of the offence." The guards were to be polite and courteous to visitors and were to be "especially watchful to protect women and children from annoyance, insult, or rudeness."[15]

The guards worked 12- or 13-hour days seven days a week. Initially they were allowed one day off per month during July, August, and September, two days off per month for the months of October through April, and an annual vacation of seven days. No mention was made of May and June.[16] During the park's early years, the guards' duties, in addition to policing the park, extended to other tasks as well. The board considered them to be "Keepers as well as Police, and ... required to do such work as may be necessary to maintain their respective grounds in good order."[17] In March 1894, Superintendent Leisen provided the Board of Park Commissioners with his assessment of the work that lay ahead during the year. His estimate, he noted, was "only for such work as seems to be most urgently required" and assumed that "many minor works may be carried out with the aid of the Park Guards, without entailing any great extra expense." Within two months, he advised that he was using guards for house repairs, sodding along drives, cutting new pathways and repairing old ones.[18] During the waning years of the 1890s, police force members not only provided security but also repaired footbridges damaged by flooding, replaced wood around the sink in one of the board's rental properties, and did other unspecified repair and maintenance work.[19] By the 1920s, the increased use of the parks had been matched by an increased number of park employees so that keeping the parks clean and maintained became someone else's responsibility.

In the 1930s, the designation for members of the park police force changed from "park guard" to "special policeman." The board also assigned three officers to motorcycle duty, making patrolling the parks easier and allowing outlying portions of the park to be visited more regularly.[20]

The park rules that the officers were charged with enforcing, from the vantage point of the 21st century, seem both familiar and quaint. In 1887 the regulations included expected prohibitions that survive. Visitors were not to "indulge in threatening, abusive, insulting, or indecent language" nor were they to "carry firearms, shoot birds, or other animals ... or in any way disturb or annoy the birds or animals." Other rules, however, have the sound of a bygone era—prohibiting, for example, turning "any horses, cattle, goats, swine, dogs or other animals loose in the Park."[21]

Not unexpectedly, therefore, rules changed with the time. By 1919 the rules banned possession of intoxicating liquor, loitering in "any prohibited place, or any comfort house for the opposite sex," and lying down on park benches or sleeping in the park.[22] There was also a prohibition against gambling, a regulation that may have arisen at the insistence of Superintendent Leisen. In 1894 Leisen called the attention of the commissioners to the card playing that was taking place in the parks. "Innocent and harmless in itself," he wrote, "it leads invariably to gambling. Furthermore it is not an out-door sport, and it seems to me it would not be curtailing the priveleges [*sic*] of the public to prohibit it entirely ... My observation shows also, that it usually attracts a rough and unruly set of boys and men."[23]

By the 1930s, automobile traffic noticeably impinged on the rules. In 1930 the commissioners banned parking in the park after dark; a year later, they forbade individuals doing auto repairs in the park; and in 1932 they prohibited use of park roads by "commercial vehicles of any kind."[24] The park guards were kept busy enforcing the rules. The captain's report book shows repeated arrests for drunkenness, an offense that most frequently resulted in a fine of $1 or $2 plus costs. Although the officers regularly dealt with assaults, disorderly conduct, and occasional gambling activities, they also retrieved lost property, helped individuals injured in the parks, stopped runaway horses, and provided assistance to a great variety of groups using the parks for picnics, concerts, or other gatherings.[25] In the late 1940s, they provided a traffic officer to keep order at South Park Drive and Van Buren Street on weekday evenings between 4:30 and 5:30 p.m. and in the early 1960s served the same function at the "bottleneck" at 18th Street and Monkey Hill.

When the 1967 change in the City Charter disbanded the Board of Park Commissioners and established the city's Department of Parks and Recreation, the city police became responsible for enforcing the rules, replacing the park police force of a captain and 25 men. A special group of employees with long ties to Brandywine Park and Wilmington's entire park system passed into history. Almost immediately there were complaints about the loss of the specially dedicated park force. The 1969–70 *Annual Report* from the Department of Parks and Recreation noted that the park police totaled 24 full-time officers with seven vehicles on a 24-hour, three-shift per day basis. In contrast, the subsequent city police coverage seemed lacking, amounting as it did to four or five men in one or two vehicles assigned to the parks but also to other duties as well. "Our safety and maintenance problems has increased each year since the park police were disbanded," observed the department.[26] Only when management of the park was transferred to the state did the park again have a force of officers dedicated to providing security within the park.

The Challenges of Administration

Like any supervisors, the park superintendents had to deal with the practicalities of "running a park business," always under the direction of the Board of Park Commissioners. In 1903, for example, when the city made eight hours the official length of the working day for city employees, the superintendent had to meet the park's needs with two fewer hours of work from his crews each day. "Since the first of July," he complained, "we, in conjunction with other city departments, have been working in compliance with the law and have been paying $1.50 for eight hours work, instead of the same amount for ten hours."[27] The work week, however, was still six days long and remained that way until 1949, when it dropped to a five-day workweek.[28] Even then, the City Council asked the Board of Park Commissioners to maintain weekly wages for 40 hours at the same level as had been paid for 44 hours. Pay for the park workers was closely tied to the pay in other city departments, although there was not yet a Park Department.[29]

In the 1920s and 1930s, the superintendent added workers to his crews as work relief programs brought unemployed workers to the park. While this increase in manpower meant that additional projects could be completed, it added to the scheduling, supervisory, and administrative duties shouldered by the superintendent. The superintendent also took responsibility for keeping the park staff supplied with the equipment and materials necessary to do their jobs. Tracking the changes in equipment provides a glimpse of technological changes experienced by Wilmingtonians. From the late 19th into the 20th century, lawn mowing was accomplished with horse-drawn mowing machines. In 1916 the board approved the purchase of a "Coldwell Threesome Horse Lawn Mower," a horse-drawn mower with three mower mechanisms, and as late as 1930, the Executive Committee instructed the superintendent to take bids on a horse-drawn mower and to select one for the park system.[30]

In 1899 the Executive Committee approved the purchase of two bicycles for the superintendent and guards, but motorized vehicles soon began to replace animal- or human-powered conveyances. By 1905 the superintendent rode an Indian motorcycle, which was replaced by a Thor three years later.[31] By 1912 the superintendent had a Ford Roadster Runabout for his use, a vehicle that cost the board $635. Subsequently, the board replaced the cars at regular intervals, and in 1932 the commissioners purchased motorcycles for the park guards, assigning three officers to

Beginning in 1992, the Friends of Wilmington Parks sponsored Hands Across the Brandywine, an annual day in the park for neighborhood school children. In 2005, youngsters explored Delaware history, measured the Brandywine's water quality, and visited the animals at the zoo.
(Courtesy of the Friends of Wilmington Parks.)

motorcycle duty. "The efficiency of the park police has been increased," the board noted in the 1932 Annual Report. "This has permitted frequent patrol of the drives and of outlying park property where no guards are regularly stationed."[32]

There were occasional odd administrative challenges as well. In 1918, for example, Superintendent Mack explored the possibility of grazing sheep in parks. In response to his inquiry, A. G. Potts of the United States Department of Agriculture's Bureau of Animal Industry wrote, advising that park land "is well adapted to this purpose" but warning that small herds were usually not profitable.[33]

THE PARK'S FRIENDS

As Brandywine Park and the Wilmington park system prepared to celebrate the 100th anniversary of the city's parks in 1983, Wilmington newspaper columnist Bill Frank remarked critically on their condition. "Oh, so much as

been neglected over the past years since the late 1960s," he wrote, "when the Board of Park Commissioners was replaced by the Department of Parks and Recreation."[34] When revision to the City Charter disbanded the board in 1967, Brandywine Park lost a steady, dedicated, and at times passionate advocate that spoke on its behalf and campaigned for its protection and maintenance. In short, it lost someone who looked out for its best interests. This situation of friendlessness continued until 1991, when a group of interested citizens formed the Friends Society of Brandywine Park (FSBP), dedicated to the restoration of the park and motivated by a love of the park's "natural beauty, recreational amenities, and impressive architecture."[35]

One of the key founding members of the organization was Sandy Poppiti, who became the Friends' first executive director in 1992. Her particular interest in nature and in American Indian lore shaped and propelled many of the initial programs. Her passion for educating park visitors, particularly children, about the natural wonders within the boundaries of Brandywine Park prompted the first "Hands Across the Brandywine" event in 1992. Intended as a fund-raiser for some of the FSBP projects, the event brought children from several local schools to the park for a day of educational activities— studying the creatures that live in the Brandywine's water, learning how water can be used to power machinery, creating a piece of art that captured the river's dancing waves, or meeting a bird of prey from the zoo.

"Hands Across the Brandywine" enjoyed sufficient success that within three years, at Poppiti's behest, the FSBP launched the Junior Naturalists group to provide year-round educational programs for youngsters and began a summer camp program. These programs focused on education, teaching campers about the ecology of the river, about the forest areas of the park, and about Indian lore—stories, traditions, symbols, music, and art. To extend education to adults, the FSBP offered guided walking tours to acquaint visitors with the park's history and organized workshops to provide public school teachers with materials and background intended to build their interest in and confidence about using the park as an educational resource.

The FSBP recognized that the park's dire condition dictated the nature of many early stewardship activities. Members spent countless hours cleaning up the park, picking up broken glass and other debris along the river, the walkways, and in the quarry area just below South Park Drive. The FSBP attempted a small project to stabilize selected portions of the Brandywine's banks, hoping to stop damaging erosion, and they devoted themselves to a forest diversity project that began the seemingly endless task of eradicating invasive Norway maple saplings.

The group also raised awareness in the community about the park's needs and encouraged Wilmingtonians to return to the park, to lend a hand in its rehabilitation, and to enjoy its many positive attributes. In April 1997, Poppiti resigned from the directorship to continue her college education. By this time, many more residents were aware of improvements in the park and had become advocates, taking a new interest in seeing it return to earlier days when it had enjoyed better care.

Nancy DeNisio, who had been with the Friends since April 1995 as an administrative assistant, moved into the position as executive director at Poppiti's departure. Many of the organization's activities continued, with volunteers participating in clean up days along the river, visitors taking history tours, and Hands Across the Brandywine bringing youngsters into the park each spring. Summer camp became a more structured, themed program, but lasted only through 1998, as growing concerns about liability exposure caused the board to end the program.

One of the projects that Poppiti had begun was the Sensory Trail, intended to provide sight-impaired visitors with a woodland trail adorned with plants that appealed to senses other than sight—leaves with inviting textures, blossoms with distinctive scents, tree bark with special tactile character, and plant material that rustled or whispered in the breeze. When DeNisio took over as executive director, she inherited the project, which had fallen

badly behind schedule and was running far over budget (and the funding had been woefully inadequate from the start). Through her skillful and tenacious outreach to community groups and local funding sources, she managed to see the Sensory Trail through to completion.[36]

DeNisio's efforts to build collaborative relationships with other organizations enabled the FSBP to achieve a number of successes that would otherwise have eluded them. By organizing community service days, the organization recruited numerous volunteers to assist with the ongoing park work, both weeding out maple saplings as part of the forest diversity project and extending the clean-up by eradicating invasive English ivy. With the assistance of two U. S. Forest Service retirees, Charlie Newlon and Duane Green, the FSBP sponsored a tree survey that identified and accounted for all the trees in the park's 178 acres. This information was vital for the creation of a management plan for the park forest. Through cooperative work with the Delaware Center for Horticulture and the YMCA's "Back on Track" program, youthful garden crews joined the FSBP to tackle several park gardens that needed attention.[37]

Educational programs continued to be a staple of what the FSBP offered to the community. Although summer camp ended, the organization used the materials created for the various camp themes and revised them to serve as educational programs for school groups that visited the park. Younger students began to learn about ecosystems when they participated in the "Wiggle Worms" program while older students applied the group's tree survey and forest management techniques when they enrolled for the "Forest Diversity" course.

In the autumn of 1998, the organization had an opportunity to work on the restoration of the Monkey Hill Pavilion, a WPA structure severely damaged by fire in the 1980s. The Junior League of Wilmington offered to work with the FSBP in a fund-raising effort so the timber framing and slate roof of the stone pavilion could be restored. The $150,000 project, which included the

The Monkey Hill Pavilion, completed in 1941, suffered arson damage in the 1980s. In 1999–2000, the Junior League of Wilmington, the Friends of Wilmington Parks, and the state Division of Parks and Recreation collaborated on the pavilion's restoration. (Courtesy of the Friends of Wilmington Parks.)

additional collaboration of the state Division of Parks and Recreation, was completed in the spring of 2000. Representatives of the three participating groups met to dedicate the once-again-handsome pavilion at the foot of Monkey Hill.

In January 1999, a severe windstorm downed nearly 100 trees along the millrace, closing the path and leaving substantial devastation in its wake. The FSBP joined forces with State Parks personnel to organize volunteers and replace the downed trees with new ones. As a result of the storm damage, the FSBP board decided to pursue funding to renovate a 17-acre area adjacent to South Park Drive. The work involved removing an additional 75 substantial trees so that native trees—oak, beech, and hickory—would have a better chance of survival. The project began in the fall of 2001 and was of particular interest to board member Charles F. Richards Jr., who raised over $400,000 to underwrite the cost of the South Park Drive restoration.[38] Completed in the spring of 2002, the project eventually

required the removal of over 400 large Norway maples and a substantial volume of English ivy and Japanese knotwood. The areas cleared were then planted with more than 200 trees, 1,277 shrubs, 9,850 perennials, and 540 flowering bulbs. In addition, work crews installed trails, steps, and walls to enhance the project area.

At the time Poppiti left the executive directorship, the organization had stretched its resources to the limit by taking on a large number of widely varied projects, few of which were receiving the attention they required. One of the big difficulties facing DeNisio and the FSBP Board of Stewards was determining which projects to abandon and which to see through to completion. DeNisio rose to the challenge, providing dedicated management and marshalling the resources (both financial and human) to finish the Sensory Trail project, which had attracted substantial community notice. She expended considerable energy building well-grounded, stable relationships with other community organizations and with potential individual and corporate benefactors. When she left the executive director's position in October 1999, she handed over to her replacement, Kim Johnson, an organization that was well prepared to move on to its next set of challenges and opportunities.

As had been the case with DeNisio before her, Johnson inherited a project that had to be completed—the restoration of the Monkey Hill Pavilion. Happily, it was well on its way with sufficient funding and reliable collaborators and was completed the following spring. The organization, now renamed the Friends of Wilmington Parks (FOWP), and its new executive director recognized the need to discriminate among possible projects and select carefully those they took on.[39]

Members bent their backs to the job, turning up on a

W-18—Rose Garden, Brandywine Park, Wilmington, Del.

[Top] Prompted by a gift from Jasper Crane's descendants, the Friends of Wilmington Parks restored the Jasper Crane Rose Garden in 2001 with 450 replacement plants which have flourished. (Courtesy of the Friends of Wilmington Parks.)

[Bottom] In the 1940s and 1950s, the Jasper Crane Rose Garden earned a reputation as one of the top public rose gardens in America. (Postcard from author's collection.)

rainy March Saturday in 2001 to dig up the old rose bushes so that they could be sold to individuals interested in planting a bit of the historic rose garden in their own yards. The rose garden had always suffered from a lack of irrigation, a need that was remedied with the installation of an underground watering system. Two leading rose producers, Conard-Pyle and Jackson & Perkins, donated 450 new rose plants of 53 varieties to demonstrate the two companies' support for public gardens. In June 2001, the FOWP gathered to rededicate the Jasper Crane Rose Garden and to unveil the new hybrid rose, "Jasper Crane."

Continuing its work in the rose garden, the FOWP next undertook the relocation and conservation of the Bringhurst Fountain, which had stood at the center of the garden since 1988. Again mustering the necessary support from foundations, political leaders, and the state Division of Parks and Recreation, FOWP built a new stone terrace overlooking the Brandywine as a suitable site for the fountain. In April 2004, a skilled crew carefully disassembled the fountain's five constituent parts so it could be moved it to its new location and reassembled. A conservator assessed its condition and proceeded with careful cleaning. Two months later, members and guests

dedicated the new terrace and celebrated the Bringhurst Fountain's refurbishment.

Many of the initiatives launched by the FSBP have continued: "Hands Across the Brandywine" remains an annual event that attracts hundreds of children and teachers to the park each spring. The organization has maintained its dedication to promoting the history of the park. Although walking tours are no longer offered on a regular schedule, FOWP worked with the Division of Parks and Recreation to make a complete inventory of the historic resources in the park. Finished in August 1999, the inventory identified all the bridges, buildings, benches, walls, pavilions, and other features that can be found within the park and provided an assessment of their significance. Nearly every FOWP newsletter includes an article exploring the history of one or more of Wilmington's state parks.

The FOWP found the state Division of Parks and Recreation staff to be congenial collaborators. In April 2002, the division allowed FOWP to host a gala event to celebrate the reopening of Rockford Tower after extensive restoration of the century-old tower to its former glory. On a pleasant spring evening, partygoers watched from atop the 115-foot tower as a full moon rose over the city and the FOWP celebration yielded $20,000 to underwrite future work. When summer 2002 brought a severe drought, park administrator Ron Crouch knew he could call on FOWP members to help with watering the new trees that had been planted that spring. The relationship between the FOWP and the Division of Parks and Recreation seems to approach the fruitful cooperation that once prevailed in relation to Brandywine Park, one in which everyone's top priority was what seemed best for the park. Although years of neglect leave many tasks on the horizon, there is much to be expected from the partnership that links state dedication to the park with the FOWP's focused and productive enthusiasm.

After replanting the rose garden, the FOWP moved the Bringhurst Fountain from the garden to a new terrace overlooking the river. Here workers anchor the decorative urn atop the relocated memorial. (Courtesy of the Friends of Wilmington Parks.)

NORTH RACE, LOOKING S.E. FROM FRANKLIN ST.
1518   Wilmington, Del.

The north millrace, laid out in 1769, had developed into a
liability and nuisance during the 20th century. It was filled with
earth in 1959-60 and paved to provide parking near the
Josephine Fountain and the zoo. (Postcard from author's collection.)

Chapter 10

What Went Away or Didn't Happen
and What We Have

Hovering in the background of the Brandywine Park story are ghosts—the ghosts of park elements that no longer survive. There are the ghosts of projects that loomed as possibilities but never went beyond the planning stages, and there are the "ghosts of Christmas future" that hint at what might lie ahead.

What Went Away

A glance at a mid-19th-century map of the park would show four millraces parallel to the Brandywine River. The south long race is the sole survivor. The north long race remained a park feature until 1959–60, when it was filled in and paved over. But what of the two short races that began at the dam at the foot of West Street and paralleled the river down to the mills of Brandywine Village?

The short race in North Brandywine Park was the first to disappear, showing up on an 1876 map but gone by 1883. The short race on the south side of the Brandywine also appeared on the 1876 map, but Board of Park Commissioners records indicate that it was filled in during the 1890s to provide the foundation for the portion of South Park Drive that runs between Market Street and West Street.

A more substantial disappearance from the park landscape occurred at the other end of the park, however, when the Board of Park Commissioners demolished a little Roman Catholic chapel near the corner of Lovering Avenue and DuPont Street in 1909. The story of the little building's link to the park began in 1886, when the Roman Catholic Diocese of Wilmington sold a parcel of land to the city as part of Brandywine Park. The chapel stood on that land. Dedicated in 1869, St. James' Chapel eventually became the sponsor in 1872 of a night school for boys who spent their days working in nearby mills and, seven years later, of "St. James Protectory," an "orphan asylum" for dependent boys.

With the construction of the Baltimore & Ohio Railroad line across the Brandywine in 1883–85, the diocese decided to relocate the congregation and sold the chapel and land to the city. Within a year of the sale, the new parish church, St. Ann's, on Union Street was dedicated. The abandoned chapel proved useful to the Board of Park Commissioners, providing space for a workshop and for storage. Park employees used it in inclement weather, especially during the winter, to repair benches, fix mowers, and perform other necessary maintenance.[1] When the B&O Railroad realigned their tracks in 1909, it was necessary to demolish the chapel building as part of the project.

[Top] *These picnickers in the early 20th century sit on a lawn in North Brandywine Park and, in the background, are a series of wolf cages on the hillside, enclosures that have long since disappeared. (Courtesy of the Historical Society of Delaware.)*

[Bottom] *St. James Chapel, built in 1869, became the property of the Board of Park Commissioners in 1886. It served as a workspace and warehouse for park operations until it was demolished in 1909. (Courtesy of St. Ann's Church, Wilmington.)*

WHAT DIDN'T HAPPEN

There were a number of ideas for the park that never got beyond the initial plans. In retrospect, it is probably a good thing. In 1929 the Board of Water Commissioners sought permission to construct a water pumping station in South Brandywine Park between the B&O Railroad and the dam. This never happened, although some years later the Water Department did erect the pumping station on the opposite bank. In the 1930s, the Levy Court and the county engineer began making plans to use Civil Works Administration (CWA) resources to build the "Brandywine Park Highway," a scenic road that would run along the river through North Brandywine Park and extend from Wilmington to the Pennsylvania state line. In 1953 the Executive Committee approved making a parking area for 25 cars at the foot of Adams Street in the area that the swimming pool had once occupied. There were also plans for a band shell in Rattlesnake Run and a boating facility with pavilions and an amphitheater along the Brandywine.[2]

One of the earliest and most tenaciously pushed projects was the rebuilding of the barley mill dam near the foot of Adams Street. It was advocated by Theodore A. Leisen, the park superintendent, as a means for additional recreation in the park. With a mill pond gathered behind the dam, park visitors could boat and swim in the summer, he claimed, and in the winter, there would be "a magnificent field for skaters." Leisen's plans went beyond constructing a mere dam, however. There was to be an eight-foot-wide walkway across the top of the dam, and on the nearby bank, a shelter would serve as a boathouse in the summer and a shelter for skaters in the winter. First proposed in 1895 and proposed annually for several years, the plan finally had to be abandoned in 1902 because the Board of Park Commissioners could not reach agreement with the Lea milling interests downstream in Brandywine Village. William Lea and Sons Company threatened to seek an injunction against the project unless there was an agreement safeguarding the company's water rights. When no agreement could be achieved, "the execution of this important work (was) blocked, and the pleasure which its completion would afford to the large mass of people, both old and young, (was) denied them."[3]

What We Have

In spite of the resources that have disappeared and the projects that never got off the drawing board, Wilmingtonians still enjoy a resource that is as valuable and as appealing now as it was when it was first established. When A. J. Clement wrote about Wilmington's parks in 1888, he singled out Brandywine Park for special notice because of its "rare features of natural beauty as to defy any improvements by art beyond rendering all parts of it safely and easily accessible." Six years later, when the *Every Evening* newspaper compiled a history of Wilmington, the editors described the park as "the resort of thousands of citizens every Sunday and every holiday. Its existence is undoubtedly as fruitful a source of wholesome moral upbuilding to the community as it unquestionably is of unmeasurable hygienic value."[4]

Although Brandywine Park has had some reversals of fortune in the intervening years, it seems to have come under the protection of thoughtful custodians and passionate advocates once again. As people return to the park in increasing numbers, it is to be expected that they would agree with the 19th-century writers. It is indeed a wonderful resource in the midst of the city and, as it has always done, continues to supply refreshment and renewal for visitors. When park users were interviewed in 1994 for

the "Brandywine Park Essential Plan," most individuals praised the park's natural setting and worried about maintenance and security.[5] As the 21st century progresses, it seems clear that the desirable aspects of the park have been secured and enhanced, and the concerns are being effectively addressed. The first members of the Board of Park Commissioners would probably agree that their work to provide a public park that "puts wholesome and rational out door enjoyment within the reach of all" has been achieved.[6]

[Left] Frame pavilions in South Brandywine Park near the dam provided shelter for visitors from early in the 20th century, but were also plagued by periodic flooding. A masonry pavilion took their place in the 1930s.

[Right] Rustic pavilions such as this cedar structure, popularly called the Bird Cage, offered a shady refuge along park paths where ladies sat to chat and youngsters found a place to play checkers on rainy days. This small pavilion along the millrace survived into the 1960s.

Appendix

INITIAL LAND PURCHASES FOR BRANDYWINE PARK
NOVEMBER 1886

NORTH BRANDYWINE PARK

Seller	Acres	Price paid	Buildings on parcel
Joseph Tatnall	63.02	$54,660	none
Robert Kirkpatrick	.14	3,500	2 frame houses
Bernard McVey	.14	2,500	2 frame houses
James Morrison	.07	1,900	1 frame house
John Wier	.07	1,400	1 frame house
TOTAL	**63.44**	**$63,960**	

SOUTH BRANDYWINE PARK

Seller	Acres	Price paid	Buildings on parcel
E. P. Morris, et al.	2.76	$1,620	none
William Bright	3.50	5,000	none
Hartmann & Fehrenbach	1.60	4,000	none
William M. Field	9.80	8,500	4 small stone houses
Philip P. Tyre	5.77	6,500	none
Daniel W. Taylor	3.40	9,500	none
Edward Betts	9.60	15,000	none
Rev. Thomas A. Becker	1.89	14,000	2 houses, 1 chapel
TOTAL	**38.32**	**$64,120**	

Source: *Annual Report 1895*, 25–26.

Endnotes

Chapter 1

[1] *Report of the Board of Park Commissioners of Wilmington, Del., for the Year Ending December 31ˢᵗ, 1895, including a General Review from 1883 to 1894* (Wilmington, Del.: John M. Rogers Press, 1896), 12. The Board of Park Commissioners began publishing annual reports in 1895, and each was titled slightly differently. In this book, they are cited hereafter as *Annual Report* and the year. Unless otherwise stated, all primary records reside in the Delaware Public Archives, Dover, Del.

[2] Laura Wood Roper, *FLO: A Biography of Frederick Law Olmsted* (Baltimore: Johns Hopkins University Press, 1973), 328.

[3] *Annual Report* 1895, 9–10.

[4] *Annual Report* 1895, 12.

[5] *Annual Report* 1895, 13.

[6] *Annual Report* 1895, 14.

[7] At the time of the first Board of Park Commissioners meeting, John P. Wales was Wilmington's mayor, Henry C. Conrad served as president of the City Council, Charles W. Talley chaired the Council's Finance Committee, and Myers C. Conwell was chief engineer of the city's Surveying Department. None of them ever served as an appointed commissioner on the board. *City of Wilmington Board of Park Commissioners Minutes of the Board of Park Commissioners Meetings* (hereafter *Board Minutes*), April 26, 1883.

[8] For Canby's commercial board memberships, see J. Thomas Scharf, *History of Delaware, 1609–1888* (Philadelphia: L. J. Richards & Co., 1888), 2:682, 741, 743, 846; *Every Evening*, March 10, 1904, 1. Unless otherwise noted, all newspapers referenced herein are Wilmington papers.

[9] Scharf, *History of Delaware*, 2:830, 835; *Every Evening*, March 10, 1904, 1.

[10] J. N. Rose, "William M. Canby (A Portrait)," *Botanical Gazette* 37 (May 1904): 385.

[11] Rose, "William M. Canby," 387.

[12] The Liverpool Museum, for example, has several Canby specimens. John Edmondson, director, Botany Department, Liverpool Museum, May 8, 2002, personal communication to the author.

[13] Jane Loring Gray, ed., "The Botanical Correspondence of William M. Canby," (n.d.), Historical Society of Delaware.

[14] Priscilla M. Thompson, "Creation of the Wilmington Park System before 1896," *Delaware History* 18, no. 2 (Fall–Winter 1978): 90, quoting from papers of Olmsted Associates, July 8, 1893, Library of Congress. Thompson's detailed account of the interaction between the Board of Park Commissioners and the Olmsted firm provides the basis for this summary.

[15] *Annual Report* 1904, 19.

[16] In 1919 the Board of Park Commissioners named the pathway along the Brandywine River from Market Street to Kentmere "Canby Walk" in honor of William Marriott Canby; *Every Evening*, February 13, 1919. In 1930 the board renamed Southwest Park, changing its name to Canby Park in honor of William Marriott Canby, first president of the board, and in honor of his son, Henry M. Canby, a board member from 1913 to 1928. *fs*, July 1, 1928, to June 30, 1932 (published together), *Annual Report* 1930, 19.

[17] Thompson, "Creation of the Wilmington Park System," 79, quoting from William Poole Bancroft's letter book no. 1, Woodlawn Trustees, Wilmington, Delaware.

[18] "William Poole Bancroft," *National Cyclopedia of American Biography*, 22:187. Other committee members include J. Taylor Gause, George H. Bates, Francis N. Buck, and George W. Bush, who were on the original Board of Park Commissioners, and Dennis J. Menton, who served on the board 1884–86 as an ex-officio member and 1886–1913 as an appointed member.

[19] Scharf, *History of Delaware*, 2:797. William Poole Bancroft's brother (Samuel Bancroft Jr.) was named after his uncle, Samuel Bancroft.

[20] *Journal–Every Evening*, February 8, 1937, 8.

[21] Deed Record U-14-229, September 28, 1899.

[22] *Annual Report* 1899, 12.

[23] *Board Minutes*, October 10, 1917.

[24] See, for example, *Board Minutes*, August 1, 1899; *Wilmington Board of Park Commisiners Minutes of the Executive Committee of the Board of Park Commissioners*, September 4, 1903 (hereafter, *Executive Committee Minutes*); *Executive Committee Minutes*, January 18, 1907; *Board Minutes*, February 12, 1908.

[25] *Board Minutes*, March 8, 1911; see also *Executive Committee Minutes*, April 18, 1916.

[26] *Board Minutes*, October 7, 1902; January 2, 1907; April 8, 1907.

[27] *City of Wilmington Board of Park Commissioners Superintendent's Diaries*, 1910 (hereafter *Superintendent's Diaries*.)

[28] "William Poole Bancroft," 187; *Morning News*, August 9, 1956, 20. Claudia L. Bushman, *So Laudable an Undertaking: The Wilmington Library, 1788–1988* (Wilmington, Del.: Delaware Heritage Press, 1988), 47–51.

[29] *Mayor's Advisory Board Minutes*, February 2, 1910, and March 2, 1910; *Board Minutes*, May 14, 1913.

[30] *Annual Report* 1895, 29.

31 *Mayor's Advisory Board Minutes*, September 6, 1916.

32 "The Woodlawn Trustees, Alias William P. Bancroft," *One-Two-One-Four*, 2:6 (September 1924):1; Carol E. Hoffecker, *Corporate Capital : Wilmington in the Twentieth Century* (Philadelphia: Temple University Press), 33. See also "William Poole Bancroft," 187.

33 William Poole Bancroft to William Marriott Canby, April 24, 1890, City of Wilmington Parks and Recreation correspondence; letter to City Council read into *Board Minutes*, January 12, 1915.

34 Because of his military rank, du Pont was accorded appropriate honors at his funeral when the organist played "Taps" at the conclusion of the service; *Morning News*, January 3, 1927, 1.

35 See John K. Winkler, *The Du Pont Dynasty* (New York: Blue Ribbon Books, Inc., 1935), 126; Joseph Frazier Wall, *Alfred I. du Pont: The Man and His Family* (New York: Oxford University Press, 1990), 174.

36 *Evening Journal*, December 31, 1926, 1. See also Scharf, *History of Delaware*, 2:683, 743.

37 *Annual Report* 1895, 29.

38 Winkler, 290–291; Wall, 391.

39 *Board Minutes*, October 10, 1941; *Board Minutes*, April 10, 1942.

40 *History of Wilmington: The Commercial, Social and Religious Growth of the City during the Past Century* (Wilmington, Del.: Every Evening, 1894), 203; *Sixth Annual Statement of the Board of Directors of the Street and Sewer Department of Wilmington, Delaware, for the Fiscal Year Ending April 30, 1893* (Wilmington, Del.: Diamond Printing Co., 1893), n.p.

41 Scharf, *History of Delaware*, 2:620, 674, 747, 893; *Morning News*, May 15, 1935, 2.

42 Scharf, *History of Delaware*, 2:694, 744, 830, 832, 833, 893.

43 *Every Evening*, June 22, 1907, 1; *Sunday Star*, October 24, 1943, 9.

44 *Board Minutes*, November 13, 1883.

45 A memorial to Thomas F. Bayard stands on Kentmere Parkway. He is shown in clothing typical of his period: a long frock coat with a cloak hanging over his arm. Effie Stillman Richie created the model for the statue in England, where the bronze was also cast. The dedication of the statue on June 22, 1907, drew 5,000 people; *Every Evening*, June 22, 1907, 1.

46 Scharf, *History of Delaware*, 2:670, 740.

47 Scharf, *History of Delaware*, 2:835–836.

48 Scharf, *History of Delaware*, 2:670, 755, 798, 867.

49 Scharf, *History of Delaware*, 2:670, 682, 744, 747, 754, 758, 670, 813, 832, 833, 835, 846; Bush obituary, *Board of Trade Journal* II, no. 4 (July 1900): 6.

50 Scharf, *History of Delaware*, 2:767–768, 771. See also J. Taylor Gause obituary, *Board of Trade Journal* I, no. 3 (December 1898): 1.

51 Scharf, *History of Delaware*, 2:832.

52 For a short but vivid portrait of Mrs. Gause, see Bill Frank, "The Energetic Mrs. Gause," *Morning News*, May 1, 1963, 26.

53 Scharf, *History of Delaware*, 2:830, 831. The Bringhurst Fountain, originally at the corner of Pennsylvania and Delaware avenues, was removed in the 1960s and returned to public view in Brandywine Park in 1988; see chapter 6 on memorials in the park.

54 Carol E. Hoffecker, *Wilmington, Delaware: Portrait of an Industrial City, 1830–1910* (Charlottesville: For the Eleutherian Mills-Hagley Foundation by the University Press of Virginia, 1974), 76–77.

CHAPTER 2

1 "Population," U.S. Census for 1850, 210; "Population," U.S. Census for 1880, 116

2 W. P. Bancroft, "An Interesting Memoir Written by Mr. W. P. Bancroft in Acknowledgement of Birthday Greetings from Some of the Older Employees on the Occasion of His Seventy-Eighth Birthday," *The Bancroft Bulletin* (1913).

3 Lisa M. Fine, *The Souls of the Skyscraper* (Philadelphia: Temple University Press, 1990), 45.

4 *Annual Report* 1895, 15.

5 *Board Minutes*, April 26, 1883.

6 *Board Minutes*, November 13, 1883.

7 *Board Minutes*, December 28, 1883; *Board Minutes*, November 13, 1883.

8 *Annual Report* 1895, 18 (quotes Olmsted to Board of Park Commissioners, December 23, 1883).

9 *Annual Report* 1895, 15–19.

10 *Annual Report* 1895, 19.

11 David Schuyler, *The New Urban Landscape: The Redefinition of City Form in Nineteenth-Century America* (Baltimore: Johns Hopkins University Press, 1986), 120.

12 The "Swinging Bridge" gets its name from the tendency of the suspension span to sway when pedestrians crossed it. It has since been stabilized and now merely bounces lightly with foot traffic, but it retains the name, which was first recorded on March 24, 1907, in the park superintendent's diary. See chapter 5 for a more detailed discussion of the park's bridges.

13 It is not apparent where the name *Rattlesnake Run* originated. It has had that name since at least 1822. In that year, a map of the Brandywine and the various flourmills at Brandywine Village records the stream's path and identifies it as Rattlesnake Run. The map, which is part of the P. S. du Pont collection at Eleutherian Mills Historical Library, is reproduced in Carol E. Hoffecker's book on Brandywine Village: Carol E. Hoffecker, *Brandywine Village: The Story of a Milling Community* (Wilmington, Del.: Old Brandywine Village, Inc., 1974), 104.

14 Board of Directors of Street and Sewer Department to Board of Park Commissioners, November 18, 1887, *Wilmington Board of Park Commissioners Letter Books, Project Files, Agreements and Miscellaneous* (hereafter *Letter Book*).

15 *Thirty-Third Annual Report, Chief Engineer of the Water Department to the Board of Water Commissioners, Wilmington, Delaware for the Year 1902* (no publication information), 7.

16 *Annual Report* 1905, 14–15; *Annual Report* 1909, 33.

17 *Executive Committee Minutes*, June 1, 1915; June 6, 1916. *Annual Report* 1915, 18; *Annual Report* 1916, 13.

18 *Sunday Star*, June 28, 1925, 8, lists five springs that survived into the mid-1920s.

19 *Sunday Star*, July 11, 1909, 1.

20 *Annual Report* 1911, 9.

21 *Evening Journal*, November 15, 1962, 3.

22 Frank R. Zebley, *The Churches of Delaware: A History, in Brief, of the Nearly 900 Churches and Former Churches in Delaware as Located by the Author* (Wilmington, Del.: William N. Cann, Inc., 1947), 36; *Annual Report* 1895, 51.

23 *Annual Report* 1918, 9; *Board Minutes*, August 12, 1927; *Executive Committee Minutes*, October 3, 1938.

24 *Annual Report* 1898, 11; *Annual Report* 1901, 12. It was called the "Sugar Bowl" because its rounded dome reminded some park visitors of the round lid of a sugar bowl.

25 *Annual Report* 1896, 9.
26 *Annual Report* 1903, 12–13.

27 *Annual Report* 1931, 27.

28 For an excellent account of flour milling along this section of the Brandywine, see Hoffecker, *Brandywine Village.*

29 It is important to note that the river actually flows in a southeasterly direction through the park, so technically what is usually called North Brandywine Park ought to be called Northeast Brandywine Park and what is called South Brandywine Park should be designated Southwest Brandywine Park if direction from the river is the starting point. To avoid confusion, however, we will keep to the usual form—North and South Brandywine Park.

30 Scharf, *History of Delaware*, 2:760.

31 Scharf, *History of Delaware*, 2:788; Hoffecker, *Brandywine Village*, 52–54.

32 *Annual Report* 1922–23, 12; Hoffecker, *Brandywine Village*, 50–51.

33 *Executive Committee Minutes*, December 28, 1959, letter of complaint; *Annual Report* 1959–60, 3. Edward R. Mack to 9th Ward Business Men's Association about the north race pollution, October 10, 1934, *Wilmington Board of Park Commissioners Correspondence* (hereafter *Correspondence*). See chapter 10 for brief account of the two short races that once paralleled the Brandywine.

34 Scharf, *History of Delaware*, 2:793–794.

35 *Annual Report* 1895, 19–20. The members of the City Council committee were D. J. Menton, R. H. Taylor, T. R. Latimer, E. C. Moore, and Merris Taylor.

36 *Board Minutes*, May 21, 1885; June 24, 1885.

37 *Annual Report* 1895, 20.

38 *Annual Report* 1895, 20, 22.

39 *Board Minutes*, May 27, 1886.

40 *Annual Report* 1895, 22, 24.

41 For a detailed account of efforts to raise funds through bond issues, see *Board Minutes*, March 2, 1897; April 6, 1897; May 4, 1897; June 1, 1897; January 14, 1898; September 2, 1898. *Superintendent's Diaries*, January 12, 1897; February 28, 1897. *Annual Report* 1898, 9.

42 Jerome B. Bell, editor of the *Sunday Star* newspaper, served from 1909, when the Finance Committee was formed, until his death in 1921. He also served on the board's Park Extension Committee for the same years. In 1909 Irénée du Pont was appointed to the board and began serving immediately on the Finance Committee, an appointment he held until he left the board in 1918. John H. Danby, vice president of Union National Bank and president of the Wilmington Fountain Society, began his board service and his term on the Finance Committee in 1915. He served the park board until his death in 1921. Contractor Thomas Melvin, appointed to the board in 1918, joined the Finance Committee in 1919 and remained a committee member through 1926.

43 See Appendix A for a list of the sellers whose land made up the initial park purchases, the acreage conveyed, and the prices paid.

44 *Annual Report* 1895, 50–53. During the same year, from mid-November 1886 to mid-November 1887, they also purchased 5.34 acres of land for Delamore Park that also came under the jurisdiction of the board. When reporting park acreage, the park board routinely included in the total the approximately 23 acres occupied by the Brandywine River, so for the sake of clarity and consistency, the acreage included in this narrative will do likewise.

45 *Annual Report* 1895, 30; Deed Record I-16-282, February 2, 1894.

46 *Board Minutes*, April 3, 1894.

47 *Board Minutes*, January 6, 1903.

48 Theodore A. Leisen, "Parks of Wilmington, Del.," *Board of Trade Journal* 1, no. 9 (June 1899): 6.

49 *Annual Report* 1895, 20.

50 *Annual Report* 1895, 29.

51 *Board Minutes*, July 6, 1897.

52 *History of Wilmington*, 241.

53 *Board Minutes*, January 14, 1914.

54 *Board Minutes*, February 10, 1922.

55 Edward R. Mack, "Wilmington's Park System," *Wilmington* 4, no. 2 (June 1929): 8.

Chapter 3

1 The Board of Park Commissioners began meeting in 1883 and acquired the first parkland in 1886. In the *Board Minutes*, the first reference to an Executive Committee is on May 1, 1888, when the Executive Committee reported awarding a contract for the construction of "three watch and tool houses." The *Executive Committee Minutes* held by the Delaware Public Archives do not begin until 1896.

2 *Board Minutes*, October 12, 1887; November 1, 1887; November 25, 1887; July 30, 1888; September 4, 1888.

3 *Board Minutes*, September 12, 1892, Washington Street Bridge site. *Executive Committee Minutes*, February 15, 1896, wall between Market and West streets; November 5, 1897, tree planting location; July 19, 1901, "Sugar Bowl" pavilion site. *Superintendent's Diaries*, March 26, 1897, swimming pool site.

4 *Executive Committee Minutes*, February 2, 1908; December 6, 1921; August 29, 1932.

5 *One-Two-One-Four*, 2:5 (August 1924): 1, 4.

6 *Board Minutes*, March 13, 1925.

7 *Annual Report* 1912, 9.

8 *Annual Report* 1917, 23; *Annual Report* 1918, 17; *Annual Report* 1920, 10; *Annual Report* 1921, 11; *Annual Report* 1922, 10.

9 *Annual Report* 1917, 23; *Annual Report* 1918, 17; *Annual Report* 1920, 10; *Annual Report* 1921, 11; *Annual Report* 1922, 10.

10 *Board Minutes*, March 13, 1925.

11 Haynes often was called "Colonel," an honorific he was entitled to use because of his service as a military aide to Gov. Preston Lea. *Board Minutes*, October 11, 1956.

12 *Morning News*, September 17, 1956, 1. *Wilmington Fountain Society Minutes*, March 17, 1924; September 13, 1933.

13 *Board Minutes*, July 14, 1933. *Executive Committee Minutes*, October 16, 1933. *Annual Report* 1934, 21. For a more complete discussion of the Jasper Crane Rose Garden, see chapter 4.

14 *Evening Journal*, July 30, 1929, 1.

15 *Journal–Every Evening*, August 8, 1935, 5.

16 *Executive Committee Minutes*, September 17, 1956. *Board Minutes*, October 11, 1956.

17 *Annual Report* 1956–57, 5.

18 *Evening Journal*, January 3, 1974, 1.

19 *Evening Journal*, January 3, 1974, 1.

20 *Evening Journal*, January 9, 1965, 1.

21 *Morning News*, January 7, 1974, 6.

22 *Board Minutes*, August 23, 1956. A more detailed consideration of the board's defense of the park against the construction of a new school is provided in chapter 4.

23 A more detailed discussion of Lee's efforts to defend the park against the construction of the highway and the I-95 Bridge and his efforts to mitigate its impact is provided in chapter 5.

24 *Evening Journal*, January 3, 1974, 1.

25 *Evening Journal*, January 9, 1965, 1.

26 *Journal–Every Evening*, August 8, 1935, 5.

27 *Board Minutes*, June 14, 1967.

28 *Annual Report* 1967–68, 2.

29 Chapter 4 discusses in further detail the board's oversight in regard to the parks infrastructure and the projects that involved collaboration with other city departments.

30 *Wilmington Board of Park Commissioners Bills and Distribution Book* (hereafter *Bills and Distribution Book*), data for 1911 provide a good overview of a year's work. *Board Minutes*, February 23, 1942.

31 *Annual Report* 1900, 15.

32 *The Parks and Playgrounds of Wilmington, Delaware* (Wilmington, Del.: Board of Park Commissioners, 1929), 27.

33 *Executive Committee Minutes*, September 18, 1933; November 20, 1933; March 9, 1934. Miscellaneous Documents, inventory of possible projects for Wilmington parks, February 7, 1935, *Letter Book*. *Board Minutes*, January 14, 1944.

34 *Annual Report* 1955–56, 5–8.

35 *Executive Committee Minutes*, June 16, 1909.

36 George Anderson to Edward R. Mack, superintendent, June 7, 1935, *Correspondence*.

37 *Board Minutes*, March 11, 1936.

38 Elizabeth Donohue to board regarding swimmers, June 3, 1935; Joseph Bancroft & Sons Company to board regarding swimmers, July 14, 1947; William A. Mikesell to superintendent regarding grazing animals, August 11, 1919, all *Letter Book*. *Executive Committee Minutes*, February 23, 1942, regarding blackout procedure.

39 *Executive Committee Minutes*, April 24, 1896.

40 *Annual Report* 1896, 7.

41 *Mayor's Advisory Board Minutes*, March 1, 1911; *Board Minutes*, May 10, 1911.

42 *Mayor's Advisory Board Minutes*, June 5, 1912.

43 *Annual Report* 1913, 8.

44 *Annual Report* 1895, 23.

45 *Executive Committee Minutes*, June 13, 1902, August 20, 1928; *Bills and Distribution Book*, July 1902; June 1903. There is no record of the monthly rental rate in 1902 and 1903, although in 1914, the house at 1601 Adams rented for $10 per month per *Board Minute Book, 1914–1919*, record inside front cover.

46 *Annual Report* 1911, 20. The rents remained unchanged as late as 1918 per the board's Rent Ledger; *Board of Park Commissioners Rent Ledger (1914–1918)*, n.p.

[47] L. Robinson to board, March 28, 1887, *Letter Book*; James H. Powell to board, May 2, 1893, *Letter Book*.

[48] Agreement between Board of Park Commissioners and Henry S. Black and his partners, Barton D. Curry and William S. Stannard, May 1894, *Letter Book*. See also Black's letters to the board, June 5, 1894, and August 7, 1894, *Letter Book*. In 1904 Robert Barry leased a refreshment stand in South Brandywine Park for $5 per month.

[49] *Executive Committee Minutes*, March 8, 1911; June 6, 1922.

[50] *Board Minutes*, March 11, 1955; April 15, 1955.

[51] Baseball—*Executive Committee Minutes*, July 30, 1962. Football—*Executive Committee Minutes*, January and February 1965; March 22, 1965; April 8, 1965; June 28, 1965; February 28, 1966; July 19, 1966. *Morning News*, September 4, 1965. *Evening Journal*, September 2, 1967.

[52] *Executive Committee Minutes*, April 8, 1904; March 22, 1954; January 14, 1957. *Board Minutes*, October 9, 1907; November 13, 1907; February 12, 1926.

[53] *Annual Report* 1905, 16. The establishment and creation of the zoo is covered more fully in chapter 8 and the Todd Memorial in chapter 6.

[54] *Annual Report* 1926, 13–14.

[55] *Board Minutes*, October 3, 1927.

[56] *Wilmington Fountain Society Minutes*, September 2, 1872. *Bills and Distribution Book*, July and August 1904.

[57] *Executive Committee Minutes*, July 8, 1909. The National Humane Alliance donated identical fountains to at least 20 other cities around the same time that it gave the fountain to Wilmington. Hermon Lee Ensign founded the National Humane Alliance, and, for that reason, the fountain is occasionally referred to as the "Ensign Fountain."

[58] *Wilmington Fountain Society Board Minutes*, September 26, 1928; October 21, 1929. *Board Minutes*, October 11, 1929.

[59] *Wilmington Fountain Society Minutes*, October 31, 1924; October 8, 1925; November 25, 1931; May 1, 1939. *Executive Committee Minutes*, March 10, 1925. *Board Minutes*, August 14, 1931. A 1937 Fountain Society map identifies the locations of nine society fountains in South Brandywine Park and seven in North Brandywine Park.

[60] *Board Minutes*, September 8, 1966; *Annual Report* 1967–68, 11.

[61] *Wilmington Fountain Society Board Minutes*, June 1, 1966.

[62] *Board Minutes*, August 13, 1913. The pools operating in various city locations in 1913 were Brandywine Pool, Delamore Pool, and Kirkwood Pool.

[63] *Board Minutes*, July 8, 1914. *Sunday Star*, June 28, 1914, 2.

[64] *Parks and Playgrounds*, 20.

[65] *Recreation in Wilmington—Summary of Findings and Recommendations: Part I of Wilmington Recreation Survey* (typescript, 1938–39), 7.

[66] *Executive Committee Minutes*, May 2, 1949; April 24, 1950.

[67] *Sunday Star*, September 18, 1921, 1; August 2, 1925, 12; October 11, 1925, 1; May 30, 1926, 1; October 17, 1926, 6. *Evening Journal*, June 21, 1965, 143.

[68] *Executive Committee* Minutes, June 26, 1923. *Board Minutes*, July 13, 1923.

[69] *Executive Committee Minutes*, September 10, 1956. *Evening Journal*, January 3, 1974, 1.

[70] *Board Minutes*, June 14, 1956; August 23, 1956.

[71] *Annual Report* 1956–57, 1–2.

[72] See chapter 5 for a full discussion of the I-95 Bridge project.

[73] *Board Minutes*, April 12, 1929; June 12, 1958. *Executive Committee Minutes*, May 26, 1958. *Journal–Every Evening*, October 29, 1959, 1.

[74] *Board Minutes*, March 11, 1965; April 8, 1965. *Annual Report* 1964–65, 16.

[75] Undated petition circa 1897–98 from 10 people near park asking board to cut grass and pull weeds on "Washington Triangle," *Correspondence*. Washington Heights Association to board, June 30, 1899, asking to borrow seats for an unspecified event, *Letter Book*; Samuel H. Baynard, president of Washington Heights Association, to Park Superintendent Theodore A. Leisen, July 2, 1900, asking to use "Washington Triangle" for neighborhood 4th of July celebration, *Letter Book*.

[76] *Sunday Star*, July 5, 1908, 1.

[77] *Board Minutes*, April 14, 1939; August 22, 1944. *Executive Committee*, December 3, 1945; November 14, 1949.

[78] Employees to board, September 12, 1894, *Letter Book*; *Board Minutes*, October 2, 1894.

[79] *Executive Committee Minutes*, May 14, 1913; November 3, 1947; September 26, 1949; October 30, 1950; November 5, 1951; November 3, 1952. *Annual Report* 1917, 14; *Annual Report* 1918, 9.

[80] *Board Minutes*, March 1, 1898; July 5, 1898.

[81] *Mayor's Advisory Board Minutes*, April 5, 1922; *Board Minutes*, October 13, 1922.

[82] Hoffecker, *Corporate Capital*, 85.

[83] *Mayor's Advisory Board Minutes*, October 5, 1921; December 7, 1921.

[84] *Mayor's Advisory Board Minutes*, June 7, 1922; *Annual Report* 1922, 11–12.

[85] *Board Minutes*, November 14, 1930.

[86] A more detailed examination of the work done under these programs is included in chapter 4. *Sunday Star*, July 31, 1938, 7; *Board Minutes*, January 12, 1934; January 11, 1935; October 11, 1935; November 8, 1935; December 13, 1935; August 11, 1939.

[87] *Sunday Star*, July 15, 1951, 12.

[88] *Annual Report* 1957–58, 4; *Annual Report* 1961–62, 15. *Executive Committee Minutes*, September 8, 1958; May 21, 1962.

89 *Superintendent's Diaries*, December 15, 1910; May 15, 1911; *Executive Committee Minutes*, June 7, 1911; August 7, 1912; April 30, 1913; May 1, 1917; February 19, 1918; *Board Minutes*, November 13, 1912.

90 *Board of Park Commissioners Miscellaneous Ledgers and Papers* (hereafter *Ledger*), March 1896; May 1896. *Bills and Distribution Book*, May 1901; March 1904. *Superintendent's Diaries*, May 1, 1909. *Executive Committee Minutes*, April 14, 1914.

91 *Park and Cemetery* magazine to Leisen, May 11, 1897, *Letter Book*.

92 C. W. Clapp, civil engineer, Greenfield, Mass., to Leisen, May 19, 1898; Fred R. Charles, assistant city engineer, Richmond, Ind., to Leisen, September 27, 1898; J. H. Griffith, *Garden and Forest* magazine, to Leisen, circa April 16, 1898, all from *Correspondence*.

93 *Board Minutes*, May 8, 1907; November 13, 1912. *Executive Committee Minutes*, February 11, 1909; March 23, 1910; June 7, 1911; August 7, 1912. *Superintendent's Diaries*, December 15, 1910.

94 Requests came to Leisen or the Board of Park Commissioners for copies of the 1899 *Annual Report* from the Boston Society of Civil Engineers; the Engineers' Club, Philadelphia; American Society of Civil Engineers, New York; George Hanson, landscape architect, Berkeley, California; Thomas Meehan and Sons, nurserymen and landscape engineers, Philadelphia; Snow and Barbour, civil and sanitary engineers, Boston; Warren H. Manning, landscape architect, Boston; Frank C. Osborn, civil engineer, Cleveland; Daniel Smiley, Lake Mohonk Mountain House, Monhonk Lake, N.Y.; Department of Parks, Paterson, N.J.; Commissioners of Lincoln Park, Chicago; Bureau of Parks, Pittsburgh; Board of Park Commissioners, Worcester, Massachusetts; Engineering Department, Lafayette, Ind.; Park Commissioners, Lynn, Mass.; Board of Park Commissioners, Chester, Pa.; Engineering Department, Dubuque, Iowa; Keney Park Trustees, Hartford, Conn.; Park Commission, St. Louis; Board of Public Works, West Superior, Wisc.; Park Commission, Buffalo, N.Y.; Office of Street and Park Commission, Manchester, N.H.; Department of Public Works, Philadelphia; Commissioners of Parks and Boulevards, Detroit; New York State Library, Albany; Metropolitan Park Commission, Boston.

CHAPTER 4

1 J. C. Olmsted to William Marriott Canby, October 22, 1887, *Correspondence*. *Board Minutes*, November 5, 1887. In December 1886, Thomas G. Janvier offered his surveying services, but he was not hired. Thomas G. Janvier to William Marriott Canby, December 28, 1886, *Letter Book*.

2 Samuel Canby," *The National Cyclopædia of American Biography*, vol. 33 (New York: James T. White & Co., 1947), 400–401; David F. Barber, *Trial and Triumph: The Story of One Community's Acquisition and Development of Its Own Water and Gas Utilities* (Omaha: Metropolitan Utilities District of Omaha, Nebraska, 1989), 79.

3 *Board Minutes*, December 3, 1889; February 4, 1890.

4 *Board Minutes*, March 4, 1890.

5 *Annual Report* 1895, 30.

6 Frederick Law Olmsted & Co. to William Marriott Canby, November 23, 1889, *Correspondence*.

7 Frederick Law Olmsted & Co. to William Marriott Canby, April 5, 1890, *Correspondence*. The Washington Street Bridge was constructed in 1893; see chapter 5.

8 *Board Minutes*, April 9, 1892; June 9, 1893. Superintendent Theodore A. Leisen to Board of Park Commissioners, March 2, 1894, *Letter Book*.

9 Throughout the early years of road building in the park, the Board of Park Commissioners benefited from close cooperation with the Street and Sewer Department. In July 1898, for example, the park paving projects used a Street and Sewer Department steamroller for eight days, at a cost of $52. The following summer, the Street and Sewer Department agreed to sprinkle the park drive on Thursdays and Fridays during the summer, although before June was out, the park board's Executive Committee had approved the purchase of a sprinkler wagon. *Executive Committee Minutes*, June 9, 1899; June 23, 1899.

10 *Board Minutes*, January 1, 1895, Theodore A. Leisen's report to the Board. *Annual Report* 1897, 7. *Annual Report* 1898, 11.

11 *Annual Report* 1904, 15; *Annual Report* 1905, 14–15; *Annual Report* 1906, 11. Elliott's Woods was the wooded area on the hill above the river and above North Park Drive.

12 See chapter 5 for a full discussion of the construction of the Van Buren Street Bridge.

13 *Annual Report* 1908, 10; *Annual Report* 1909, 15.

14 *Annual Report* 1919, 11. *Mayor's Advisory Board Minutes*, April 5, 1922.

15 *Board Minutes*, October 13, 1922. *Executive Committee Minutes*, December 12, 1922. *Annual Report* 1922, 13.

16 *Board Minutes*, January 14, 1955; this document also records one of the first uses of the name "Monkey Hill" in an official record of the Board of Park Commissioners.

17 *Ledger*, May 1898. *Executive Committee Minutes*, July 17, 1903. *Board Minutes*, September 18, 1903. *Annual Report* 1908, 11.

18 *Annual Report* 1901, 16. *Board Minutes*, April 10, 1912; September 10, 1913; July 7, 1914. *Bills and Distribution Book*, August 1901. *Executive Committee Minutes*, September 18, 1903; July 30, 1913. *Annual Report* 1913, 9.

19 The Levy Court was the county agency then responsible for roads and bridges.

20 *Board Minutes*, September 12, 1892.

21 *Board Minutes*, August 10, 1893.

22 *Board Minutes*, August 10, 1893.

23 *Board Minutes*, January 7, 1896; February 4, 1896. *Executive Committee Minutes*, February 15, 1896.

24 *Superintendent's Diaries*, September 22, 1904; December 29, 1904.

25 Delaware Safety Council to Park Superintendent Edward R. Mack, December 11, 1920, *Letter Book*.

26 *Executive Committee Minutes*, January 3, 1922. *Annual Report* 1929, 9.

27 *Annual Report* 1930, 18; *Annual Report* 1932, 37; *Annual Report* 1934, 31. *Board Minutes*, December 9, 1932. *Executive Committee Minutes*, June 19, 1933.

28 *Board Minutes*, September 11, 1964.

29 *Annual Report* 1896, 10. *Executive Committee Minutes*, September 11, 1896. *Board Minutes*, October 6, 1896.

30 *Annual Report* 1899, 14.

31 The board built other later walls in connection with roads. In 1908 the commissioners also had a retaining wall built to support North Park Drive where it passed below the zoo, and in 1912, at the upper end of the North Long Race, they had a wall constructed to "secure the bank and roadway ... from further danger from floods"; *Executive Committee Minutes*, July 31, 1908; August 12, 1908. *Annual Report* 1912, 9.

32 *Annual Report* 1898, 11, 14.

33 *Executive Committee Minutes*, July 18, 1901; July 26, 1901.

34 *Executive Committee Minutes*, November 6, 1903; November 20, 1903. *Annual Report* 1904, 14–15.

35 *Board Minutes*, July 30, 1888; October 1, 1889.

36 *Board Minutes*, July 2, 1894; September 4, 1894.

37 *Board Minutes*, September 4, 1900. *Executive Committee Minutes*, December 7, 1900; October 8, 1908. *Superintendent's Diaries*, December 12, 1911 refers to replacing light bulbs along South Park Drive, first actual reference to tending lights on the drive. *Annual Report* 1908, 11. *Executive Committee Minutes*, August 10, 1910; July 12, 1911; December 6, 1911. *Annual Report* 1911, 8.

38 *Board Minutes*, April 4, 1905. *Executive Committee Minutes*, February 16, 1906.

39 *Executive Committee Minutes*, October 1, 1908, March 12, 1913, note lighting for "comfort houses." See also *Annual Report* 1908, 12. *Executive Committee Minutes*, June 19, 1912, record lighting the Elliott's Woods pavilion. *Executive Committee Minutes*, August 8, 1922, refer to installation of lights at picnic grounds. Delmarva Power & Light to Superintendent Edward R. Mack regarding adding lights to Rodney Street tennis courts, May 22, 1934, *Letter Book*.

40 *Board Minutes*, May 1, 1888. *Annual Report* 1896, 10. There were plans in 1893 to build a toilet at the recently completed Washington Street Bridge, but it is unclear whether the toilet was ever constructed. *Wilmington Board of Park Commissioners Maps and Drawings, Field Book Index*, 1893.

41 *Annual Report* 1904, 13.

42 *Executive Committee Minutes*, April 25, 1902. *Board Minutes*, May 6, 1902; October 3, 1905. Negotiations for transfer of management of the comfort stations took three years.

43 *Annual Report* 1905, 17.

44 *Board Minutes*, July 11. 1905; November 12, 1937. *Annual Report* 1914, 8.

45 "Call for sealed proposals for comfort station in South Brandywine Park," bids due November 24, 1930, *Letter Book*. *Board Minutes*, November 14, 1930. *Executive Committee Minutes*, November 24, 1930. *Annual Report* 1931, 27. Per *Executive Committee Minutes*, August 22, 1907, there were repairs to a comfort house near Rattlesnake Run, but it is unclear where along the course of the run the facility stood.

46 "Call for sealed proposals for comfort station in North Brandywine Park," bids due August 24, 1931, *Letter Book*. *Annual Report* 1932, 12. *Board Minutes*, October 9, 1936, March 12, 1937.

47 In 1935 the Federal Emergency Administration of Public Works compiled a "National Inventory of Works Projects" that included among its recommended allocations $15,000 for comfort stations for Wilmington's parks, describing the projects as "in much frequented parks and ... needed from a sanitary point of view." "National Inventory of Works Projects, Prepared by Federal Emergency Administration of Public Works in cooperation with the State Planning Boards," February 7, 1935, *Letter Book*.

48 The 1931 Rattlesnake Run toilet measures 11 feet 8 inches by 19 feet 4 inches; the 1932 zoo toilet measures 17 feet by 22 feet 5 inches; the original portion of the Baynard Stadium toilet measures 18 feet 8 inches by 25 feet 9 inches.

49 *Annual Report* 1908, 12. *Annual Report* 1911, 10. Lest it be imagined that the Board of Park Commissioners was the only government body concerned about public toilets, it is worthwhile to note that in 1919 the City Council had a Committee on Public Comforts that inquired of Park Superintendent Edward R. Mack whether there would be "public comforts in the new park," the "new park" being Rodney Square: "The Committee of Council, on Public Comfort" to Superintendent Mack, November 17, 1919, *Letter Book*.

50 *Board Minutes*, February 10, 1928.

51 *Board Minutes*, September 5, 1893. *Annual Report* 1895, 32.

52 *Annual Report* 1895, 32. *Executive Committee Minutes*, October 7, 1909.

53 Theodore A. Leisen report to board on the pavilion, October 1, 1895, *Letter Book*. *Annual Report* 1895, 32.

54 *Superintendent's Diaries*, February 3, 1897. *Annual Report* 1897, 10.

55 Superintendent's report to board, July 1, 1895, *Letter Book*. *Annual Report* 1895, 47.

56 *Board Minutes*, August 6, 1901.

57 *Sunday Star*, April 13, 1902, 6. *Annual Report* 1901, 12.

58 Interestingly, a 1905 article in the April issue of the Wilmington *Board of Trade Journal* reported that local businessman Alfred Gawthorp, visiting a villa in Port Antonio, Jamaica, had seen a "pagoda" that was "an exact reproduction" of the Brandywine Park pavilion. The superintendent in charge of the villa provided a souvenir booklet that included an illustration of the Wilmington structure. Although the Jamaican structure appears to have been of stone on a concrete foundation, the similarities must have seemed especially striking to Mr. Gawthorp, whose relative, J. Newlin Gawthorp served on the Board of Park Commissioners at the end of the 19th century. Certainly, the existence of a second pavilion raises tantalizing questions about the link of the two. "Copying After Wilmington," *The Wilmington Board of Trade Journal* VII, no. 1 (April 1905), 11.

59 *Board Minutes*, April 8, 1949.

60 *Annual Report* 1958–59, 6.

61 *Annual Report* 1911, 8.

62 *Sunday Star*, July 31, 1938, 7. In recent years, the open spaces around the perimeter of the shelter have been entirely filled with concrete block to create a storage building.

63 *Sunday Star*, January 10, 1937, 14; March 24, 1940. *Annual Report and Statement, City of Wilmington, Delaware, 30 June 1941*, 70.

64 *Annual Report and Statement, City of Wilmington, Delaware, 30 June 1939*, 61.

65 *Board Minutes*, June 10, 1938.

66 *Board Minutes*, August 12, 1938; May 12, 1939. *Annual Report and Statement, City of Wilmington, Delaware, 30 June 1939*, 61.

67 *Sunday Star*, June 15, 1941, 9.

68 *Annual Report 1895*, 47.

69 *36th Annual Report, Chief Engineer of the Water Department, to the Board of Water Commissioners, Wilmington, Delaware for the Year 1905*, 11. Chapter 5 covers the bridge's history, including its recent reconstruction.

70 *Annual Report 1895*, 47

71 *Board Minutes*, May 3, 1892; January 1, 1895.

72 *Executive Committee Minutes*, November 5, 1897; April 14, 1899. The five park properties were Brandywine, Rockford, Eden, and Kirkwood parks and Kentmere Parkway.

73 *Ledger*, February 1898. *Bills and Distribution Book*, May 1900. *Executive Committee Minutes*, April 3, 1903.

74 *Executive Committee Minutes*, November 16, 1900; January 26, 1906; January 25, 1907.

75 Lewis & Valentine Co. to William Poole Bancroft, March 7, 1919, *Letter Book*.

76 *Sunday Star*, November 9, 1944. *Executive Committee Minutes*, July 12, 1948; September 13, 1948. Mrs. Ross D. Pittsbury to board, August 22, 1949, *Letter Book*.

77 *Executive Committee*, September 9, 1957.

78 *Annual Report 1960–61*, 6.

79 *Parks and Playgrounds*, 12. *Board Minutes*, November 18, 1929; December 13, 1929. *Every Evening*, December 9, 1929, 4.

80 *Sunday Star*, April 6, 1947, 12.

81 *Evening Journal*, January 21, 1931, 1.

82 *Board Minutes*, May 1, 1935; April 8, 1938. *Journal–Every Evening*, March 25, 1946. Annual Report 1954–55, 12. See chapter 6 for an account of J. Ernest Smith's donation of the Josephine Fountain in memory of his wife.

83 *Journal–Every Evening*, May 14, 1946, 7. In addition to working in Brandywine Park, PWA workers put their efforts into the construction of P. S. du Pont High School, the renovation of Wilmington High School, and the erection of an addition to Howard High School. *Annual Report 1964–65*, 8.

84 *Sunday Star*, January 13, 1935, "Special Business Pre-View Section,"12.

85 In addition to his gardening interests, McFarland is probably best remembered as an advocate for city planning, the establishment of the National Park Service, and the preservation of renowned natural areas such as Yosemite and Yellowstone parks. For a survey of McFarland's life and work, see Ernest Morrison, *J. Horace McFarland: A Thorn for Beauty* (Harrisburg: Commonwealth of Pennsylvania, Pennsylvania Historical and Museum Commission, 1995).

86 *Annual Report 1934*, 21. R. Marion Hatton, "Wilmington," *The American Rose Annual* (Harrisburg, Pa.: American Rose Society, 1935), 153.

87 *Journal–Every Evening*, May 20, 1946, 1. *Morning News*, December 2, 1969, 1.

88 Hatton, "Wilmington," 153. *Journal–Every Evening*, May 14, 1946, 7.

89 *Journal–Every Evening*, July 17, 1951, 18.

90 During the 1950s, the Board of Park Commissioners developed another rose garden. Planted at Kirkwood Park, the second garden also received donated plants from the rose nurseries.

91 Personal communication from J. Benjamin Williams to Friends of Wilmington Parks Executive Director Kim Johnson, 2001.

92 *Board Minutes*, April 14, 1939; May 10, 1940; July 29, 1940; August 11, 1950. *Executive Committee Minutes*, September 22, 1952. *Annual Report and Statement, City of Wilmington, Delaware, 30 June 1941*, 70.

93 *Board Minutes*, July 24, 1917; August 8, 1917.

94 For a detailed history of the church, see Anne Morris Mertz, *The First Presbyterian Church of Wilmington, Delaware* (Wilmington, Del.: National Society of the Colonial Dames of America in the State of Delaware, 1984).

95 Robert Penington to Mrs. Peter T. Wright, July 20, 1917, National Society of the Colonial Dames of America in the State of Delaware Archives.

96 Pierre S. du Pont to Mrs. Charles R. Miller, May 29, 1917, National Society of the Colonial Dames of America in the State of Delaware Archives.

97 Meeting Minutes, November 12, 1917, National Society of the Colonial Dames of America in the State of Delaware Archives. *Every Evening*, March 1, 1918, 12.

98 A footnote to the story of the little church that moved to the park is the story of how the graveyard that stood next to it for over a century also moved. In 1916, when the Presbyterians sold the land on which the church stood, they included the adjacent cemetery as part of the parcel. Local surveyor Francis A. Price began laying out plots in the Wilmington and Brandywine Cemetery to receive remains moved from the Market Street graveyard. In 1917, as remains were disinterred for removal to new graves, Price's crew kept careful records of the project. In February 1917, he prepared a plan showing "the division into lots of … Wilmington and Brandywine Cemetery for reception of remains from First Presbyterian Church Graveyard." According to Price's note on the plan, "The number at the top of each lot indicates its number with reference to Section XXVIII. The number in the lower part of each lot indicates the number of the grave (as shown on the plan of the First Presbyterian Church Graveyard made by Francis A. Price, July 1904) from which the remains placed in this lot were taken." Price and Price Collection, New Castle County Department of Land Use.

99 Postcard in Author's collection.

CHAPTER 5

[1] Scharf, *History of Delaware*, 2:794. Jessup and Moore continued in operation until 1939, when Container Corporation of America bought the company. Container Corporation ceased operations in the mid-1980s; *Morning News*, May 26, 1939, 31.

[2] *Journal–Every Evening*, September 9, 1950, 6.

[3] Edward Hungerford, *The Story of the Baltimore & Ohio Railroad, 1827–1927* (New York: G. P. Putnam's Sons, 1928), 149–151.

[4] Passenger service ended in 1958. *Morning News*, April 22, 1958, 21.

[5] *Annual Report* 1909, 15.

[6] *Board Minutes*, June 6, 1905. *Superintendent's Diaries*, March 24, 1907.

[7] *Board Minutes*, January 2, 1906; February 12, 1908; May 13, 1908.

[8] *Annual Report* 1908, 12. *Annual Report* 1910, 11. *Board Minutes*, August 10, 1910.

[9] *Executive Committee Minutes*, July 3, 1912; July 24, 1912; September 18, 1912; December 24, 1912.

[10] *Executive Committee Minutes*, May 4, 1915. Because it was roughly a continuation of Du Pont Street, the bridge initially had been called the "Du Pont Street Bridge."

[11] *Annual Report* 1920, 12.

[12] *Washington Street Bridge Commission General Files*, Frederick W. Carpenter, Executive Officer, report to Washington Street Bridge Commission, August 12, 1920.

[13] *Board Minutes*, November 13, 1912. *Sunday Star*, December 3, 1933, 1.

[14] *Board Minutes*, December 5, 1905. Interestingly, when the bridge was completed, the Board of Water Commissioners mounted on it a plaque identifying the men who served on the Board when the bridge was constructed. The Board of Park Commissioners through the Executive Committee, on the other hand, made an unqualified decision that there would be no tablet listing their names; *Executive Committee Minutes*, November 2, 1906.

[15] In 1900 Theodore A. Leisen recommended a bridge across the Brandywine at the foot of Clayton Street. His description of that bridge was remarkably like the design of the Van Buren Street Bridge with three large arches in the river flanked by 30-foot arches and smaller arches over the sidewalks. *Annual Report* 1900, 11. By 1906 Leisen was chief engineer for the Water Department; *Water Commissioners Annual Report* 1906, 10.

[16] *Water Commissioners Annual Report* 1905, 11.

[17] *Water Commissioners Annual Report* 1906, 10.

[18] U. S. Department of Transportation, *Highway Statistics Summary to 1975* (Washington, D.C.: U.S. Government Printing Office, 1975), 48.

[19] The one change was a slightly higher and more solid balustrade used in the replacement bridge to meet 20th-century safety code requirements.

[20] *Levy Court New Castle County Minutes*, August 19, 1892; June 27, 1893.

[21] *Evening Journal*, August 9, 1921, 1. Per the plaque on the bridge itself, the official name is Washington Memorial Bridge.

[22] *Washington Street Bridge Commission Meeting Report*, July 12, 1921.

[23] *Every Evening*, December 23, 1921, 1.

[24] *Washington Street Bridge Commission Meeting Report*, May 22, 1922.

[25] *Report of the Washington Street Bridge Commission to the General Assembly of the State of Delaware* (Wilmington, Del.: Star Publishing Company, 1923), 31.

[26] Scharf, *History of Delaware*, 2:670

[27] Scharf, *History of Delaware*, 2:670; Harold E. Cox, *Diamond State Trolleys: Electric Railways of Delaware* (Forty Fort, Pa.: By the author, 1991), 5. In the early years of the 20th century, the trolley company briefly offered funerals by trolley along this route. They provided a special funeral car divided so there was space for the casket and flowers in one end of the car and accommodations for mourners at the other end.

[28] *Evening Journal*, March 19, 1928, 11.

[29] *Evening Journal*, September 28, 1927, 1.

[30] P. A. C. Spero & Company, *Delaware Historic Bridges Survey and Evaluation* (Dover: Delaware Department of Transportation, 1991), 160.

[31] Harrington, Howard and Ash, of Kansas City, Missouri, designed the Market Street Bridge. Interestingly, they were among the unsuccessful designers who submitted plans for the Washington Memorial Bridge earlier in the decade.

[32] This discussion will be limited to considering the Board of Park Commissioners' handling of the I-95 Bridge in the park. For a more detailed discussion of the politics behind the creation of the highway itself and its impact on the city, see Hoffecker, *Corporate Capital*, 142–53.

[33] *Annual Report* 1956–57, 1–2.

[34] *Board Minutes*, September 15, 1968.

[35] *Annual Report* 1959–1960, 2.

[36] *Annual Report* 1960–61, 6.

[37] *Board Minutes*, May 9, 1963.

[38] Initially identified as the FAI-2 Highway, the Board of Park Commissioners first referred to the interstate as I-95 in the minutes of their April 9, 1964, meeting.

[39] *Board Minutes*: June 14, 1962; October 11, 1962; November 8, 1962; January 8, 1963; April 11, 1963; June 11, 1964; December 9, 1965.

[40] *Annual Report* 1898, 11–12.

[41] Leisen to board, April 3, 1894, *Letter Book*.

[42] *Executive Committee Minutes*, November 16, 1900. *Board Minutes*, May 6, 1902.

[43] *Annual Report* 1909, 33.

[44] *Executive Committee Minutes*, July 17, 1896; August 17, 1896; September 11, 1896.

45 *Progress in Delaware* 1, no. 12 (Works Progress Administration publication of work in Delaware, February–March 1937): 4.

CHAPTER 6

1 Gause would later be one of the original members of the Board of Park Commissioners.

2 *Wilmington Fountain Society Minutes*, September 2, 1872. Scharf, *History of Delaware*, 2:830.

3 The motto "Kindness to God's Creatures is a Service Acceptable to Him" is also inscribed around the base of the Charles Parks' statue that replaced the Bringhurst Fountain near the intersection of Pennsylvania and Delaware avenues.

4 Delaware Avenue Community Association archives, 1977–88.

5 Emerson Wilson, *Forgotten Heroes of Delaware* (Cambridge, Mass: Deltos Publishing Company, 1969), 172.

6 *Every Evening*, July 7, 1898, 1; September 1, 1898, 1; December 29, 1898, 3.

7 *Sunday Star*, April 24, 1904, 1. *Wilmington Fountain Society Minutes*, Superintendent's Report, December 5, 1904.

8 *Wilmington Fountain Society Minutes*, October 8, 1925; March 18, 1926.

9 "Our Murdered President," *Board of Trade Journal* III, no. 6 (September 1901): 8.

10 *McKinley Monument Committee Minutes*, January 18, 1902; February 1, 1902; November 19, 1906.

11 In the 1920s, Wilson chaired the committee that raised $30,000 for the Caesar Rodney monument on Rodney Square. The committee commissioned James Edward Kelly to sculpt the equestrian statue that has become so emblematic of Wilmington and Delaware; *Wilmington Journal–Every Evening*, January 7, 1939, 3.

12 *Board Minutes*, April 1, 1902. *Executive Committee Minutes*, December 5, 1907. *Annual Report* 1908, 11.

13 *Sunday Star*, September 6, 1908, 1.

14 *Morning News*, September 18, 1908, 1–2.

15 *Annual Report* 1961–62, 16. *Executive Committee Minutes*, August 27, 1962. *Evening Journal*, July 10, 1962, 8. *Board Minutes*, July 1, 1963.

16 *Morning News*, November 12, 1925, 1.

17 *Evening Journal*, May 16, 1932, 1.

18 It is interesting to note that "1918" is used on the pier and "1919" on the bronze plaque; the war ended in 1918, but the plaque may have been intended to honor those who died as a result of the war in the year following the end of hostilities.

19 *Prospect Park Memorial*, New York Department of Parks and Recreation Monuments Catalogue.

20 See Robert T. Silver, *Outdoor Sculpture in Wilmington* (Wilmington, Del.: Wilmington Arts Commission, 1987). The Roman Bronze Works, which cast the statue of "Winged Victory" in 1925, also cast the 1921 sculpture that Todd gave to Brooklyn. Established in 1897, the foundry cast the works of most major sculptors working in bronze during the 20th century. In 1908 the foundry cast the bas-relief panels of the McKinley Memorial at West Street and South Park Drive.

21 *Board Minutes*, October 9, 1931, notes Smith's letter of October 6, 1931, identifying the original fountain and naming it the Josephine Fountain and naming the tract with the cherry trees Josephine Gardens" *Annual Report* 1932, 37.

22 Silver, 42.

23 New Castle County Council Resolution No. 83-027, approved February 8, 1983.

24 *News Journal*, February 12, 1998, B1.

CHAPTER 7

1 *Annual Report* 1913, 15.

2 *Wilmington Board of Park Commissioners Park Police Captains' Diaries* (hereafter *Captains' Diaries*), June, July, and August 1914.

3 George H. Burris, captain of tournament, Delaware Anglers and Gunners Assoc., to Edward R. Mack, superintendent, April 3, 1920, *Letter Book*. *Executive Committee Minutes*, April 18, 1922; April 30, 1923; April 29, 1924.

4 *Board Minutes*, April 14, 1922; April 13, 1923; May 9, 1924; June 10, 1927. *Executive Committee Minutes*, May 19, 1925; April 26, 1926.

5 *Sunday Star*, October 15, 1933, 12.

6 *Executive Committee Minutes*, July 20, 1931; June 7, 1937; June 5, 1939; June 2, 1941. *Board Minutes*, June 14, 1940.

7 *Morning News*, May 3, 1940, 20.

8 *Journal–Every Evening*, January 12, 1944.

9 Clipping from *Sunday Star*, April 9, 1945, *Wilmington Board of Park Commissioners Scrapbook* (hereafter *Scrapbook*).

10 *Executive Committee Minutes*, March 30, 1953; March 29, 1954; March 20, 1961; April 9, 1962; February 24, 1964. *Annual Report* 1954–55, 8. *Annual Report* 1955–56, 8. *Annual Report* 1956–57, 5. *Annual Report* 1957–58, 4.

11 *Executive Committee Minutes*, March 27, 1950; July 31, 1950; April 26, 1954; April 18, 1955; March 12, 1956; July 29, 1957; July 28, 1958; July 11, 1960; August 7, 1961; February 13, 1962; August 5, 1963; August 9, 1965; July 18, 1966.

12 YMHA/YWHA, *Executive Committee Minutes*, June 26, 1944; May 13, 1946; May 10, 1948; May 8, 1950; May 26, 1952; May 3, 1954. Scouting, *Board Minutes*, May 14, 1919; November 11, 1938. *Executive Committee Minutes*, June 1, 1931; April 22, 1940; January 27, 1941; June 22, 1942; August 24, 1942; June 24, 1946; August 23, 1948; March 17, 1952; May 10, 1954; March 7, 1955; May 28, 1956.

13 C. M. Dillon, state adjutant, American Legion Delaware Branch, to Edward R. Mack, superintendent, November 9, 1919, *Letter Book*; C. M. Dillon, state adjutant, American Legion Delaware Branch, to Edward R. Mack, superintendent, November 14, 1919, *Letter Book*. *Executive Committee Minutes*, October 19, 1964; October 18, 1965; October 17, 1966.

14 *Executive Committee Minutes*, July 5, 1926; March 27, 1928; August 9, 1943; June 9, 1944; May 15, 1950.

15 *Executive Committee Minutes*, July 9, 1897. *Board Minutes*, September 2, 1902.

16 *Executive Committee Minutes*, May 15, 1912; May 25, 1914; May 9, 1916; May 15, 1917; April 30, 1918; July 1, 1919; May 3, 1921; May 29, 1923; June 7, 1926; June 13, 1927; June 17, 1929; June 13, 1930; June 1, 1931; June 20, 1932.

17 *Annual Report* 1914, 12.

18 *Executive Committee Minutes*, May 24, 1926; June 7, 1926.

19 *Executive Committee Minutes*, May 29, 1933; February 6, 1956; May 27, 1957.

20 *Executive Committee Minutes*, April 14, 1914; July 20, 1915. *Sunday Star*, April 26, 1914, 1.

21 *Executive Committee Minutes*, November 14, 1927; September 19, 1949.

22 *Captains' Diaries*, undated letter inside front cover of book for 1915.

23 *Executive Committee Minutes*, January 7, 1896. *Superintendent's Diaries*, January 1897 entries.

24 *Annual Report* 1910, 14.

25 *Annual Report* 1919, 13.

26 *Executive Committee Minutes*, July 8, 1909. *Annual Report* 1912, 10. *Annual Report* 1913, 10. *Annual Report* 1914, 9. *Annual Report* 1915, 19. *Annual Report* 1917, 14.

27 *Board Minutes*, May 13, 1927; June 12, 1931.

28 *Board Minutes*, May 1, 1935.

29 *Executive Committee Minutes*, June 9, 1899.

30 *Board Minutes*, May 1, 1935. *Executive Committee Minutes*, January 8, 1951; October 25, 1954.

31 *Annual Report* 1913, 9.

32 *Annual Report* 1921, 13. *Annual Report* 1922, 12.

33 *Executive Committee Minutes*, May 10, 1926. *Board Minutes*, October 14, 1927.

34 *Executive Committee Minutes*, March 21, 1955. *Annual Report* 1963–64, 18.

35 *Board Minutes*, August 12, 1898.

36 *Annual Report* 1899, 17. *Executive Committee Minutes*, July 1, 1946.

37 *Board Minutes*, August 11, 1944. *Morning News*, August 12, 1944. At the time, the Brandywine Pool was not operating; there were four public pools in Wilmington—Price Run, Kirkwood, Canby, and Kruse. *Executive Committee Minutes*, August 18, 1947; August 9, 1948.

37 After Price Run Pool opened in 1925, the five municipal pools operating in Wilmington were Brandywine Pool, Delamore Pool (opened 1905, replaced by Canby Pool 1930), Kirkwood Pool (opened 1909, closed 1947), Walnut Pool (opened 1914, replaced by Kruse Pool, 1931), Price Run Pool. Black Wilmingtonians used the Walnut Pool and its replacement, Kruse Pool, until 1956 when all the city's public swimming pools were integrated.

38 *Morning News*, June 18, 1943; August 12, 1944. *Annual Report* 1959–60, 3.

39 *Annual Report* 1954–55, 2.

40 *Annual Report* 1895, 16.

41 *Annual Report* 1899, 18.

42 *Executive Committee Minutes*, April 18, 1907; March 27, 1912. *Board Minutes*, May 8, 1907. *Annual Report* 1916, 14. *Annual Report* 1919, 11. *Annual Report* 1957–58, 4.

CHAPTER 8

1 *Board Minutes*, January 6, 1891; October 1, 1895. *Every Evening*, March 25, 1913, 12. *Journal–Every Evening*, May 4, 1936, 8.

2 *Annual Report* 1904, 11.

3 *Annual Report* 1905, 16.

4 "The New Zoological Garden," *Board of Trade Journal* VII, no. 1 (April 1905): 5.

5 *Annual Report* 1923, 12. *Annual Report*, 1924, 10.

6 *Every Evening*, August 2, 1930, 3.

7 Broad Ripple Zoo to Edward R. Mack, park superintendent, October 21, 1935, *Letter Book*.

8 Clipping from *Morning News*, November 19, 1943, n.p., *Scrapbook*.

9 Clipping from *Morning News*, November [ca. 1944], n.p., *Scrapbook*.

10 *Executive Committee Minutes*, January 24, 1955. *Annual Report* 1955–56, 12.

11 *Mayor's Advisory Board Minutes*, June 7, 1922. In the minutes, Baynard notes that the increased appropriation was due to the activities of the local Elks lodge, which had campaigned for several years for greater support for the Zoo from the city.

12 *Executive Committee Minutes*, February 1, 1954; January 24, 1955.

13 *Executive Committee Minutes*, November 1, 1921. *Mayor's Advisory Board Minutes*, November 2, 1921. *Board Minutes*, November 11, 1921.

14 *Executive Committee Minutes*, January 24, 1922.

[15] Clipping from *Journal–Every Evening*, July 21, 1943, n.p., *Scrapbook*.

[16] *Annual Report* 1926, 14.

[17] *Board Minutes*, February 12, 1932.

[18] *Every Evening*, August 2, 1930, 3.

[19] *Executive Committee Minutes*, August 1, 1927. *Board Minutes*, August 12, 1927. *Annual Report* 1927–28, 13. *Annual Report* 1929–30, 18. *Annual Report* 1955–56, 3.

[20] Clipping from *Journal–Every Evening*, June 29, 1943, n.p., *Scrapbook*.

[21] Clipping from *Journal–Every Evening*, March 25, 1946, n.p., *Scrapbook*.

[22] *Board Minutes*, May 8, 1953. *Executive Committee Minutes*, February 1, 1954; April 12, 1954. *Annual Report* 1955–56, 14.

[23] *Board Minutes*, December 12, 1952. *Annual Report* 1954–55, 13.

[24] *Annual Report* 1955–56, 15.

[25] *Executive Committee Minutes*, May 23, 1955. *Annual Report* 1956–57, 5.

[26] *Executive Committee Minutes*, September 19, 1955.

[27] *Annual Report* 1957–58, 3.

[28] *Annual Report* 1954–55, 13.

[29] *Executive Committee Minutes*, December 19, 1961; March 20, 1961; November 13, 1961; December 4, 1961.

[30] *Annual Report* 1932, 13.

[31] *Executive Committee Minutes*, December 27, 1962; January 2, 1963. *Board Minutes*, January 10, 1963.

[32] *Annual Report* 1963–64, 13.

[33] *Executive Committee Minutes*, January 24, 1966.

[34] *Executive Committee Minutes*, January 25, 1967.

[35] *Friends Society of Brandywine Park Newsletter* (Autumn 1997): 4.

CHAPTER 9

[1] Edward Tatnall to "W" (probably William Marriott Canby, president of the Board of Park Commissioners), December 23, 1886, *Letter Book*.

[2] *Board Minutes*, June 2, 1903; November 3, 1903; September 10, 1906.

[3] *Board Minutes*, September 10, 1906.

[4] *Wilmington Fountain Society Board Minutes*, October 8, 1925.

[5] *Wilmington Fountain Society Board Minutes*, September 26, 1928; April 11, 1929; October 21, 1929. *Board Minutes*, October 11, 1929. *Annual Report* 1930, 18.

[6] *Morning News*, March 22, 1944, 1.

[7] *Board Minutes*, April 14, 1944.

[8] *Board Minutes*, May 12, 1950.

[9] *Board Minutes*, March 13, 1953.

[10] *Executive Committee Minutes*, October 20, 1954. *Annual Report* 1957–58, 5.

[11] *Annual Report* 1957–58, 1.

[12] John B. Quinn, Annual Report of the Director of Parks and Recreation to the Board of Park Commissioners, June 30, 1957, *Annual Report* 1956-57.

[13] *Board Minutes*, May 27, 1886, newspaper clipping included in minutes for that date. No attribution for paper provided.

[14] *Annual Report* 1895, 30.

[15] Rules for guards inserted inside front cover of *Executive Committee Minutes* book for July 1, 1909 through April 22, 1919.

[16] *Executive Committee Minutes*, September 9, 1904.

[17] *Annual Report* 1896, 12.

[18] Leisen to Board of Park Commissioners, March 2, 1894, and May 1, 1894, *Letter Book*.

[19] *Annual Report* 1896, 12. *Superintendent's Diaries*, January 2, 1897.

[20] *Board Minutes*, June 12, 1931. *Annual Report* 1932, 13.

[21] *Board Minutes*, October 12, 1887.

[22] *Board Minutes*, November 11, 1914; February 10, 1909. *Executive Committee Minute* book, July 1, 1909 through April 22, 1919, rules inserted inside front cover.

[23] Leisen to board, April 3, 1894, *Letter Book*. *Executive Committee Minutes*, June 1, 1906, gambling prohibition.

[24] *Board Minutes*, May 9, 1930; May 8, 1931; January 8, 1932.

[25] *Captains' Diaries*, 1906–19.

[26] *Annual Report* 1969–70, 15.

[27] *Annual Report* 1903, 11.

[28] *Board Minutes*, October 14, 1949.

[29] *Board Minutes*, August 9, 1946.

[30] *Board Minutes*, March 29, 1916. *Executive Committee Minutes*, March 31, 1930.

[31] *Executive Committee Minutes*, May 12, 1899; June 16, 1905; October 1, 1908.

[32] *Annual Report* 1932, 13.

[33] A. G. Potts to Edward R. Mack, July 5, 1918, *Correspondence*.

[34] Bill Frank, "Clean up the city's parks," *Sunday News Journal,*
March 6, 1983.

[35] *Friends Society of Brandywine Park Newsletter* (fall 1993). The odd name,
Friends Society of Brandywine Park, arose from the founding members' desire
to avoid the name *Friends of Brandywine Park, Inc.* They labored under the
misapprehension that "Inc." had to be added to the group's name if they
incorporated as a nonprofit organization. Wanting to avoid "Inc." as too
formal, they reworked various possible name configurations until Friends
Society of Brandywine Park was chosen.

[36] Subsequent maintenance problems and low usage led the Friends and
the Division of Parks and Recreation to forego any future maintenance
efforts.

[37] *Friends Society of Brandywine Park Newsletter* (Autumn 1997): 4.

[38] MBNA provided a $150,000 grant for the project, and the
Longwood and Welfare foundations provided grants that, when
combined, matched the MBNA gift.

[39] In May 1998, when the state Division of Parks and Recreation
assumed management of Brandywine Park, along with Rockford Park,
Kentmere Parkway, Alapocas Woods, and H. Fletcher Brown Park, the
FSBP elected to change its name to Friends of Wilmington Parks and to
assume stewardship over all the collective Wilmington State Parks.

Chapter 10

[1] *Superintendent's Diaries,* March 16, 1904; December 3 and 5, 1904;
September 23, 1907. *Annual Report* 1909, 15–16.

[2] *Wilmington* magazine 4, no. 1 (May 1929): 28; *City of Wilmington Street and
Sewer Survey Engineer's File,* 1931–32; *Executive Committee Minutes,* June 22,
1953; January 1, 1957; *Annual Report* 1960–61, 7.

[3] *Annual Report* 1895, 47; *Annual Report* 1899, 17; *Annual Report* 1900, 17.
Board Minutes, August 5, 1902; September 2, 1902. *Executive Committee
Minutes,* November 4, 1902.

[4] A. J. Clement, *Wilmington, Delaware—Its Productive Industries and Commercial
and Maritime Advantages* (Wilmington, Del.: Delaware Printing Co., 1888),
24; *History of Wilmington,* 52–54.

[5] New Castle County and the City of Wilmington, *Brandywine Park
Essential Plan—Research Report Part 1: User Perceptions* (August 1994): 6–7.

[6] *Annual Report*

Bibliography

PRIMARY SOURCES

Bancroft, W. P. "An Interesting Memoir Written by Mr. W. P. Bancroft in Acknowledgement of Birthday Greetings from Some of the Older Employees on the Occasion of His Seventy-Eighth Birthday." *The Bancroft Bulletin* (1913).

Brandywine Park Century Plan, collaborative effort of New Castle County and the City of Wilmington, comprehensive master plan for Brandywine Park; jointly published by New Castle County and the City of Wilmington, September 1996.

Brandywine Park Essential Plan: Executive Summary, collaborative effort of New Castle County and the City of Wilmington, plan to guide the growth of Brandywine Park and address existing maintenance and restoration needs in the park; jointly published by New Castle County and the City of Wilmington, December 1994.

Brandywine Park Essential Plan: Research Report Part 1: User Perceptions, collaborative effort of New Castle County and the City of Wilmington, plan to guide the growth of Brandywine Park and address existing maintenance and restoration needs in the park; jointly published by New Castle County and the City of Wilmington, August 1994.

Brandywine Park Essential Plan: Site Analysis & Program Report, collaborative effort of New Castle County and the City of Wilmington, plan to guide the growth of Brandywine Park and address existing maintenance and restoration needs in the park; jointly published by New Castle County and the City of Wilmington, May 1994.

City of Wilmington. *Annual Report and Statement, City of Wilmington, Delaware*, 1939–1941. Historical Society of Delaware.

City of Wilmington. *City Executive Board Minutes*, 1907–9. After 1909, the board was renamed the Mayor's Advisory Board. Delaware Public Archives.

City of Wilmington. *Mayor's Advisory Board Minutes*, 1909–22. Prior to 1909, the board was called City Executive Board. Delaware Public Archives.

City of Wilmington. *Street and Sewer Survey Engineer's File*, 1923–38. Delaware Public Archives.

Deed Record U-14-209, dated September 29, 1899. New Castle County Recorder of Deeds.

Delaware Avenue Community Association archives, maintained by the organization.

McKinley Memorial Committee. *Minutes*, 1901–3. Part of Wilmington Board of Park Commissioners *Letter Books, Project Files, Agreements and Miscellaneous* record group. Delaware Public Archives.

National Society of the Colonial Dames of American in the State of Delaware archives, maintained by the Colonial Dames in Wilmington.

New Castle County Levy Court. *Minutes*, 1892–93. Delaware Public Archives.

The Parks and Playgrounds of Wilmington, Delaware. Wilmington, Del.: Board of Park Commissioners, 1929. Historical Society of Delaware.

Price and Price Map Collection, New Castle County Department of Land Use.

Recreation in Wilmington—Summary of Findings and Recommendations: Part I of Wilmington Recreation Survey. 1938–39, typescript, Delaware Public Archives.

United States Department of Transportation. *Highway Statistics Summary to 1975*. Washington, D.C.: U.S. Government Printing Office, 1975.

Washington Street Bridge Commission. *General Files,* 1919–23. Delaware Public Archives.

Washington Street Bridge Commission. *Report of the Washington Street Bridge Commission to the General Assembly of the State of Delaware.* Wilmington, Del.: Star Publishing Company, 1923.

Wilmington Board of Directors of the Street and Sewer Department *Annual Reports,* 1893–1908. Historical Society of Delaware.

Wilmington Board of Park Commissioners *Annual Reports,* 1895–1934; 1954–67. Delaware Public Archives.

Wilmington Board of Park Commissioners *Bills and Distribution Book,* 1900–1918. Delaware Public Archives.

Wilmington Board of Park Commissioners *Contracts and Specifications,* 1901. Delaware Public Archives.

Wilmington Board of Park Commissioners *Correspondence,* 1887–91; 1897–98; 1919–20; 1934–35. Delaware Public Archives.

Wilmington Board of Park Commissioners *Letter Books, Project Files, Agreements and Miscellaneous,* 1883–1930. Delaware Public Archives.

Wilmington Board of Park Commissioners *Maps and Drawings,* 1893, including "Index to Field Books of the Park Engineer." Delaware Public Archives.

Wilmington Board of Park Commissioners *Minutes of the Board of Park Commissioners Meetings,* 1883–1967. Delaware Public Archives.

Wilmington Board of Park Commissioners *Minutes of the Meetings of the Executive Committee of the Board of Park Commissioners,* 1896–1967. Delaware Public Archives.

Wilmington Board of Park Commissioners *Miscellaneous Ledgers and Papers,* 1895–98. Delaware Public Archives.

Wilmington Board of Park Commissioners *Park Police Captains' Diaries,* 1909–16. Delaware Public Archives.

Wilmington Board of Park Commissioners *Parks Maintenance and Improvement Books,* 1925–1944. Delaware Public Archives.

Wilmington Board of Park Commissioners *Rent Ledger,* 1914–18. Delaware Public Archives.

Wilmington Board of Park Commissioners *Scrapbook,* 1943–46. Delaware Public Archives.

Wilmington Board of Park Commissioners *Superintendent's Diaries,* 1897, 1904, 1907–13. Delaware Public Archives.

Wilmington Board of Park Commissioners *Time Books,* 1900–1903. Delaware Public Archives.

Wilmington Board of Water Commissioners, Annual Report of the Chief Engineer, 1872; 1902–07; 1909–10; 1913–16; 1920–21; 1922–23. Historical Society of Delaware.

Wilmington Department of Parks and Recreation *Annual Report,* 1968–70; 1972–73; 1976–77. Delaware Pubic Archives.

Wilmington Fountain Society *Board Minutes,* 1871–1968. Historical Society of Delaware.

Periodicals

Evening Journal (Wilmington, Del., newspaper) 1921–74.

Every Evening (Wilmington, Del., newspaper) 1898–1930.

Friends of Wilmington Parks *Newsletter* (1993–2004).

Journal-Every Evening (Wilmington, Del., newspaper) 1935–56.

Morning News (Wilmington, Del., newspaper) 1908–83.

News Journal (Wilmington, Del., newspaper) 1983–98

One-Two-One-Four, publication by local lumber company, Brosius and Smedley, produced monthly for members of the Wilmington building trades. The name, *One-Two-One-Four,* was the company's telephone number and the name of the publication changed to *Four-One-Two-One* when the company phone number changed in 1930.

Progress in Delaware. Works Progress Administration publication about WPA work in Delaware. 1935–1937.

Sunday Star (Wilmington, Del., newspaper) 1901–51. This newspaper was variously called *Sunday Morning Star, Delmarva Star,* and *Sunday Star.* In the interests of simplicity, *Sunday Star* is used throughout this narrative.

Wilmington (magazine) 1929.

SECONDARY SOURCES

Barber, David F. *Trial and Triumph: The Story of One Community's Acquisition and Development of Its Own Water and Gas Utilities.* Omaha, Neb.: Metropolitan Utilities District of Omaha, Nebraska, 1989.

Boyer, M. Christine. *Dreaming the Rational City: The Myth of American City Planning.* Cambridge: MIT Press, 1983.

Bushman, Claudia L. *So Laudable an Undertaking: The Wilmington Library, 1788–1988.* Wilmington, Del.: Delaware Heritage Press, 1988.

Calvert, Monte A. "The Wilmington Board of Trade, 1867–1875." In *Delaware History* 12, no. 3 (April 1967): 175–97.

Clement, A.J. *Wilmington, Delaware—Its Productive Industries and Commercial and Maritime Advantages.* Wilmington, Del.: Board of Trade, 1888.

"Copying After Wilmington," *The Wilmington Board of Trade Journal* 7, no. 1 (April 1905).

Cox, Harold E. *Diamond State Trolleys: Electric Railways of Delaware.* Forty Fort, Pa.: By the author, 1991.

"Death of J. Taylor Gause," *The Wilmington Board of Trade Journal* 1, no. 3 (December 1898).

"Death of George W. Bush," *The Wilmington Board of Trade Journal* 2, no. 4 (July 1900).

Department of Commerce. Bureau of the Census. *U. S. Census for 1850,* "Population."

Department of Commerce. Bureau of the Census. *U. S. Census for 1880,* "Population."

Fine, Lisa M. *The Souls of the Skyscraper.* Philadelphia: Temple University Press, 1990.

Frank, Bill. "The Energetic Mrs. Gause," *Morning News,* May 1, 1963.

Gray, Jane Loring, ed., "The Botanical Correspondence of William M. Canby," typescript, Historical Society of Delaware, undated.

Hatton, R. Marion. "Wilmington" in *The American Rose Annual.* Harrisburg, Pa.: American Rose Society, 1935.

Heckscher, August. *Open Space: The Life of American Cities.* New York: Harper and Row, Publishers, 1977.

History of Wilmington: The Commercial, Social and Religious Growth of the City during the Past Century. Wilmington, Del.: *Every Evening* newspaper, 1894.

Hoffecker, Carol E. *Corporate Capital: Wilmington in the Twentieth Century.* Philadelphia: Temple University Press, 1983.

Hoffecker, Carol E. *Wilmington: A Pictorial History.* Norfolk, Va.: Donning Company Publishers, 1982.

Hoffecker, Carol E. *Wilmington, Delaware: Portrait of an Industrial City, 1830–1910.* Published for the Eleutherian Mills-Hagley Founcation by the University Press of Virginia, 1974.

Hungerford, Edward. *The Story of the Baltimore & Ohio Railroad, 1827–1927.* New York: G. P. Putnam's Sons, 1928.

Leisen, Theodore A. "Parks of Wilmington, Del." In *The Wilmington Board of Trade Journal* 1, no. 9 (June 1899).

Leisen, Theordore A. "Parks, Squares and Driveways." In *Industrial Wilmington,* compiled by George A. Wolf. Wilmington, Del.: Board of Trade, 1898.

Lubove, Roy. "The Roots of Urban Planning." In *The Urban Community: Housing and Planning in the Progressive Era.* Englewood Cliffs, N.J.: Prentice-Hall, 1967; reprint, Westport, Conn.: Greenwood Press, 1981, 1–22.

Mack, Edward R. "Wilmington's Park System." *Wilmington* 4, no. 2 (June 1929).

Mertz, Anne Morris. *The First Presbyterian Church of Wilmington, Delaware.* Wilmington, Del.: National Society of the Colonial Dames of America in the State of Delaware, 1984.

Morrison, Ernest. *J. Horace McFarland: A Thorn for Beauty.* Harrisburg: Commonwealth of Pennsylvania, Pennsylvania Historical and Museum Commission, 1995.

Munroe, John A. *History of Delaware.* Newark: University of Delaware Press, 1979, 1984.

"The New Zoological Garden." *The Wilmington Board of Trade Journal* 7, no. 1 (April 1905): 5.

"Our Murdered President." *The Wilmington Board of Trade Journal* 3, no. 6 (September 1901).

P. A. C. Spero & Company. *Delaware Historic Bridges Survey and Evaluation.* Dover: Delaware Department of Transportation, 1991.

Prospect Park Memorial. New York: New York Department of Parks and Recreation Monuments Catalogue, 1998.

Roper, Laura Wood. *FLO: A Biography of Frederick Law Olmsted.* Baltimore: Johns Hopkins University Press, 1973.

Rose, J. N. "William M. Canby (A Portrait)." *Botanical Gazette* 37 (May 1904): 385–87.

"Samuel Canby," in *The National Cyclopedia of American Biography,* volume 33. New York: James T. White & Co., 1947.

Scharf, J. Thomas. *History of Delaware, 1609–1888,* 2 vols. Philadelphia: L. J. Richards & Co., 1888.

Schuyler, David. *The New Urban Landscape: The Redefinition of City Form in Nineteenth-Century America.* Baltimore: Johns Hopkins University Press, 1986.

Silver, Robert T. *Outdoor Sculpture in Wilmington.* Wilmington, Del.: Wilmington Arts Commission, 1987.

Thompson, Priscilla M. "Creation of the Wilmington Park System Before 1896." *Delaware History* 18, no. 2 (Fall–Winter 1978): 75–92.

Wall, Joseph Frazier. *Alfred I. du Pont: The Man and His Family.* New York: Oxford University Press, 1990.

"William Poole Bancroft," in *The National Cyclopedia of American Biography,* vol. 22. New York: James T. White & Co., 1932.

Wilmington City Directory for 1869–70. Wilmington, Del.: Commercial Press of Jenkins & Atkinson, 1869.

Wilson, Emerson. *Forgotten Heroes of Delaware.* Cambridge, Mass.: Deltos Publishing Co., 1969.

Winkler, John K. *The Du Pont Dynasty.* New York: Blue Ribbon Books, 1935.

Zebley, Frank R. *The Churches of Delaware: A History, in Brief, of the Nearly 900 Churches and Former Churches in Delaware as Located by the Author.* Wilmington, Del.: William N. Cann, 1947.

Name Index

Author Susan Mulchahey Chase moved to Delaware from the Midwest in 1986. In 1995 she earned a Ph.D. from the University of Delaware from the College of Urban Affairs and Public Policy. A consulting historian, she has prepared histories for the Delaware Division of Parks and Recreation, IA Holdings Corporation, the Delaware Heritage Commission, and the Tyler Arboretum and has contributed to the 75th anniversary history of Tower Hill School and the 90th anniversary history of the Rotary Club of Wilmington.

She has consulted on urban revitalization projects in Rock Hill, South Carolina; Paterson, New Jersey; and Florence, South Carolina. She also served on the Rockwood Advisory Committee that guided restoration of Rockwood, a Victorian house museum in Wilmington.

She has been park historian for the Friends of Wilmington Parks since 1994. She regularly writes articles on aspects of park history for the Friends' newsletter and leads tours in the park. She lives near Brandywine Park with her husband and two dogs and counts it as one of the city's outstanding assets.

She suggests that you, dear reader, use the balance of this page for your own observations of the park and its many features.